How To REALLY Use LinkedIn

Bert Verdonck, Michael (Mike) Clark & Caleb Storkey

Billions of people can be talking about you.

With most of the world now spending hours a day on LinkedIn, Twitter, Instagram, Facebook and other favorite networks, there are potentially billions of people...

Wanting to know if they can trust you.

Wondering what kind of people work for you.

Willing to talk you up or tear you down.

Either you are an active participant in these conversations and making the strongest case for your organization . . . or you are leaving it to others less interested in your amazingness.

Which option are you taking? In the advice of Richard Branson:

> "Embracing social media isn't just a bit of fun,
> it's a vital way to communicate, keep your ear to the ground
> and improve your business." [1]

And interestingly, when we hear from CEOs like Richard Branson, Mark Zuckerberg and Marissa Mayer, we find that we have an opinion about Virgin, Facebook and Yahoo. We have formed judgements – based in good part on the *social credibility* of these leaders. Another CEO who knows this well is BRANDfog's Ann Charles:

> "In today's hyper-connected, information-driven world,
> CEOs and senior executives alike are expected to have
> an active social presence. Brand image, brand trust,
> and a company's long term success depend on it." [2]

---

1 http://www.forbes.com/sites/williamarruda/2014/08/10/why-social-savvy-ceos-thrive-and-anti-social-ones-wont-survive/
2 https://www.linkedin.com/pulse/thoughts-ceo-reputation-social-media-robin-young

Social credibility is becoming the calling card of our digital era.

And *social credibility* is what this book is about. Our goal here is to quickly move beyond "needing to understand" the new social business imperative to "needing to actually execute" – where so many companies falter.

That's the "REALLY" part of the book title, as explained by Scredible CEO, Colin Lucas-Mudd:

> "Your team can REALLY follow through because we fill
> the gaps in your social business knowledge base
> with strategies that practically execute themselves."

We have worked in the social business industry since 2004 – the very year the term *social media* escaped its origins at AOL.

- We have since trained 65,000+ individuals in 650+ companies in 10 languages on three continents.
- Our first two editions of *How to REALLY Use LinkedIn* were bestsellers with 250,000+ in print.
- Among our book buyers are the staff and management team of LinkedIn itself.

When you complete this book and share it with your organization, we encourage you to schedule a follow-up *Strategic Assessment Session* with one of our Master Trainers, gratis.

StandOut with LinkedIn™

PRAISE FOR THE 2ND EDITION

"Scredible's LinkedIn training is highly valued and highly rated within Deloitte."
Nancy Bulens–Learning Officer, Deloitte

"This enlightening exploration of social media and latest communication skills provides meaningful, easy-to-read ideas."
Dr. Nido Qubein–President, High Point University

"Native English speakers will know the saying, 'Cometh the hour, cometh the man'. In the case of this book we could correctly say, '*Cometh the technology, cometh the book*'. *How to REALLY use LinkedIn* is an essential reference work for any businessperson seriously interested in the power of social networking. It's far more useful than an operating manual. Here you'll find excellent strategies..."
Chris Davidson–Managing Editor, Professional Speakers Journal

"Two weeks from finishing our 1st sales training session with Scredible, I *secured a £500k client* using their techniques – thank you!"
Wayne Murray–Client Services Director at Pure

"How to REALLY Use LinkedIn is a must for all professionals wishing to enter the next era of networking."
Erik Van Den Branden–PwC Belgium

"Well-structured insights and tips throughout to increase the effectiveness of your network—a big help to reach your goals easier and quicker."
Frank Opsomer–Channel Partner Manager Hitachi Data Systems

"Through applying the Scredible LinkedIn strategies, I've put more than £400,000 into my pipeline and closed >£150,000 in sales."
Kevin Joseph–Sr. Business Development Manager, Winmark Europe

"We've created new leads and new opportunities and we now have a pipeline in the area of £60,000 of new business."
Terry Carney–Director at Sales Remedy

"Attended the Social Selling program... got key actions I can take to find a *vast reservoir of leads*, more than I will ever be able to service."
David Klaasen–Managing Director at Inspired Working

"It is great to read a book that is this practical and gives examples to help you obtain your networking goal."
Mary Roll–Career Services Manager International MBA Program, Vlerick Leuven Gent Management School

"If you take networking seriously, use LinkedIn. If you take LinkedIn seriously, read this book."
Edgar Valdmanis–Marketing & Projects Director at The Norwegian Computer Society

"Must-read for anybody who wants to grow their business through networking."
Ivan Misner–NY Times Bestselling author and Founder of BNI

"Finally, someone *explaining why LinkedIn is useful*. As a typical Gen Xer, I was starting to become frustrated to hear more and more people talking about the advantages and the fun of being LinkedIn. Once I got it, I immediately made a profile and started connecting."
Hubert Vanhoe–Vice-President, USG People Belgium

"As a how-to guide, this book contains everything you may need to know about LinkedIn. I've personally found it very useful indeed."
Mike Southon–*Financial Times* columnist and co-author of *The Beermat Entrepreneur*

"*How to REALLY use LinkedIn* will not only give you *clear strategies to increase your network efficiency* with the use of LinkedIn, but it will also explain the sense and purpose of networking. A must for every professional!"
Vincent De Waele–Business Transformation Director, Mobistar (Orange)

Special Offer

"How to REALLY Use LinkedIn" is available at significant discount when purchased in quantity for client gifts, sales promotions, and premiums. Special editions, including co-branded or custom covers, as well as excerpts, can also be created in large quantities for special needs. For further information:
connect@reallyconnect.com

"How To REALLY Use LinkedIn" Third Edition
Bert Verdonck, Michael (Mike) Clark & Caleb Storkey
Copyright © 2019 Bert Verdonck & Michael (Mike) Clark
All Rights Reserved.
Publisher: Really Connect Ltd, 25 New Road, Chatteris, Cambridgeshire,
PE16 6BJ, United Kingdom.

Authors: Bert Verdonck, Michael (Mike) Clark & Caleb Storkey

Publicatiecoördinatie: Bianca Kroon, www.auteurscollege.nl
Vormgeving: Jo-Ann Snel, www.ophonkdesign.nl

The web addresses (URLs) referenced in this book were live and correct at the time of the book's publication, but may be subject to change.

Library (Legal Depot)
ISBN: 978-1-9996295-4-0

This is the work product of Really Connect Ltd. We are not affiliated with LinkedIn and are not paid commissions on our referrals of their business. If you want to learn more about our relationship or receive an introduction to your LinkedIn representative, feel free to drop us a line.
connect@reallyconnect.com

FOREWORD

Here's to the Change Makers!

Change Makers are those that don't settle for the status quo. They see the future coming at a pace of knots and they work relentlessly to equip others to get ready for it. Without Change Makers, more companies would stay stuck in the past and be destroyed by the disruptive nature of cash-fuelled tech start-ups today.

This book is for you, Mr or Mrs Change Maker! We've seen your work first hand in many organizations. We've worked with your corporate brothers and sisters to conspire to inspire transformation across hundreds of companies. Our vision is to inspire other Change Makers to step up and accept the challenge that their organization presents in their transformation into being a Social Business.

What we've noticed over the years is that for companies to see true transformation into social businesses, or even just making a shift from the "dark ages" to realising they have to adapt, this often comes down to someone driving that change. That is why this book is dedicated to those folks who are brave enough to take ownership of this challenge and tackle it head on.

We hope this book provides both inspiration and practical strategies for you.

Keep working your magic. The world needs more leaders like you to shape the future.

> "Don't ask yourself what the world needs.
> Ask yourself what makes you come alive,
> and go do that, because what the world needs,
> is people who have come alive."
> *Howard Thurman*

TABLE OF CONTENTS

SOCIAL FUTURE COMING AT 100 TERABYTES AN HOUR

On top of Gordon Moore's Law...

In which the number of transistors in an integrated circuit will double every 18 months – allowing the design of new products that we absolutely must have.

Updated with Gilder's Law...

In which bandwidth will grow at least three times faster than computing power – bringing amazing new digital products to billions of people.

And broadened with Metcalf's Law...

In which the value of a network is proportional to the square of the number of connected users – so the more people who join in, the more valuable the service.

We'd like to humbly add Really Connect's Law...

In which each time we double the total amount of information in the world, we halve our understanding of it – effectively tossing us into a state of overwhelm.

We are creating an estimated 16 Zettabytes of new information every year, with IDC Data Age 2025 report predicting this will rise to 163 Zettabytes by 2025.[3] And if you're not sure what an Zettabyte is, it's one trillion gigabytes. Oh yes... that much! Even with massive computers, we struggle to understand it all.

Always-on technologies make demands on us with unrelenting and merciless speed. Our smartphones are constantly at our side, with studies

---

3   https://www.seagate.com/files/www-content/our-story/trends/files/data-age-2025-infographic-2017.pdf

showing millennials checking them an average of 150 times a day.[4] Every minute in social media we knock out another...

- 17,361 LinkedIn profile views[5]
- 456,000 tweets[6]
- 31,250,000 Facebook messages
- 44,146,600 YouTube videos viewed
- 46,740 posts uploaded on Instagram
- 1,800,000 snaps created[7]

We've reached the point where we are expected to consume content and offer opinions on a nonstop basis – at 100 terabytes an hour, as we only half-joke. But it turns out that our brains have built-in limits. We are banging up against our design capabilities. We can only give and take so much before we literally blow circuits.

How do we deal with the relentlessly accelerating pace?

For those of us in business, there is only one way to manage this faster-better-quicker pace. That's with *focus*. A way to *focus* that's equal to the input.

And there's the rub.

Focus has become the hardest thing, making it a valuable commodity. We know that *time* used to be most the most valuable commodity. Many of us can easily complete these sentences: *You may delay, but... time waits for...*

But now we need a *focus* that is equal to the challenge of a terabyte pace.

We know this instinctively. It's part of the reason the successful movie turned TV series with Bradley Cooper, *Limitless*, is so popular. Who doesn't secretly wish for a single pill that opens every synapse so that the brain can soar? Such a "pill" may be in our future. But for now, and still lacking the alchemic shoehorn to add hours to our day, we are confronted

---

4   https://www.inc.com/john-brandon/science-says-this-is-the-reason-millennials-check-their-phones-150-times-per-day.html

5   https://www.cio.com/article/2915592/social-media/7-staggering-social-media-use-by-the-minute-stats.html#slide8 and https://www.statista.com/statistics/195140/new-user-generated-content-uploaded-by-users-per-minute/

6   https://www.statista.com/statistics/195140/new-user-generated-content-uploaded-by-users-per-minute/

7   http://uk.businessinsider.com/everything-that-happens-in-one-minute-on-the-internet-2017-9

with so many inputs that our thoughts can jumble and analysis becomes a challenge.

Focus – it's the thing now

So that's what guides this book. It's why we capitalize the REALLY in the title *How to REALLY Use LinkedIn*. Because there are plenty of good books on using LinkedIn and optimizing for social business. It's important to note that due to the continuous changes on the LinkedIn platform, we recognise the limitations of a printed book. We'd encourage you to look at the digital resources at the end of the book. The thing we most need is *focus* – the ability to rise above shiny object syndrome and zero in on just what REALLY needs doing, to succeed in our social business future.

We're looking to provide focus where it matters.

Social business = continuous learning

The workplace is not only moving at terabyte speed, it is transforming radically.

The traditional employer-employee relationship has been shattered. The old model of "employees as family" doesn't work, where employees find it hard to trust employers and businesses face continuous and relentless change. But neither does a model of "employees as free agents."

LinkedIn founder Reid Hoffman offered some insights in a book authored with Ben Casnocha and Chris Yeh called *The Alliance*. They argued that we can no longer think of employees as either *family* or as *free agents*. Think of them instead as *allies*.

This alliance between a company and employees who come together for a specific project or vision requires that everyone be "in learning mode" all the time, to keep up with the pace of technology and stay on script with the mission.

Indeed, the average organization is spending an average of $1,252 a year per employee on training costs.[8] They are doing it because they know they have to.

The McKinsey management consultants drove that nail home with a 2015 study of what the most successful companies are doing to improve their business capabilities. As per Fig. 1.1, what the top-performing companies know they need to focus on is:[9]

Improving employee skillsets continually.

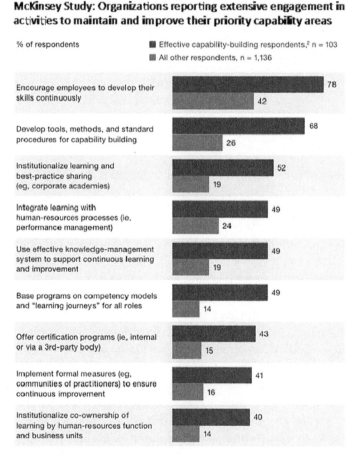

McKinsey Study: Organizations reporting extensive engagement in activities to maintain and improve their priority capability areas

% of respondents — ■ Effective capability-building respondents,[2] n = 103
■ All other respondents, n = 1,136

Activity	Effective	All other
Encourage employees to develop their skills continuously	78	42
Develop tools, methods, and standard procedures for capability building	68	26
Institutionalize learning and best-practice sharing (eg, corporate academies)	52	19
Integrate learning with human-resources processes (ie, performance management)	49	24
Use effective knowledge-management system to support continuous learning and improvement	49	19
Base programs on competency models and "learning journeys" for all roles	49	14
Offer certification programs (ie, internal or via a 3rd-party body)	43	15
Implement formal measures (eg, communities of practitioners) to ensure continuous improvement	41	16
Institutionalize co-ownership of learning by human-resources function and business units	40	14

Fig. 1.1 Mc Kinsey study of most capable organizations

8   https://www.yourerc.com/blog/post/3-ways-to-calculate-a-training-and-development-budget-for-your-organization.aspx
9   http://www.mckinsey.com/insights/organization/building_capabilities_for_performance

Another study by famed Kleiner Perkins Internet expert, Mary Meeker, corroborated the McKinsey findings. In her Internet Trends report, she looked at the Millennial Generation which is now the largest segment of the workforce in most countries. Aged 18 to 35, they bring a fresh face with ideas and preferences that bear only passing resemblance to the concerns of the Baby Boom Generation, 80 million of whom will retire this decade.

In her investigation of Millennials in the workplace and what they desire on the job, Ms. Meeker found that Millennials are very clear on the kind of future they are entering and what their biggest need will be, as per Fig. 1.2.[10]

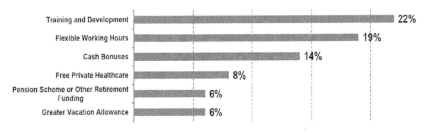

Which Three Benefits Would You Most Value From an Employer?
% Ranking Each 1st Place, Global

Training and Development	22%
Flexible Working Hours	19%
Cash Bonuses	14%
Free Private Healthcare	8%
Pension Scheme or Other Retirement Funding	6%
Greater Vacation Allowance	6%

Fig. 1.2 KCPB's Mary Meeker on the Millennials top workplace desires

Millennials put the highest value on receiving the training and development they need to focus, to ally with organizations, to compete at terabyte pace and confront the reality of their future, their time.

Of course, the Millennials are a very human bunch. They also hope their perks will include flexible working hours and cash bonuses! But the on-the-job perks once coveted by Boomers fall far down the scale.

Other perks had fewer than 8% of Millennial respondents indicating interest. In order downward is healthcare, retirement plans, vacation allowances, housing assistance, company car, assistance with student loans, maternity/paternity benefits, subsidized travel costs, free childcare, low interest loan assistance, time off for charity work, and a zero-benefits for higher-wages swap.

10 http://www.kpcb.com/internet-trends

The long-tail of Boomers pales in comparison with the top desire of Millennials:

> Getting the real-time on-the-job training and skills development they need to keep pace in a fast-changing world.

And the old training won't do.

As explored in *Futureproof*, a book by Caleb and Minter Dial, they argue the need for leaders to adopt a mindset of Responsibility, in relation to learning. It's not simply waiting for the Corporate Training Programme, but creating learning habits, tools and environments. It's about understanding the ways that each of us learns. And good training companies have embraced the disruptive nature of education and are finding increasing innovative ways to enable learning. On one end there's video. Millennials have demonstrated a preference for digital and visual training tools over the traditional analogue tools of Baby Boomers. This generation is both video-literate and video-motivated. Which is why Cisco is confidently predicting that 82% of Internet traffic will be video by 2021.[11] But additionally, Machine Learning will significantly impact Human Learning. In short, better-focused training is a top priority of successful companies.

Millennials offer up a social manifesto

What's more, the newest workforce segment has done something that no entry-level group of employees has ever done before. Through their actions they have put something of a manifesto to senior management:

> *We want to text more than talk, use video more than meet, use our own devices when we want to, work remotely if we please, get constant training to stay current, get almost daily performance feedback, and switch jobs if we're not happy.*

Big demands?

Absolutely! But here's the thing: The companies that are listening and acting in socially accommodating ways are also **outperforming** their disengaged

---

11 http://www.cisco.com/c/en/us/solutions/collateral/service-provider/ip-ngn-ip-next-generation-network/white_paper_c11-481360.html

peers on every business metric that matters. Gallup's 2013 "State of the Global Workplace" study found that socially engaged companies are:
1. Holding their employees longer
2. Having fewer morale problems
3. Attracting the best talent out of college
4. Experiencing fewer work-related accidents
5. Enjoying more loyal, committed customers
6. Most importantly, showing higher profitability.

So this broad "social" movement is not just something the Millennials are driving. Professionals of all ages are recognizing the value of socially aware workplaces and constant training to prepare for fast-arriving technologies, and capitalize on them. We are seeing social business rise into a mature model. And there is a core organizing principle behind this movement...

Identifying the Core Value of Social Business Success

To look at today's most admired companies is to see some interesting things. Figure 1.3 shows *Fortune's* list of the world's most admired enterprises, as of February 2018. [12] Some 3,900 executives did the ranking. What do these companies all have in common?

THE TOP 10

ALL STARS		INDUSTRY
1	Apple	Computers
2	Amazon	Internet Services and Retailing
3	Alphabet	Internet Services and Retailing
4	Berkshire Hathaway	Insurance: Property and Casualty
5	Starbucks	Food Services
6	Walt Disney	Entertainment
7	Microsoft	Computer Software
8	Southwest Airlines	Airlines
9	FedEx	Delivery
10	JPMorgan Chase	Megabanks

Fig. 1.3 Top 10 most admired companies

12 http://fortune.com/worlds-most-admired-companies/

Certainly a lot of considerations go into a ranking of "admiration." *Fortune* has a number of hard attributes, such as financial soundness and investment value. And softer attributes as well, such as people management and social responsibility. But in doing any kind of ranking, there is the human element. Humans do these rankings. As humans, we place a higher value (or rank) on things we believe in, higher ideals, greater aspirations, bigger feats of wonder. Indeed, the word admire comes from the Latin *mirari*, meaning *to wonder*.

Our yearning for a higher-level aspirational ideal in companies becomes even more important to us amid the pounding noise of social media. With so much noise, we have a need to admire companies that break through it all with a crisp message that resonates in our lives.

That is what all of the top companies on Fortune's list do, even if their "social responsibility" ranking is not in the top one or two.

We see them as socially credible companies because they have presented themselves as socially credible companies.

Indeed, we believe that...

Social credibility is the new "calling card"

Intel gets this idea. They came up 45th on *Fortune's* list of most admired this year. They are a less public brand and so, understandably, not ranked higher. But they are a company that has continued to thrive when so many other microchip companies fell into the dustbin of history. And why?

One explanation comes from Ekaterina Walter who began her social career at Intel and has since authored several fascinating books, most recently *Think Like Zuck*. She says of the Intel difference:

> *"When I was at Intel we activated the internal brand love by educating our employees and allowing them to not only talk about their passion towards technology, but to engage our customers and build relationships with them."* [13]

---

13 https://www.forbes.com/sites/williamarruda/2014/08/10/why-social-savvy-ceos-thrive-and-anti-social-ones-wont-survive/#2244dec36beb

Yes, Intel gets it. They understand that to continue being a great business, they must be a socially credible business. Even though Intel sells through B2B channels, the company recognizes that every employee can be a public-facing spokesperson in social business, advocating for the brand, cheerleading for the brand, apologizing for the brand from time to time, but always actively representing the company credibly.
This is the essential innovation of social business.

There are plenty of iconic brands, but the *Fortune* most admired are ranked in good measure for how they are perceived in the global social business conversation.

They are thought to be credible and trustworthy in that conversation, and are rewarded with category-topping accolades that manifest across harder attributes such as market share, revenue growth, and stock appreciation.

In the digital era, then, a company's social credibility has become something of a secret ingredient that can make marginal companies good and good companies great.

> Note: To superstar business writer Jim Collins, it may be time to update your *Good to Great* and *Great by Choice* once again!

Google affirms importance of social credibility

Google's behind-the-curtains activity reinforces the value of social credibility.

A recent algorithm update impacted 90% of paid search engine activity. The search giant effectively buried the "bad searches" (keyword stuffing, duplicated content, manipulated hyperlinks) which had been the bread and butter of the SEO industry for years.

In search rankings, Google for a while has now considered the *quality, originality,* and *relevance* of the content, as well as *engagement* with the content.

> The greater the viewer engagement,
> the higher the ranking in the organic listings.

It's the way in which others engage with your content that leads to your social credibility. This engagement is measured by Google's algorithms, and it cannot be gamed or held for long if inauthentic. Millions of people who are participating in the global conversation see to that, in a massive on-going fact-check campaign.

In this book we'll show you how to weave genuine and authentic social credibility into everything you and your company do.

Social business is no longer an option, but some resist

Among the social business holdouts in the executive suites, some are quick to point out what can go wrong. There are plenty of examples of companies who posted first and saved the thinking for later, such as...

1. British Embassy in US Mocks History – Embassy staffers tweeted a photo of a cake topped with a miniature White House and sparklers, with the words: "Commemorating the 200th anniversary of burning the White House. Only sparklers this time!" Nobody was amused.
2. American Apparel Oblivious to History – For a Fourth of July post, a no doubt young and ignorant social media assistant at American Apparel posted to Tumblr an image that was meant to be artistic fireworks – but it was actually the 1986 photo of the Challenger space shuttle exploding.

With stories that lack judgement like these, it's understandable why some would hesitate. But what is the larger cost of that hesitation?

Surely when the telephone came along, there were fears about using it. You can imagine people asking: *"What will people do on the phone? ... Will they just say anything? ... Not everyone should be allowed to have one, right?"*

But people quickly learned all the advantages of using the telephone.

Then the Internet came along and with it a chorus of voices calling it a waste of time, a terrible distraction. Some still call it that. But the advantages it brings certainly rival and even surpass the telephone when harnessed intelligently.

The talented Shawn DuBravac, President at Astra Insights, captured the reality of our place in time most eloquently in his book *Digital Destiny*:

"Whether or not we enter the digital age is not a choice anymore. Once man invented the sail, he could not go back to just using the oar. Once man invented the steam engine, he could not pretend that horses were the only way to travel. And once man discovered atomic energy, he had to come to grips with the benefits and risks of this new invention – from power plants to bombs. Digital technology resides in the same realm as these transformational technologies, and we cannot undo what has been done. This is our digital destiny. This is not what might happen if we choose this road over another. This is what will happen regardless of which road we take."[14]

So yes, in social business there are risks of mistakes and missteps. But the greater mistake is surely inaction. For the future is departing now...

A great opportunity to capitalize on a new way of work

In the first edition of this book, published in 2009 when social media was still a "personal plaything" to most, our goal was simply to show people how to create the Best LinkedIn Profile and begin networking more effectively.

Today the foundation of social business has solidified. Companies are building an employer social brand; they are selling and recruiting on this foundation. We have come a long way. Yet too many companies have yet to take full advantage and move forward into our shared social business future.

Let's bring everyone forward.

Measuring the Return on (Social) Investment

We can now measure the value of a socially credible footprint – that is, the value of organizing as a social business. We can know its worth. We call this measure "Return on (Social) Investment" and it is predicated on a "social credibility loop" that drives initial consumer interest in the

---

14   Shawn Dubravac, *Digital Destiny*, Regnery Publishing, 2015, p. xxii (https://www.regnery.com/books/digital-destiny/)

company, continues to aid in product discovery and acceptance, drives sales conversion numbers, builds up brand loyalty and a corps of social champions, and, ultimately, impacts bottom line performance. (See Fig. 1.4.) To make it even more tangible, we will introduce some hard and soft key performance indicators (KPIs) later in this book.

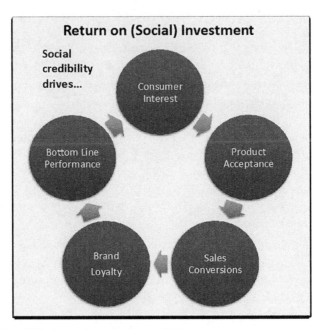

Fig. 1.4 Social credibility drives value across the organization

(Social credibility drives) consumer interest

You learn a lot about consumers by being honest and forthright with them. This can be a scary idea to some old-school marketers. But when you approach people in an open, supportive and credible manner, you learn what they truly think about your business. Not what they say in focus groups to please you. What they REALLY think. Armed with this information...

- You can create content that speaks very directly to the interests and concerns they've expressed.
- You can test various promotions (in A/B format) across the social business channels to continually hone your message and increase sales.

(Social credibility drives) product acceptance

In the old economy, companies pushed out products – testing, perfecting, papering over any faults. Companies profited by controlling access to information. Seldom now.

In movies, for example, a studio could spend "*x*" on opening weekend advertising and project "*y*" gross. But in 2017 over Memorial Day weekend in the US, sales for the long awaited adaption of *Baywatch* had already began to slump. Pulling in a dismal $23million which was nearly $20 million less than predicted, these results were influenced by audiences and critics who had immediately taken to social media to criticise it.[15]

Movies are not as different from consumer products or B2B widgets as one might think. If there are product issues, or pricing concerns, your buyers are usually going to know about them. Or if an issue is successfully covered up for a while, such as Volkswagen's circumventing the emissions control standards, consumers will find out soon enough.

Then the fallout is immense.

Credibility is the big key to consumer acceptance of products.

(Social credibility drives) sales conversions

Every social business connection is an individual getting to *know* you, wanting to *like* you, hoping to *trust* you before interacting commercially with you or your organization. This is a process that unfolds on the click path to your website or walk to your storefront.

Each successive touchpoint with a connection, each new interaction that happens in the way the individual prefers – each of these moves the relationship toward a sales event.

The more socially credible activity you dedicate yourself to, the more inbound traffic you receive, the more conversions you enjoy in a loop of credibility.

---

15 http://www.vulture.com/2017/12/2017s-biggest-flops-made-a-case-against-cinematic-universes.html/

(Social credibility drives) brand loyalty

Brand loyalty is a soft metric, and can be difficult to measure. But Forrester Research has been able to quantify this loyalty in terms of:

- Repeat purchases
- Lower switching rates
- Increased word-of-mouth
- And similar revenue-centric metrics.[16]

In Forrester's six-year study period, loyalty programs based on a credible customer focus drove revenue increases of $3 billion for telecom companies, $2 billion across the airlines, and $1 billion for hotel chains, to name three in the study. These are impressive revenue numbers for a metric once considered soft and fluffy.

When brands are seen as genuinely responsible corporate citizens, people take pride in following the brands on social channels, actively showing a loyalty to these brands. A confirming brand study, made by social business authority Jay Baer of Convince & Convert, found that 53% of Americans who follow brands socially are demonstrably more loyal to those brands.[17]

It just makes sense.

(Social credibility drives) bottom line performance

Companies committed to a credible customer experience are also outperforming on bottom-line measures such as stock market valuation. According to a Watermark Consulting analysis of stock performance from 2007 to 2012:[18]

- Customer-focused companies chalked up 43% total returns versus 14.5% for the S&P Index.
- Companies that lacked credible customer experiences lagged far behind the market with negative 33.9% returns.[19]

---

16 Maxi Schmidt-Subramanian, Forrester Research, "The Business Impact of Customer Experience, 2013," June 10, 2013 (https://www.forrester.com/The+Business+Impact+Of+Customer+Experience+2013/fulltext/-/E-RES97721?objectid=RES97721)

17 http://www.convinceandconvert.com/social-media-research/53-percent-of-americans-who-follow-brands-in-social-are-more-loyal-to-those-brands/

18 https://www.forrester.com/How+Customer+Experience+Impacts+Company+Stock+Performance/-/E-PRE10229

19 J. Picoult, Watermark Consulting, "The Watermark Consulting 2013 Customer Experience ROI Study," April 2, 2013 (http://www.watermarkconsult.net/blog/2013/04/02/the-watermark-consulting-2013-customer-experience-roi-study)

This completes the loop of five mission-critical KPIs driven by social credibility, and measurable as Return on (Social) Investment. And we know for certain...

If you are not delivering on these KPIs, your competitors are!

No doubt you have some level of interest or involvement in social business. Otherwise you wouldn't be reading this book. But being involved and REALLY knowing how to excel in social business are two different kettles of fish.

As a successful company you need to be delivering on all five mission-critical KPIs that drive social credibility, otherwise your competitors can step in to poach your customers and tie your prospects into social relationships you can't break open.

Going forward, companies that are not strategically increasing social business traffic and conversions will increasingly find the marketplace treating them as an afterthought.

Customers, prospects, partners, business alliances – they'll all be suspect of companies that are not actively positioning as socially credible players. Companies that do not take social business seriously may in fact be contributing – often unwittingly – to the starkest corporate statistic of all: The average lifespan of today's enterprise is plunging.

Plunging faster by the year.

Analysts at Deloitte have studied the "topple rate" – the measure of how fast companies forfeit their lead positions in their industries.[20] This topple rate has increased by almost 40% since 1965, and the tenure of companies on the S&P 500 has fallen from 75 years in 1937 to just 18 years today.

Companies are rising up and falling quicker due in large part to their inability to keep pace with rapidly changing technologies.

When confronted with "big changes" to the status quo, companies typically react by first trying to improve or automate their existing processes,

---

20 https://www2.deloitte.com/insights/us/en/topics/strategy/shift-index.html

hoping that will delay the reaper. Instead they should now be assessing their business models . . . since an entire new wave of disruptive startups are not only challenging industries, they are also threatening to eliminate many companies altogether.

These threats aren't hype. As the daily headlines show us, the challenges are raw and real. But there are ways businesses can respond to be Futureproof.

Media influencer, Jeff Jarvis famously stated, *"Print is where words go to die"* and the *San Francisco Chronicle* was the epitome of a legacy major metropolitan newspaper, standing by while the digital revolution ate its lunch. Located just a few blocks from Twitter's HQ, the *Chronicle's* newsroom could have been the movie set for *His Girl Friday* or *All The President's Men* with a few more computers littered about.

But then their circulation figures plummeted 50%.

They responded by launching . . . a technology incubator.

Audrey Cooper, the first female managing editor in the paper's 152-year history, cooked up the idea. She told MediaShift writer Rachele Kanigel:

> "We hope to eventually get to the point where instead of being a newspaper company that produces websites, we think of ourselves as a digital company that also produces a newspaper."[21]

Ms. Cooper put together an offsite boot camp for her reporters. She shock-trained them in social business techniques. She went all-in on aligning with the digital future in order to save the *Chronicle* from extinction.

Most impressively, Ms. Cooper understood the awesome innovating power of today's technologies. By experimenting with drone photography, trying crowdfunding and creating her own incubator, she tapped the DNA of digital. She took hold of today's highly networked technologies and turned them into a force multiplier for the *Chronicle,* leaning into the disruption rather than fleeing it. Thanks to her efforts, the *Chronicle* is on a more profitable path today.

---

21 http://mediashift.org/2014/01/sf-chronicle-launches-incubator-2/

Another of our clients, BNP Paribas is a French multinational bank that has been running a rather hip media campaign, with the tagline:

IN A CHANGING WORLD,
BY THE TIME YOU MASTER THE GAME,
THE RULES HAVE CHANGED.

BNP Paribas is positioning itself as the bank for a rapidly changing world, a bank that can help companies adapt to constantly fluctuating environments, turning change into opportunity.

This kind of positioning should stead the bank well in a time of disruptive change and keep it relevant as other enterprises fall away.

This positioning – which BNP Paribas executed across print, broadcast and online mediums – is also an excellent example of how marketing strategies are evolving dramatically. By having it on employees' LinkedIn profiles, they took it that one step further; enabling the message to be owned by employees instead of it only remaining a corporate message.

Old-time marketing no longer delivers the goods

Before we get started on marketing, please don't let us refer to what happened to Cambridge Analytica[22]. And of course, GDPR[23] has had a significant impact on all marketing activities.

At the same time, let's just say it because it feels good:

The cold call is dead. May it RIP, with IBM's preference study indicating that 97% of cold calls simply don't work.[24] Sure, there are still unscrupulous marketers who pester and annoy consumers with their robodialers, presumably on the theory that a 3% success rate is worth trying. But the financial returns for cold calling have turned icy. More so as the same study also revealed that 75% of people are more likely to use social media in their future purchasing decisions.. Not only cold calls, but the earliest forms of "online marketing" are also losing appeal as social business

---

22 https://en.wikipedia.org/wiki/Cambridge_Analytica
23 https://en.wikipedia.org/wiki/General_Data_Protection_Regulation
24 https://leighfarnell.com/research-cold-calling-sales/

marketing ascends. General brand advertising works well enough online. But companies that try to slam interruptive advertising down the throats of online consumers are finding that the numbers seldom pencil out. Specifically:

- Consumers are even more adept at tuning-out online ads than offline.
- Search engine marketing has been overtaken by Google's own advertising.
- Email messaging doesn't work until after the customer is on board.

So marketers are casting their nets – socially.

One approach builds "social engagement" right into a marketing campaign, as an integral component. Another approach makes "social business credibility" a campaign all its own.

Both approaches are driven by the foremost B2B statistics of our time, from the research firm IDC (Fig. 1.5):[25]

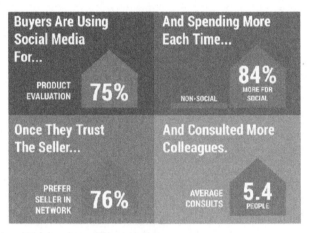

Fig. 1.5 The internet truly has changed the way we buy

Both consumers and B2B buyers now enjoy near perfect access to information through social media's many channels. As a result:

- Most of the purchasing process is complete before a salesperson becomes involved.
- Most of a purchasing decision is informed by social media, particularly LinkedIn, Facebook, and Twitter.

25 https://business.linkedin.com/content/dam/business/sales-solutions/global/en_US/c/pdfs/idc-wp-247829.pdf

- B2B buyers who use social media for buying support have bigger budgets, and make more frequent purchases, than buyers who do not use social media.
- Numerous experts can be, and often are, drawn into a buying decision and their online advice and opinions are widely shared.

In short, consumers have gained the firm upper hand in the purchasing dynamic. These consumers:

- Fully expect to go searching for, and to receive, relevant interactions on the social business channels.
- Have the means and desire to broadcast their approval and disapproval using social media.
- Are quite willing to switch vendors if they think they may snag a better deal.

In their studies of this dynamic and its potential staying power, the analysts at Accenture concluded:

> "Digital channels will continue to outpace traditional channels such as in-store or print advertising as go-to resources."[26]

Path to our social business future

This transition to the networked social business future has become a top priority for every company seeking a competitive edge in today's marketplace.

But the process of reinventing a company is no small feat, and there is so much to do – while still running the business. So it's a question of where to focus first, and what to prioritize moving forward.

Often the biggest hurdle is the team itself.

As Clayton Christensen catalogued so ably in the original bible of modern business, *The Innovators Dilemma*, the things that got you here won't allow you to go there.

---

26 Accenture Interactive, "Turbulence for the CMO: Charting a Path for the Seamless Customer Experience," May 2013

A team that is highly skilled in the existing business model will be committed to it and not the best at adopting a new business model, however urgent the need.

But fortunately the changes required by social business are not onerous – because quite frankly, business has always been social. This is true for the obvious reason that people are involved. Even if you make a specialty lubricant and sell it based on a 100-page request for proposal (RFP), you are still selling to people.

Social people, by any definition.

So it's not really a matter of reinventing the organization, but of understanding how the human elements of the organization can be organized around principles of social credibility using the very best social technologies. To begin:

1. You need a roadmap brief.
2. You need to have a well-defined starting point.

First, the broad strokes of a social business roadmap:

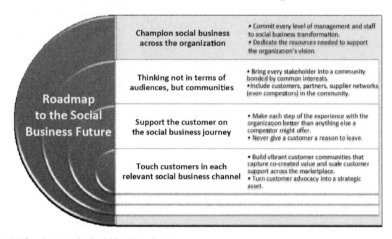

Fig. 1.6 Roadmap to the Social Business Future

Fig. 1.6 offers a condensed view of the journey every social business takes, a journey that can take several years to achieve at scale. Fortunately, it is possible to complete this entire journey from a single, well-defined starting point. An Archimedean lever to move your organization into an entire world of social business opportunity.

Lifting Your Organization: The Lever is LinkedIn

What's the first thing we do when meeting someone in business? Look them up on LinkedIn, right? We all do this.

Yet most people still spend less time reading and comparing their own LinkedIn Profile than they do reading and comparing labels at the supermarket...

Why is this? Where's the disconnect, when a Harvard study has clearly quantified the ways in which people interact with companies now:[27]

> *"Customers are, on average, 37% of the way through a purchase process by the time they reach the solution-definition stage, and 57% of the way through the process before they engage with supplier sales reps."*

And according to SiriusDecisions[28], the latter has gone up to 67% lately.

LinkedIn is simply the most effective channel and platform for advancing the modern social business. See Fig. 1.7 for a summary of the global capabilities LinkedIn delivers; then answer the question posed...

Spending 17.5 billion hours of time...

Fig. 1.7 Social business activity on LinkedIn

27 https://hbr.org/2015/03/making-the-consensus-sale
28 Webcast: www.brainshark.com/siriusdecisions/Marketing_Organization_2017

Is your business harnessing your fair (or unfair) share of all this social business activity? Do you REALLY know?

LinkedIn is the modern agora, only on a global scale. There has never been a single place where professionals from literally every global industry are congregating in the same place at once.

It doesn't matter whether you want to use LinkedIn to find sales prospects, get a job, recruit new employees, forge and maintain connections, or build your online and physical presence. There are ways to achieve all of these goals on LinkedIn.

The other big online networks – Twitter, Facebook, and Google+ specifically – are also useful social business channels. But Step 1, 2, and 3 for every serious organization *of any size* is LinkedIn, LinkedIn, and LinkedIn.

This has been true since we wrote the first edition of *How To REALLY Use LinkedIn* back in 2009, though LinkedIn has come a long way since then in the value it provides. (We believe we have, too).

We now have 250,000+ copies in print, making it the world's bestselling book on social business. Along the way, we've trained 65,000+ professionals in 10 languages on four continents based on the strategies in *How To REALLY Use LinkedIn*.

In this 3rd edition, the book has been updated with all the important changes on the LinkedIn platform as well as looking to where LinkedIn is headed, and to help open up new opportunities for professionals.

How LinkedIn helps you and your organization today

Here is a summary of LinkedIn strategies that can be applied to any organization.

In the Fig. 1.8 matrix, you see that there are three kinds of LinkedIn strategies that can be pursued (passive, active, and proactive) and five levels of the organization that can be involved (the organization itself, senior management, the sales team, HR and recruiters, and the rest of the team).

	PASSIVE STRATEGIES	ACTIVE STRATEGIES	PROACTIVE STRATEGIES
Organization	**Branding, Job Openings & Followers** ◎ Company Profile ◎ Showcase Pages ◎ Career Pages	**Branding, Ads, Job Posts, Interaction** ◎ Marketing Solutions (fee) ◎ Sales Solutions (fee) ◎ Talent Solutions (fee) ◎ Company Status Updates	**Market, Hire, Sell:** ◎ Marketing Solutions (fee) ◎ Sales Solutions (fee) ◎ Talent Solutions (fee)
CEO, Managers	**Branding & Lead Generation** ◎ Personal Profile ◎ Rich Media	**Branding, Visibility, Interaction** ◎ Status Updates ◎ Influencer Program	**Find:** ◎ See below (all co-workers)
Salespeople	**= All Co-workers +** ◎ Case Studies ◎ Targeted Content	**= All Co-workers +** ◎ Follow Prospects & Companies ◎ Sales Navigator (fee)	**= All Co-workers +** ◎ Sales Navigator (fee)
Recruiters	**= All Co-workers +** ◎ Talent Brand ◎ Targeted Content	**= All Co-workers +** ◎ Recruiter (fee) ◎ LinkedIn Referral	**= All Co-workers +** ◎ Recruiter (fee) ◎ Build Talent Pipeline
All Co-workers	**Branding & Lead Generation** ◎ Personal Profile ◎ Rich Media + call-to-action	**Branding, Visibility, Interaction** ◎ Group Managers (internal & external + alumni Groups) ◎ Active member of internal and external Groups ◎ Content contribution ◎ Status Updates & Share information ◎ Events preparation and follow up	**Find:** ◎ New customers ◎ New employees ◎ New partners ◎ New suppliers ◎ Project members ◎ Internal and external expertise

Fig. 1.8 LinkedIn Strategy Matrix for Organizations

> There are great benefits to be gained at each level of the matrix, with often the greatest benefit coming from the proactive behavior of all co-workers.

It is in the proactive strategies that the entire team takes that LinkedIn can be leveraged most powerfully to move the organization's social business ahead.

We discuss these strategies in depth ahead. But first, since it matters greatly...

What does the future hold for LinkedIn?

The social business sector is fast moving. Staying relevant and vital is a constant challenge for every company, and LinkedIn is no different.

LinkedIn is constantly upgrading the platform, fixing weaknesses, adding new tools to meet emerging professional needs, acquiring new companies to remain vital and continue expanding CEO Jeff Weiner's vision of becoming an "economic graph"[29] of the world's professionals.

LinkedIn's forte at door opening – business networking – is the starting point but far from insufficient for achieving the economic graph. LinkedIn aims to do much more than bring people together. The Sunnyvale (ex-Mountain View) company also wants to help their members obtain the skillsets needed to land jobs.

So in 2015, LinkedIn purchased Lynda.com to address this larger vision. Lynda is a storied learning platform that offers more than 100,000 training videos by subscription. It's self-paced, focused learning related to business, technology, software and creative skills.

With the integration of Lynda, now being rebranded as LinkedIn Learning[30], it becomes easier for HR officers and recruiters to source properly credentialed and trained candidates on LinkedIn, saving time over the more traditional winnowing process.

As Scredible CEO Colin Lucas-Mudd told *Personnel Today* when the Lynda acquisition was announced:

> *"With this move LinkedIn can use its data and expert knowledge to effect real change in the continuing education of its professional base . . . the combined products we can expect to see have the potential to deliver better qualified and prepared candidates, while reducing investment in wasted screening and interviews."*[31]

Even prior to Lynda, LinkedIn was the go-to source for recruiters looking to find top candidates, with 97% of US recruiters onboard.[32]

But as anyone involved in hiring knows, it's often common to run into "nearly perfect" job candidates. These candidates may have the experience. They may be a good cultural fit. But they lack one crucial bit of knowledge required for the job. Now with LinkedIn Learning, LinkedIn can proactively communicate with members and tell them what courses or knowledge would be ideal for them in order to obtain a particular job.

29   https://www.youtube.com/watch?v=M86okhXTwfU
30   https://www.linkedin.com/learning/
31   http://www.personneltoday.com/hr/e-learning-linkedin-buys-lynda-biggest-acquisition-date/
32   https://www.bullhorn.com/news-and-press/press-releases/recruiters-still-not-leveraging-facebook-social-recruiting-candidates/

LinkedIn can improve this functionality even more with the addition of adaptive training modules that deliver just the precisely calibrated bits of training that a member needs, just when needed, in the learning style that works best.

This, we believe, is coming.

Now let's preview the levels you rise through, with the LinkedIn lever, to social business success...

Rising up to Social Business Leadership

We first began training people in social networking in 2004. "Networking Coach" was one of the brands back then, because the real transformation we could see coming was the move from a pipeline–oriented business model to a networking–centric business model.

But the concepts that we and other training leaders shared then were little different from today. Our challenge has always been to break down something that looks simple, but is not, into something that is simple.

On its face, social business looks like child's play – be social, make friends; who didn't learn that in grade school?!

But social business is far from easy to master in this day and age and that is because of this day and age. There are so many inputs, as we know, so our daily routines become a process of elimination, to somehow sift through the torrents of inputs to get to the core of what matters most. That is the task we all face.

To help, we've organized the rise to social business leadership into to a simple pyramid schema, and a colorful one at that (if you are reading on a screen:)

This Social Business Capability Maturity Model™ (Fig. 1.9) illustrates in a simple graphic what an organization must go through to build up to a position of social business leadership.

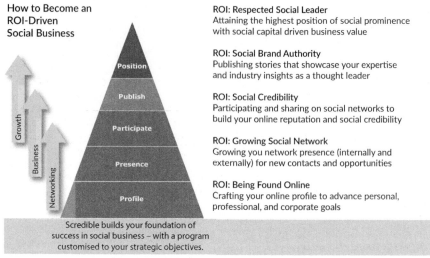

How to Become an
ROI-Driven
Social Business

ROI: Respected Social Leader
Attaining the highest position of social prominence
with social capital driven business value

ROI: Social Brand Authority
Publishing stories that showcase your expertise
and industry insights as a thought leader

ROI: Social Credibility
Participating and sharing on social networks to
build your online reputation and social credibility

ROI: Growing Social Network
Growing you network presence (internally and
externally) for new contacts and opportunities

ROI: Being Found Online
Crafting your online profile to advance personal,
professional, and corporate goals

Scredible builds your foundation of
success in social business – with a program
customised to your strategic objectives.

Fig. 1.9 Social Business Capability Maturity Model

We'll summarize the rise to the top, and develop it in detail in chapters to come. As we proceed, you will get a clear idea of what level you and your organization have already attained on the pyramid.

For those just starting out at the first level, it's all about the Profile.

PROFILE > ROI > Being Found Online

Crafting a Profile that advances personal, professional, and corporate goals.

The first step in social business is to build a Profile of yourself on LinkedIn, as well as on other social networks – depending on your business interests. Sounds easy enough, and it is.

But creating a professional-looking StandOut Profile that's so distinctive it grabs attention – that is not so easy.

Crafting a StandOut Profile is a game of margins. Add the right data to one section of your Profile, and the right rich media to another section, and soon you've created a margin of difference for yourself. It's essential to find a way to StandOut, to be found for your expertise, to showcase your projects, to advance your cause and to accomplish your business goals. This is our focus in Chapter 4.

Another way of looking at your Profile is:
- What is the cost of not being found among the 178 million daily searches?
- If people are looking for you, but don't find a reason to stop at your Profile, what happens next?

Most people will continue on and find your competitor's Profile. Either way, the opportunity is lost!

PRESENCE > ROI > Growing Social Network

Growing your network presence for new contacts and opportunities.

With your Profile optimized, people will find you, and reach out to you. It will begin to happen right away, amazingly, due to the sheer scale of LinkedIn, and then it will grow over time at a pace you will learn to manage.

A growing network presence will benefit you outside of your company, and inside as well. Many people are shocked at how much they learn about their co-workers from browsing LinkedIn.

This process of growing your network is the crucial second level of the pyramid. Without this, no further progress can be made. This can be the most exciting level, because of all the new contacts and opportunities that come. We will be exploring this in detail in Chapter 4.

PARTICIPATE > ROI > Social Credibility

Participating on social networks to build your social credibility.

With a profile and presence, you are set up to begin participating intelligently in the global social conversation and making an impact that you can track and measure.

At this level, you are posting articles about subjects surrounding your expertise, in ways that are meaningful to your clients and customers.

You are showing up in Google search results, gaining a social ranking score, and receiving a noticeable increase in requests to connect with current colleagues, new client prospects, old college chums – some of immediate value, some you're not so sure about.

As you engage and find shared interests with your connections, you are organically building your social credibility – the calling card of social business.

Importantly, you are building this credibility in communities of people who share common interests. You are not building audiences. That marketing language is increasingly dated. There are no audiences in social business – only communities. Audiences are one-way concepts. You speak, they listen or read passively. No more. Not even TEDtalks has audiences; they have people who come together as a community to share with thought leaders. In an interactive way. A social way.

This third level of the Social Business Capability Maturity Model is the highest level that most people in the company attain. There is great benefit to both individuals and the company at this level.

But some will have the ambition and business needed to continue to...

PUBLISH > ROI > Social Brand Authority

Publishing stories that showcase your expertise as a thought leader.

At this fourth level you move into the exalted ranks, the 5% of LinkedIn users who are authoring articles to post to their own Profiles, and to LinkedIn. These articles have the potential to reach broad numbers.

This is how you and your organization can impact your domain, deepen your relationships with your communities, showcase the thought leadership of your executives, and successfully do so, rather inexpensively. These strategies are outlined in Chapter 5.

POSITION > ROI > Respected Social Leader

Attaining the highest position of social prominence, driving business value.

In the most capable social businesses, the CEO has attained this top level – since the CEO is the face of the organization and most visible in shepherding and driving its business value. But others in the organization can and should aim for this level, as well. And having reached it, the people in your industry look to you for thought leadership and see you, correctly, as a respected social leader.

Return on (Social) Investment increases on up the pyramid

As you rise in the Social Business Capability Maturity Model, the opportunities for your organization increase – at first incrementally, then exponentially with best practice execution. Here is a summary of opportunities we'll unfold in case studies and tutorials in coming chapters.

Revenue Opportunities
- Shortens the buying cycle from greater customer engagement.
- Increases the average order size from greater customer approval.
- Introduces company's product to new communities from customer pass-along.

Sales Opportunities
- Better qualifies communities with deeper and broader segmentation capabilities.
- Generates more leads deeper in the sales funnel from tailored messaging.
- Reaches more people with marketing messages because of lower cost-per-action (CPA).

Engagement Opportunities
- Improves customer loyalty by encouraging positive word of mouth.
- Creates a core of influencers who extend brand recognition.
- Turns critics into advocates, using tailored messaging.

Cost-saving Opportunities
- Lower marketing costs from higher uptake and organic reach.
- Lowers customer service costs from efficient communications.
- Streamlines internal messaging for productivity gains.

Fig. 1.10 Opportunities from the Rise to Social Business Leadership

Here's to the Change Makers!

What we've noticed over the years is that for companies to see true transformation into social businesses, or even just making a shift from the "dark ages" to realizing they have to adapt, this often comes down to someone driving that change. That is why this book is dedicated to those folks who are brave enough to step up and take on board that challenge.

If you're reading this book, then it's likely you're someone who has that capacity to become (or continue being) the catalyst to inspire transformation with your organization. If this is you, then the next chapter will identify some of the challenges you're up against, but more importantly, we'll share how you can tackle them.

Let's get moving.

SOCIAL BUSINESS IMPLEMENTATION – MISTAKES AND CONSEQUENCES

"Vision without strategy is hallucination."
Gino Wickman, Traction Author.

From our experience of working with such a depth and breadth of medium-to corporate-sized companies, we've seen the full spectrum of what Change Makers are up against when it comes to them wanting to take advantage of social business strategies. As well as seeing the challenges, we've also worked with Change Makers who have overcome their internal and often political barriers to implement widespread roll-out. On numerous occasions, we've seen such depth of buy-in that social business training is rolled out across thousands of staff and adopted at high levels.

On one occasion, we worked with a client that had over 15 regions across Europe who all had separate LinkedIn and social selling agendas. There were pockets of companies doing things and other regions that were averse to it and not seeing the value at all. What we'll be sharing in this chapter is how we were able to get alignment throughout the different regions and cultures. We'll also share how the support of the leadership was secured so that support for wide-scale rollout across their 3,000+ sales staff was secured. By applying the principles that we learned in previous large scale engagements, we were able to replicate these in this project.

Dead Projects

In our opinion, this chapter is the most important of all the chapters in this book. So much time, energy and resources are wasted in the corporate world working on dead projects.

You know the type…

You have dozens of people from different departments and suppliers all working on something over months (or sometimes years) and the project was doomed to fail from the beginning. It consumes resources, often into the tens, hundreds, thousands or even millions. It becomes a black hole on people's CVs, not to mention the acceleration of grey hairs for most people involved.

So, if you're in this camp when it comes to your LinkedIn, social business or digital implementation campaigns, then we hope that this section of the book will help you navigate the territory so you can avoid the land mines and bring your strategy to life.

Just a quick note before we jump into it… when it comes to being a social business, there are different levels to consider. Some companies have a B2C angle, others have a B2B side of the business. A third group have both. Getting an overall social business strategy in place means that you're able to engage with your end users and build strong brand credibility and loyalty with them (B2C). However, the training that's most frequently deployed by us comes in the form of training businesses to engage with other businesses (B2B). For the purpose of this chapter, this is the type of training that we'll be referring to.

Problems & Implications of Implementation

We've identified six core problems when it comes down to poor implementation.

1. No Social Business Strategy

Too often we've seen companies turning a blind eye to social media and not appreciating the value it has for their organization. As we shared in the previous chapter, this is dangerous as it results in them missing the point that it's about engaging with their buyers, talent and community, and meeting them where they are at now.

This results in implementers doing a tick box exercise. In an attempt to show they are doing something, they get someone lower level to search around for a supplier to run a 60 minute workshop for their 100 staff with expectations that they'll be experts by the end. At the same time, this same mandate has been passed down across one or multiple departments from the same company as they're doing the same tick box exercise. However, because they're doing this as a formality, each training session ends up with similarly unimpressive outcomes.

The root cause is that there is no organization-wide direction or strategy, which involves multiple departments. The net impact is that divisions, leaders and managers end up creating their siloed projects. They progress with their project until somewhere along the line, they come across another team who's been applying the same approach. This is where it becomes interesting from an outsider's perspective and it really shines the light on the culture of the organization.

Organizations with a collaborative approach find ways to work together and bring greater alignment, even if that means delaying their projects for the greater cause. Organizations with a bureaucratic and political culture find ways to expedite their projects at the others' demise, some steal ideas to include in their training or even sabotage the projects of their competitors – sorry, colleagues.

Even if it doesn't get this dramatic, the splintered effect of a lack of unified strategy causes untold amounts of wasted time, resources and energy as people start projects that don't get completed or they recreate the wheel multiple times. Where did we hear that before…

2. Lack of Internal Structure

The word "silo" has become an institutionalized term in the corporate world. It is really short for, *"we're bloody ignorant of what others are doing and because we couldn't be bothered to take the time to find out, we'll just crack on doing what we do. And, then we'll act surprised, upset and even angry when we find out other departments were doubling up on our activities, or could have helped us in some way."*

Left Hand / Right Hand Syndrome

A classic case of siloed organizations comes down to the fact that the left hand doesn't know what the right hand is doing. A simple question like "Who is managing your LinkedIn Company Page?" remains unanswered. All of this results in departments being at odds with each other, departments and regions being marginalized and an overall lack of transparency, which leads to a fragmented social strategy. This creates friction between departments and even the adoption of new approaches and technologies that impede future implementation.

When there are poor internal structures, it will cause communication flow issues between people and departments. If you're looking to create a social business, at the heart of it all is having different departments working collaboratively. If your systems and structures don't allow for free-flowing information, then this will exacerbate the situation and cause more friction and less flow between key stakeholders.

3. No Leadership Buy-in

One of the most prevalent resistors to change that we've encountered over the years has come down to leaders not understanding social media and not being aware of the impact of their communication biases. Often when you don't understand topics and you have a lot on your plate, you push those items to the bottom of the list. It's not until they are brought to the surface and you are given an open forum to raise your questions and voice your concerns, that you can begin to understand that topic better.

This is what we've experienced countless times. In the early years of helping C-suite leaders of billion dollar brands, our trainers would spend days in board rooms raising the awareness of leaders so they understood what social media meant to them and their companies. We would help them understand how the digitally connected world now wants to engage with their company, find out who their manager would be, what the purpose of the company is and give them a glasshouse experience of peeking into their organization, its culture, products and services.

Once leaders finally realized that the world has changed and the way they used to do business has shifted, it was like the elephant in the room could finally leave. They would realize that just because they didn't understand why people need to view someone's LinkedIn profile before their meeting, or look up their Tweets, or read their blogs or even check out their company Snapchat feed, these are now important aspects to how the ecosphere of people in their brand community now want to engage with them.

The trump card always came down to this... If prospects, talent and customers want to interact with your brand through these mediums, but they can't, what does it mean? What does it tell them about the organization? Some dare to even ask if that company still exists!

In any case, they go to a brand that does!

Once leaders connect how social media is linked to sales, recruitment, customer service and even how they are perceived as a leader, the penny drops.

However, until you reach that moment of realization, you're pushing it uphill. The consequences of this are quite dire. This would lead to leaders not taking part in or supporting the social projects and this lack of support would show up in them having poor LinkedIn profiles or no profile at all. It meant that they would push the project down to a department and make them responsible without involving other key players, which further fuels the poor structure syndrome we just explored.

We often see someone who's been lumped with a project and doing their best to enrol others, but because there isn't C-suite support others would put it much lower on their to-do lists. Some budget would be made available to run training for a certain group, but in some ways it ends up just being a box-ticking exercise. As you can imagine, the results of the training are watered down, especially once teams realize the manager isn't taking an active role and their CEO doesn't even have a LinkedIn profile.

We are sure you can see where this is headed...

Teams learn some skills, but due to a lack of top-down prioritization there would be minimal changes in behaviour. Time is limited outside of the training sessions and there isn't support internally to spend the time on the areas that would bring change elsewhere. As we have come across this issue repeatedly, it has forced us to make the workshops as practical as possible so that people will make changes and take actions in real time to see results and give them motivation to continue. However, unless there's reinforcement outside of the training room, the level of progress isn't comparable to when there is.

The worst impact of all of this is that leaders would then become sceptical about LinkedIn, employer branding, social selling and social recruiting strategies because they've 'tried that before and it didn't work'. This creates a culturally negative perception that forms barriers for future leaders who want to take up this battle. But anyone with any sense of objective reality could look at this situation and realize it was doomed to fail even before it began. In these situations, the question has to be asked, why did they bother flogging the dead horse in the first place?

This is highlighted by a client of ours, Bradley Hancock, Head of Digital at Old Mutual Global Investors:

"At various stages throughout my career, I've seen digital and social business projects given the bare minimum level of attention, just enough to suffice the board and let them know something's being done in that space. It has never played out as a successful strategy. In every one of the examples I can think of, every project failed to reach a level where it achieved the goal of moving the needle and getting staff members embracing social and digital strategies so that there is a tangible uplift from it.

That's why at the heart of what I do, is work with Senior Leaders to get them on board and support any initiatives I'm going to roll out. If I don't do that, then I may as well not even bother starting the project in the first place.

Really Connect and I are on the same page with this, and that's why I constantly work with them on my projects as they consistently get leaders, teams and co-workers singing from the same hymn sheet and their projects just work. My only advice would be, if you're going to roll this type of project out, get everyone on board, especially your leadership team."

4. Silo City – Marketing & Sales/HR Competing not Collaborating

We come from a small business background. And in that environment, you don't have the luxury of wasting resources. If you waste them you'll soon be out of business. You must sweat every asset as much as you possibly can. What we observed in the corporate world is that teams of people work on projects and due to the siloed nature of their organization, or because departments compete against each other and don't want to share best practices, digital assets are created, but sit somewhere dormant. It's like the best kept secret!

This often results in situations such as marketing creating content for sales people to use, but the sales people don't know those assets exist. So, they resort to traditional means of sales tactics. Over time, this creates a carcinogenic relationship between sales and marketing where they become spiteful and resentful of each other. Sales people say, "Marketing doesn't produce good enough leads or content for us to leverage". Marketing teams say, "Why do we bother creating stuff for sales when they don't use it anyway?".

To whatever degree this plays out in any company, it's not good.

The net impact is that there's wasted energy, time and resources. Constant duplication of activities and collateral, which leads to results and targets not being achieved.

That's bad enough, however, as there's not a symbiotic and fluid relationship where constructive feedback is passed back and forth, each department stays isolated and they perpetuate the production of inadequate content. This happens across different departments, but let's stick with the current example. What this typically looks like is the following...

Sales will create a campaign focused on outreach to new or existing clients to make them aware of a new product. To get best results from a socially-led campaign like this, you need to engage with content and insights which educate prospects that they have a problem they weren't aware of. However, marketing will go off and create features-led content about how great their new widget is and use complex language that doesn't mean much to anyone outside the company. If the sales team is aware of it, they'll use it, but it won't land with impact and the campaign is seen as a failure.

This is totally avoidable! We'll explore how in the next section.

5. Ad Hoc Training

This pretty much says what it does on the tin. We won't delve into this too much further as the nub of the problem has been highlighted in point 3 just covered.

What we will expand on, is that a mistake leaders often make when it comes to social or digital skills training is the lack of appreciation of what it takes to learn these new skills. When it comes to digital it's not just new skills, it's new behaviors which means breaking old habits and forming new ones.

For these reasons, leaders often underestimate the fears and concerns people have when it comes to getting them to improve their profile and stick their head above the parapet and actually take a stance on something. For many, this is the first time they're posting, commenting or sharing. This is why having a joined up strategy is essential. These people need positive reinforcement from others, especially their leaders, that this is OK to do.

So, when training is done in isolation or without accountability support of their managers and leaders, then the training becomes forgotten soon after it's completed.

If you're delivering this type of training, for the sake of people's sanity (and your own), don't provide ad hoc training; it's best to enrol your senior leaders first. We'll share more on this soon.

6. Not Tracking or Measuring

It is fair to say that this can be a tricky beast to deal with. But as we covered in the opening chapter, it's well worth tackling, as the results are immense. As we shared in Forrester's six-year study, billions of dollars were attributed from brand loyalty in the airline, telecoms and hotel industries. This is great on the B2C side of the business, but how do you get those types of results and even track them from the B2B side of the business?

This is where it becomes a little challenging, but there are simple and advanced ways of doing it.

Up until recently, tracking tangible results from sales and recruiter social activity is a bit like having two people running around a conference of 1,000 people asking them for their feedback of the conference whilst using a clip board and pen. Times have improved, however, the biggest issues when it comes to tracking results stem from three core aspects:
1. Culture
2. Technology
3. Accountability.

Culture

It's amazing how many large corporations have a culture of not actively reporting on results. Many companies will track the end metric of revenue generated, however, they aren't asking their sales people to track progress on leads or even where their leads sources come from.

Often they're relying on the credibility of their brand. Or their systems are old and have become overly complicated so tracking these types of numbers is difficult. Instead they revert to tracking the bare minimum. However it plays out, when there is a culture of not tracking the activity that leads to results, it's difficult to put in place measurements. People aren't use to it and it requires shifting something much bigger and outside the scope of the project.

Technology

If running a small business is like driving a speed boat in terms of how nimbly you can adapt to change and shift direction, then many corporates are comparable to a 3,000 person cruise liner that needs hundreds of kilometers to change direction. If you then try to change the control panel the captain uses to initiate that change of direction, that's what it's like when asking some corporates to use technology to track their sales team's or recruiter's results.

Many companies suffer from legacy technologies that have had numerous applications built to solve particular problems that have crept up over the years. The long term impact to this patchwork-type approach is that many leaders would rather swallow a mouthful of nails than tackle using their technology to track their results, so they revert to basic statistics like the Social Selling Index (SSI). Although this is basic, it's still better than nothing.

Accountability

Even if you face challenges in culture and technology, if your company is committed to making this work, then you can make massive strides by implementing various forms of accountability into your training. Too often we see so much effort being put into setting up a training roll-out, yet what isn't considered is the actual follow-through and hand-holding for people outside of the training room. This is so essential as it's where the rubber hits the road. Without this, participants fall back into their normal daily routines before their new habits are formed.

The impact of this becomes quite obvious. The less people apply what's taught, the less people actually keep track of whatever results they are creating from the training and there's little or no tangible output from the training.

If your business suffers from one or more of these issues, then this will seriously hamper your ability to track the return on investment (ROI). This means you'll have less weight in the board room unless you can find a solution to this. The less you can demonstrate tangible returns, the more likely you'll be overlooked for that next promotion. Luckily for you, we'll be looking at how you can avoid this outcome in the next section.

If we objectively look at this list of problems and implications, we're sure you'll agree that some (or many) of these are faced frequently in your organization. These problems aren't exclusive to just LinkedIn or social business training; many will be relevant across broader training disciplines. The key to this is to be aware of what you're up against, so you can navigate your internal minefields to avoid the land mines and create a plan that takes these elements into consideration so you stand the best chance of success.

We're frequently shocked by the number of companies that don't treat the implementation of their social training programs with this level of fortitude and foresight. If there were more Change Makers who were willing to step up and take the time to zoom out from their 10-foot perspective and look at this from a 10,000-foot helicopter view and then create a plan, not only would their projects succeed, but their careers would thrive as well.

With that being said, let's jump into the next section as we tackle some of these issues to help you do just that! Develop an implementation plan to nail your social business training roll-out.

Social Training Implementation – How To Succeed

Let's delve into a methodology that we've created with proven results for large scale LinkedIn and social business training across many of our largest clients. In each case that we'll be citing, there were more than 20 offline and online training engagements for each client, across all levels of employees from C-suite to co-workers, typically across multiple regions like the UK and Europe, even North America, MENA and Asia. It involves the upskilling of anywhere between 1,500 to 7,000 people.

From this depth of experience we've been able to distil six core areas that must be addressed for successful organization-wide training implementation. Our belief is that it's better to slow things down and get things aligned instead of progressing and not addressing potentially catastrophic barriers that were predictable and avoidable in the first place. Sometimes slowing things down allows you to speed up in time. Remember the good old adage, "You must learn to fly before you can soar with eagles."

And, even if you do take more time to get a new piece of technology embedded or get alignment between departments, you can still progress some fronts, such as educating your board and winning their support.

So, let's jump into it, shall we?

1. Create an Organization-wide Social Business Strategy

Every organization is unique and comes with its own prickly special surprises. What is an obstacle in one company is a blazed pathway in another. So, as a super-diligent Change Maker who's looking to maximize impact as successfully as possible, before you embark on training up your team, take a full stock pile of all the elements that will work for and against you.

So we're clear on this, we mean a FULL list. Not just a list of things inside your remit of control, we're talking about that 10,000-foot helicopter view where you consider the full landscape with all its valleys, ravines, mountains, lakes and traffic jams. If you can see the full picture and can map out what you're up against, then you've got the making of a plan that's worthy of enrolling others.

This is the key part, enrolling others. This can also be the time-consuming part too if your stakeholders don't understand social media. This is where you may slow your project down so it adds another month, quarter or more to your timeline. However, if you don't get the right people to buy in, then they are likely to be the people that will block your progress just as you're about to accelerate.

This is paramount, especially if you have offices spread across different regions that need to get involved. We've done numerous training roll-outs across anywhere from three to 19 regions across Europe. Before we embark on the project, we get leaders from the different regions onside and get their input on what needs to be addressed in their local regions. Armed with this knowledge we're more informed, and most importantly, we have the support from the leaders in place as they have helped to develop the plan.

Who are the key stakeholders you need to get on board to help co-create the best social business strategy? And we are talking about formal and informal stakeholders…

2. Create Supportive Internal Structures

With your leadership plan in place, you can now start mapping out what structures will support your roll out and what structures are missing that will hinder it. When we say structure, this could be anything from business units and how they communicate, through to how clearly plans are created and communicated to managers and their teams. It can include an assessment of what technologies exist to support communication flow, who's in control of social channels, how reporting happens and which departments can contribute to populating social channels. This includes clarity about who needs to sign off on content before it can go out. How about compliancy? Has GDPR been properly implemented? Who is in charge?

Overall, the structures are the conduit that allows the flow of information to others who need to be involved. Poorly designed structures will have multiple departments replicating reports, poor communication flow and unclear boundaries over who and which departments can control the various social channels.

On the flip side, supportive structures streamline communication flow, have clear governance protocols (that support social media activity) in place that are visible and people are aware of them, teams work in collaboration to share best practices and there is clarity of objectives, outcomes and tracking of results. This stage involves delving into the next level of detail in your plan so you raise awareness of how teams, departments and regions can collaborate more effectively together, work with each other and share feedback on progress.

When we first started running LinkedIn training programs, often just sales or just recruitment would be involved in the design and delivery. But as social media has permeated into every area of business, that approach is just no longer acceptable. This is why we recommend to all of our clients that they form special project groups of leaders from different departments who all get together and share what's important for their respective areas of remit. We encourage sales and marketing teams to have regular meetings to share insights and feedback on what gets best engagement from posts and prospects' reactions to topics in sales meetings. Yes, we are talking about proper content planning here!

It's this collective flow of information between departments that begins to break down the silo nature of business, so everyone works towards unified goals.

3. Leadership Buy-In – Cultural Assessment

As you can see throughout this book so far, we're being quite critical of the siloed nature of organizations. To be fair though, we do understand how many companies came to be this way.

Although the flow of information from one division to another has always been important, up until recent years it was possible for departments to report into the CEO and live inside their bubble being focused on the objectives that were set for them. Digital transformation has radically accelerated the tools and technologies that increase communication and information flow between people and departments. It lifts the veil of secrecy of what teams are working on and it challenges the siloed nature norms that have become so institutionalized.

This can be problematic if the culture of that organization does not support this new era of openness and transparency. People will fight against it and leaders will lose positions if new approaches aren't upheld. There was one stage when we were in business and of the 20 clients we were working with at the time, over 10 of them were going through some form of 'restructure', which is the corporate code for…

"How we used to work is being disrupted and we're figuring out what the new landscape looks like."

In this new landscape, leaders must look to the future and appreciate that becoming a social business presents an opportunity to reinvent their brands and pioneer new channels to engage with their audiences. It creates the perfect atmosphere to do what only a few other organizations are doing.

Progressive-thinking C-suite leaders are seizing the opportunity to turn their faceless brands into personalities to engage with their communities. Here's an interesting exercise to illustrate the point. What are some of the most iconic brands you can think of?

Most people will think of Apple, Virgin, Tesla, Microsoft, Google, Amazon… Here's the more important question, why?

The answer is simple, each of these brands have a figurehead leading the charge! And the change! Each of the respective founders of these brands has made it their mission to create a public figure as they recognize that people form stronger bonds with people than they do with brands.

A company that knows this too well is called Dent Global. They have had over 3,000 small and medium sized companies go through their world-renowned business growth accelerator, Key Person of Influence. They identified this trend of people connecting with people versus brands back in 2010. Since then they have shown small business and corporate leaders how they can transform their stories and experiences into meaningful digital assets that connect and engage with their target audiences.

Doing this differentiates them from their competitors and positions them as an authority in the marketplace. Their clients have seen remarkable results, which is why they have expanded into seven cities over four continents at time of writing.

There are five key areas that leaders of brands and business units need to focus on. Mastering these five areas is proven to make your organization stand out in your crowded space. We invite you to take their Key Person of Influence Scorecard so you can assess your current level of influence. You'll then receive a detailed report giving you specific recommendations to improve in each area. You'll also get a free digital copy of their best-selling book, Key Person of Influence.

2. Social Business Implementation – Mistakes and Consequences

You can take the scorecard here (for FREE):
http://www.keypersonofinfluence.com/aff/uk/?p=a37260&w=kpiscorecard

Successful companies, now and in the future, will be the ones that lead with their personality, not their brand. When it comes to rolling out wide-scale LinkedIn and social business projects, there are three levels which your leadership team can play at. You must get them to the first level for your project to stand any sustainable chance of success.

Stage 1: Passive

At the very least you need to get your leaders to understand why this roll out is being done, help them understand the wider implications and how it touches different areas of the business, address any concerns they have and inspire them to get their support and backing. Without this minimum level of support you'll be struggling as it means you have resistors who will thwart any progress you make. Even if they don't go to the next level, but they are open and supportive, you can leverage that support to win over other department leaders and gain momentum.

Stage 2: Active

The next level is to get as many C-suite leaders to play a passive to active role. You may only get one or two in the beginning, but that can be enough to start with.

After running LinkedIn profile training workshops for well over 25,000 people, what we've learned is that when it comes to senior leaders, do as much of the heavy lifting as possible! We found that actually re-writing the LinkedIn profiles on their behalf gets the best results. Don't expect them to do it, otherwise the project will never get off the ground. Just take charge, write it for them.

We ended up developing a Profile Makeover service where we have a team of experts who will write up a profile for leaders as it was the most efficient and effective way.

If you'd like to know more about that service and to get tips on how to create an engaging LinkedIn profile, we've created a 22-Point LinkedIn Checklist for you. You can access that here: https://how-to-really-use-linkedin.com

61

Stage 3: Proactive

This is where you're asking them to stick their heads above the parapet and start creating a voice. In the early stages they might just share content from marketing or other thought leaders, however, in time as they become more engaged, you want your leaders sharing their thoughts and insights on the market they operate in.

As we shared, a number of our major clients have gone through radical transformation over the past 36 months. One of them in particular is known for their classic products, they are a household name and everyone knows them for what they've traditionally done. However, their industry has evolved massively and they have a new area of business and an evolving business model.

We have been working closely with them for several years and they have finally reached the realization that they need to turn their business unit leaders into key persons of influence, or thought leaders to give the brand greater recognition. As a result, they are now getting involved in online and offline conversations that are integral to shaping the new industries they're in. It's making their brand more personal and it's changing the culture of the organization (which once had draconian social media policies that basically castrated anyone for being socially active) as the staff are taking notice of their leaders sharing their views and improving their profiles.

This is exactly what proactive leaders of our new age should be doing. They have decades of experience in the market and they have invaluable insights to contribute. So, get as many of them on that band wagon as possible.

Understand that this will be a journey for most of them. If they haven't done this before, then be patient and encouraging. And don't forget to take as much of the legwork out of the process as possible for them.

If you need any help, you know where to find us!☺

4. Content, Collaboration & Campaigns

As addressed earlier, too much time, energy and resources are wasted in the needless divide between marketing and sales, and between marketing and most divisions that require content production. Traditionally, marketing and communications have been the source of information release from a company. So it's now mission critical for whatever departments require content that a consistent dialogue is formed and evolved.

Marketing and communications role has shifted from being the source of information, to supporting others to ensure the right themes, tone and messages are shared. As more and more companies embrace sharing tools that encourage employee advocacy, the role of marketing and communication is to work with staff at all levels so that they share appropriately, all within the brand guidelines, and minimize mistakes.

Social media is not about posting your job adverts, product features or brand messages (the classic mistakes many make). Yes, those things need to be factored into the equation, but if you lead with them it's a surefire way to lose the interest of your followers. Social media and the internet have shifted the ways in which people consume information. So, your messages that are released from a HR, Sales, Leadership or Customer Service perspective need to address topical pains, provide fresh insights and look to engage conversation.

The best way to do this is for your teams to form special project groups where key people from these divisions allocate roles, share feedback and results and explore ways to improve engagement. In this capacity, marketing aids the communication flow and it ensures that the sales people, recruiters and leaders are making use of the content that's being created for them. Having this consistent flow of communication ensures your messages change nimbly (despite how big your cruise liner is) to meet market interests and lead conversations.

A final note on this is that we've found with our clients, the more you can structure your content release behind campaigns, the better you can rally your team behind a meaningful project. Campaigns will have a start and finish date, so you can set targets and create a content plan that your teams can leverage. This often gets people focused and they're clear on their roles, compared to just an open sharing of information with no end date in mind.

We'd invite you to rally your sales and recruitment teams or even an employee advocacy project around a specific campaign and get everyone geared up to post and share content with clear objectives. You can then celebrate your successes at the end, whilst shifting behaviors and creating new habits in the process.

One of our major financial services companies applied a campaign as just outlined. Training was rolled out to a pilot group of 100 people. Within four weeks of the training being completed there was a 70% increase in confidence of using social platforms, 54% increase in content being shared by employees, network growth sizes increased by 22% and millions of pounds of new opportunities in the pipeline. This project then won the support for wider scale implementation across 1,500 employees. And for those who love the Social Selling Index (SSI score), it went up by 33% on average in less than 1 month.

5. Learning & Development Plan

Now that you have your social plan in place, you've navigated your internal landscape so you're clear what you're up against, you've enrolled your leaders so they're on board and you have special project groups in place to ensure communication flow is in place to assist the roll out, now you can begin training your team. With these bases in place, the level of clarity which you communicate inside the training room inspires certainty, authority and clarity of direction for them.

At this juncture, it's important that the training incorporates creating awareness for the wider plan and all the great work you've been doing behind the scenes. Share with the delegates your wider social business strategy, how departments will play together, the role that leaders will take (involve them in the training if possible), where content is coming from and then spell out the roll that they play in this. This will communicate volumes in terms of them following through.

Just as for leaders there are three levels they can play at, the same three levels are at play for all co-workers. These three levels map directly to the Social Business Capability Maturity Model (Fig. 2.1).

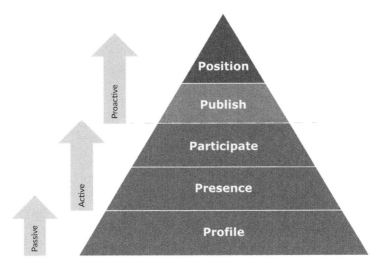

Fig. 2.1 Social Business Capability Maturity Mode

Stage 1: Passive

The biggest mistake people make with their LinkedIn (and pretty much all of their social) profile is they consider it a passive billboard instead of a proactive tool. And, most people's billboards are like one of those out of date, tatty old billboards that hasn't been updated in years. No, we are also not talking about those three billboards outside Ebbing, Missouri.☺

We'll cover profile tips later in the book so we won't go over this now. However, what we will mention is that your LinkedIn profile is not an online CV. It should be customized to speak in the language of your target audience. You know it's completed when you can say with confidence, "sure, visit my profile to get a sense of who I am and how I can help you". You should be proud to direct people to your profile. Are you?

Stage 2: Active

This is where you start connecting with the right people and begin liking, commenting, sharing and even posting content. Training in this area should be practical, address concerns and provide examples of good and bad practice. Essentially, you're saying it's OK to share and this is how you can get best results.

This is also why it's critical to have marketing's support, so the content is ready, relevant and available.

Stage 3: Proactive

Training in this space supports lead generation if it's for sales people and building talent pipeline for recruiters through the use of engaging audiences with content. For people in client facing roles, you may share premium profiles or advanced tools at this stage. Fundamentally, once you know how to 'press the buttons' on LinkedIn, you reach a natural limit where it's all about engaging your target audiences. This is where the real magic and the challenge lie.

This is why having relevant content is so essential. If your content is features led, then it's bland and not appealing. But, if it evokes the awareness of problems people didn't realize they had, then it equally evokes a response, which leads to a conversation, then you're on the right path. The goal we set for our clients is to start online conversations that lead to offline appointments.

At the top end of this spectrum, you have colleagues stepping into Social Champion roles and possibly Thought Leadership roles. Social Champions share content regularly and have a voice on their market, but they may not have the experience or clout to be deemed a thought leader; it is often their aspiration to become one. Thought Leaders have the experience and are actively sharing their views via social channels.

Some further tips to consider when running these types of sessions:
- Governance. If you have social policies, then this is a great opportunity to make people aware of them in the training. We could write another book on this topic alone, but in the pursuit of keeping it brief, we'll suggest that your policies should encourage the right behaviors for use when being active and not scare people with long lists of what they can't do.
- Accountability. Make sure you've thought through how the training will be brought to life outside of the training room. Who will hold people accountable? How will you support people if they have questions? When will people have to report on their results?
- Include KPIs and targets. We'll cover this in the next section, but all we wanted to say here is that it's important to let your team know

what they are shooting for and make sure they know how to track their results.

6. Monitoring & Key Performance Indicators (KPIs)

Monitoring and tracking results is an absolute must when it comes to widespread social business implementation. This gives you visibility of the output from the training and allows you to leverage the results to get further buy-in and support for further implementation. Although it has been tricky to track the actual activity and results from designated sales and recruitment folks when it comes to their actions, there are a lot of things that can still be done to ensure you can determine the net impact. The starting point comes down to assessing your organization on the three variables discussed in the previous section: culture, technology and accountability.

We'd advise that you look at these three elements and determine what level of support you'll receive and what obstacles you're up against. Then, start to look at what is feasible to track and how that can be done.

Assuming you've done that piece of work, then we'd like to share a few of the things that can be done based on our experience of working with hundreds of teams. The starting point is to look at your KPIs in terms of soft vs hard.

> "In God we trust, all others must bring data."
>
> William Edwards Deming

Soft & Hard KPIs

Soft KPIs measure the amount of usage and engagement on LinkedIn (and by extension also on other social media). These are essential early on in the campaign to ensure the team is changing behavior on LinkedIn or any other platform they're being trained on.

Hard KPIs measure the more tangible bottom line numbers such as pipeline value and revenue generated or money saved from direct sourcing of candidates.

Below are some examples of soft and hard KPIs for LinkedIn:

Soft KPIs

- » Number of completed profiles
- » Number of connections
- » Number of views of profiles (over a 90-day period)
- » Number of 'Recent Activity' updates (over a two-week period)
- » Your Social Selling Index Dashboard score (http://linkedin.com/sales/ssi)

Hard KPIs

- » Number of InMail and/or LinkedIn emails sent
- » Increased conversion rate emails
- » Number of appointments generated
- » Number of proposals created
- » Number of sales/hires
- » Revenue made/saved

Setting a KPI on the number of shares or status updates will be a piece of cake for your super users to obtain, but will certainly scare mid-range and laggards. Relative KPIs taking into account which group an employee fits into will be important, even crucial for success.

When looking at KPIs, it's important to take into consideration that the hard KPIs happen over a delayed period of time, especially if your sales or hiring cycles take months or years. In the absence of hard KPI metrics, it's important to track the learning, skills development and behavioral changes that take place within your sales teams. This is where soft KPIs come into play.

For LinkedIn, their Social Selling Index (SSI) is a good starting point. Your personal SSI score can be found here: http://linkedin.com/sales/ssi. You can even check your teams' performance if you have access to LinkedIn's Business Solutions. A score of 80 should be a minimum for sales and recruitment people.

Fundamentally, if your internal culture is not supportive of tracking results, then you can look at this list of KPIs and determine what is possible to

Current Social Selling Index

Your Social Selling Index (SSI) measures how effective you are at establishing your professional brand, finding the right people, engaging with insights, and building relationships. It is updated daily. Learn more

Fig. 2.2 Bert's Social Selling Index

track with your teams as you progress. You may want to allocate someone to follow through and ask people on a regular basis what their results are.

To make this more sustainable, we would encourage you to work with your managers and find ways to regularly track the soft and hard KPIs. The more your training delegates are reminded to keep track of their results, and there are resources we provide through the training work we deliver, the more likely they will be measured. Over time, new behaviors will be embedded, but in the early stages, keep it as simple and easy as possible so that it fits in with your current ways of operating (e.g. with a couple questions at your regular team meetings).

If technology is your bed bug, then it's likely you're in between systems or your systems are just so archaic, it's not worth the blood bath to work with them. If this is the case, then manual tracking can be effective. Again, work with your managers and make sure they know what they're tracking.

In the early stages it will be the soft KPIs, but as they progress and their networks increase in size and their SSI scores increase, your teams will start to see more appointments as a result. This is where you'll want to have a simple way to get them to keep score. Heck, if you just kept a spreadsheet with the value of each opportunity that's in the pipeline as a result of the training, this will do a lot to win over people that are 'on the fence'. Oh, and share these with the team. Sharing is caring, and it's also good for business!

A global financial services client of ours was able to track £20 million in new opportunities within weeks of completing training with us. This was a key factor in other departments wanting further training. Success breeds success.

If you have a well-embedded system that allows you to easily tag lead sources (e.g. such as LinkedIn) and you can automate the tracking function, then this is nirvana. There have been some great developments with LinkedIn Sales Navigator, providing insights on activity of teams and integrating into CRMs like Salesforce and MS Dynamics. This will allow for much better analysis of both soft and hard KPIs, but the success of this will still come down to accountability.

Accountability is where the rubber hits the road. The more prepared you are ahead of your training to educate and provide training to those who will be holding your teams accountable, the better informed they are of their role in holding their teams accountable to their actions and results. We recommend working with managers and even key people across departments who will play a role in this. Make sure they're clear on what their role is inside and outside of the training room. Brainstorm with them the best ways to track results and how to fit these into their ways of operating with minimal impact.

Once you have all of this information at hand, the trainer can introduce these concepts into the training room and people will know what they're accountable to and when they are required to provide updates with their results.

In this chapter we helped you understand the importance of getting everyone on board with the vision and have a proper strategy and vision in place. Then you can get on with the social training implementation. Obviously you should start with the basics like having a great profile, as people do look you up. So, how do you get started on that? Read all about it in the next chapter!

TELLING THE STORY OF A FASCINATING PERSON . . . YOU

3

SUMMARY: There are 178 million searches done every day on LinkedIn – that's a lot of searching by people looking to make a professional connection. Either you have a StandOut Profile that makes a powerful first impression to these searchers, or you lose out on your share of the 178 million. Learn how to increase pageviews, and get found by the right people, by maximizing the number of proven response drivers that are embedded in your LinkedIn Profile.

178 million searches a day. That's a lot of potential opportunity. But it's a double-edged sword. Because while a lot of people could find you, they have to do a lot of searching to find you. Unless you turn the odds in your favor.

- If you are a lawyer in London, you are among 29,800 lawyers on LinkedIn.
- If you are a marketing whiz in the Milwaukee area, you are among 2,800 others on LinkedIn.

And on it goes. With so many of your competitors on LinkedIn, you need to StandOut or get passed over. Searchers need to be instantly intrigued, interested, and convinced that you can best solve their problem or satisfy their need.

They have a job to fill, a contract to let, a deal to do, a project to research, time to kill – some objective that brings them to your page. And arriving there, they want to discover a Profile that is *not only* relevant to their objectives, *but also* a delight to read, as if they were reading the story of a fascinating and unique person – because they are!

They are reading about you!

Since LinkedIn is updating their platform nearly daily, we decided to remove the entire chapter from this book. Of course, you are entitled to get it for FREE! Simply go to https://how-to-really-use-linkedin.com/profile for the latest version.

Difference Between Pedestrian and Powerful = 12x

LinkedIn has a big storehouse of data on its members. They track closely on data such as 'page views' because they want those page views to increase. In this regard, LinkedIn's corporate objectives align perfectly with its members' objectives.

LinkedIn shares this page view data with members in the *Who Viewed Your Profile* tab. We'll look at this and you'll be able to see the number of views you've received in the last 90 days, and then extrapolate to 365 days.

How many page views should you hope to receive by following the strategies coming up? Well, the average LinkedIn Profile gets one view per day[33].

An average Profile is easily recognized as being unattended, incomplete, error prone or just plain boring.

By contrast, a well-crafted professional Profile can average three to five views per day.

When a Profile is architected by experts, it can net 12x the views – leading to many new business opportunities.

And when a professionally architected Profile is then integrated into a complete LinkedIn strategy, the pageview opportunities can be exponential.

---

33 http://expandedramblings.com/index.php/by-the-numbers-a-few-important-linkedin-stats/2/

Profile Quality	Views Per Day
Incomplete, poorly written, doesn't inspire	1-2
Thorough, well-written	3-5
Architected by experts	12-24
Integrated into complete LinkedIn strategy	100+

Fig. 3.1 How LinkedIn Profile pageviews increase

In this Chapter, we aim for 12x returns for you and your organization. In later Chapters, we get into the exponential.

The All-Star Profile Creator

In our training, we use the 22-Point LinkedIn Checklist to help clients position powerfully for the opportunities they seek. By following these 22 guidelines, summarized here in Fig. 3.2, you'll be able to craft a StandOut Profile that rivals the ones we create in training.

Levels of LinkedIn Profile Strength

Scredible StandOut All-Star Profile Creator

Passing the 6-second scan test
1. Your PHOTO is professionaly produced.
2. Your NAME cannot be confused with anyone else's.
3. Your HEADLINE clearly states what you do.
4. You have customized the link to your PUBLIC PROFILE.
5. You have made it easy to CONTACT you.
6. Your SUMMARY is nothing short of fascinating.
7. Your expertise is amplified with RICH MEDIA.

Highlighting your talents
8. Your EXPERIENCE is unfolded in terms of results.
9. Your PRIOR EXPERIENCE is neatly described.
10. You have listed all of your EDUCATION.
11. You have added your own SPECIAL SECTIONS.

Unfolding your character
12. You have added SKILLS to be endorsed for.
13. You have included some PERSONAL INTERESTS.
14. You have included your VOLUNTEER work.
15. You have added links to FREE TIPS & ADVICE.
16. You have added CONTACT DETAIL.

General Profile Tips
17. You have a KEYWORD RICH profile.
18. You have SEQUENCED your profile optimally.
19. You have profiles in several LANGUAGES (if appropriate).
20. You have spiced up your profile for easy READABILITY.
21. You have observed LinkedIn ETIQUETTE.

Fig. 3.2 Program for achieving a StandOut All-Star Profile

Having an All-Star Profile increases your visibility and impact not only on LinkedIn, but also on the web. Google and other search engines index the information from the public sections of your LinkedIn Profile. Since LinkedIn has a high Page Ranking in Google (indicating that LinkedIn is a popular website) the indexed Profiles appear high in search results.

In Fig. 3.3 you can see an example, using Bert Verdonck, to see how LinkedIn Profiles rise to the top of Google search results. That's valuable for branding.

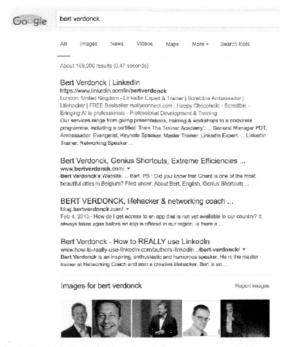

Fig. 3.3 How LinkedIn Profiles index highly in search engines

If your Profile is currently rated by LinkedIn (in the upper right of your profile dashboard) as a *Beginner*, let's take it to at least *Intermediate*, and then onto *Advanced* or *Expert*. With focus, you can then aim for a rare *All Star* ranking and see a sharp increase in the number of people reaching out to you, and opportunities ensuing.

Let's begin!
Be sure to login to LinkedIn,
so you can follow along on your screen.

First give some thought to your goals for your career and business. Make some notes about your expertise, the skills people seek you out for, where you would like your career or your organization to be going.

Have your resume handy, but don't plan on using it directly. A resume is more of a backwards-oriented view of you. Your LinkedIn Profile will be more of a forwards-oriented view, reflecting not only where you've been but also where you want to go.

A LinkedIn Profile has default settings and an order in which the sections of the profile appear as you scroll down the page. But this order can change, and you can change it yourself, as well. So we will go through the All-Star Profile Creator in a logical order, knowing that your own order may be different.

When making changes to your Profile, it's best to turn off network notifications. Otherwise your connections will be notified every time you click *Save* – which is not your intention. (Some people might even kick you out of their network!)

To turn off network notifications, as per Fig. 3.4:
- Go to your *Me-button* on the top navigation
- Choose *Settings & Privacy*
- Click on *Privacy* in the middle.
- Scroll down to *Sharing profile edits*
- Move the slider to *No*.
- When you're finished editing, toggle it back to *Yes*

Fig. 3.4 When working on your Profile, turn off notifications

Since LinkedIn is updating their platform nearly daily, we decided to remove the remainder of this chapter from this book, otherwise your book would be out of date by now ☺

To download the latest version of this chapter,
including the 22-point checklist,
go to https://how-to-really-use-linkedin.com/profile

We are covering these topics:
- The full 22-point Profile checklist
- Controlling Privacy & Setting Preferences
- Measuring your LinkedIn engagement

Of course, you are entitled to get it for FREE!

Simply go to https://how-to-really-use-linkedin.com/profile for the latest version. We update this chapter frequently, so check out the newest version, if it's been a while…

Additionally we provide a LinkedIn Profile makeover service. You can find more details about this by following the link above.

ONLINE NETWORKING BECOMES AN ARTFORM

4

We all know the importance of networking. The rub isn't in the understanding of it, but in the "doing" of it. And doing it efficiently, even enjoyably. That's our objective in this chapter, beginning with a little motivator:

How many of these networking tactics you are currently employing? Tick them off:

❑ Hold regular conversations with current customers
❑ Meet a steady number of new prospects on 'familiar ground'
❑ Get a stream of referrals to pre-qualified prospects
❑ Enjoy word-of-mouth recommendations from third parties
❑ Get introduced to potential employees or colleagues, even without asking
❑ Get to know mentors who can help with your career
❑ Gain insights into people and companies who could become partners
❑ Have reliable sources of intel on your industry's hot trends and news
❑ Gain plainly more visibility as an individual and as part of an organization
❑ Make connections that can reach people you can't reach alone
❑ Receive invitations to top events as a participant, speaker, host
❑ Simply find like-minded people whose company you enjoy
❑ Ask questions and receive the help you need

And lastly for good measure...

❑ While others try schmoozing and blanketing the room with their business cards and end up going nowhere because they don't truly understand the tactics of effective modern networking, you will be going to the top (because you've learned how to REALLY network)

How did you do? If you ticked off 10 or more of the 14 boxes, then skip ahead to the next chapter. You already know your stuff. Otherwise, let's continue...

It Begins With The "KLT Factor"

Let's imagine for a moment that you are on holiday (always a good thing, right?)

You are sitting next to someone at the bar, on the bus or at the beach. At one point you start talking to each other. How long does it take to build a feeling of trust?

Ten minutes, maybe?

How can it happen so fast?

Because you've found something in common. It could be the new place you're at together, or the school you both went to, the similarity in your jobs or someone you both KNOW.

As soon as you find out that you are from the same city, have the same hobby or studied at the same university, something changes! This stranger now seems more familiar.

You LIKE him or her more.

You continue the conversation. You invest in the relationship. After all, you share something in common!

Soon you may become real friends. Maybe you'll never see each other again, but almost always, there is an elevated level of TRUST when the holiday is over. If you were to meet again, you would get back to a similar level of trust fairly quickly.

Now a simple question:

> Since this relationship-sparking dynamic works so well in your
> personal life, why not apply it in your professional life?

When you put it to work, you are putting what we shorthand as the "KLT Factor" to work – the "Know, Like & Trust Factor". It's how you connect with the people you want and need to connect to.

Fig. 4.1 Taking the KLT Factor to work

There's an old Irish line...

> "People do business with people
> they want to do business with."

Networking expert Bob Burg famously updated it for the Internet era...

> "All things being equal, people do business with,
> and refer business to people they Know, Like, and Trust."

So in order to increase the business you do, it makes sense to concentrate on raising your KLT Factor with the people from your network.

What does this mean in practical business terms?

The 'Know' Part

What do people in business know about you? What is your background? What are your interests on a professional and personal level? Which organizations do you belong to?

To raise the 'Know' part, it is important to complete your Profile on LinkedIn as fully as you can (achieving a balance; not swamping readers in detail!).

Make it easy for people to find you, to learn more about you, and to see where you might connect on either a professional or a personal level.

The 'Like' Part

Being liked is the simplest formula of all: Listen to what people want, and give it to them. Think about what you can share with other people. Answer questions in LinkedIn Groups. Listen to what others are looking for and provide answers. After a while, you not only appear on people's radar (the 'Know' part), but they also start to like you. And think about it: If you have two nearly equal suppliers, which will you do business with, someone you like or someone you don't? Exactly!

The 'Trust' Part

There are two dimensions of trust:
- Trusting your expertise. This can be raised when answering questions in LinkedIn Group discussions in your field of expertise. By giving solid answers you will be perceived, correctly, as an expert. Also, by asking people to post recommendations on your LinkedIn Profile, you increase the trust part.
- Trusting your behavior. You can be counted on to behave well when you get an introduction or referral. Here again, having recommendations from people who describe your working attitude helps to raise trust.

Stephen Covey wrote about this in his book, *The Speed of Trust*[34]:

> "Trust can also be transferred via an intermediary."

LinkedIn becomes the intermediary for transferring trust. It's a safe (as safe as exists) way to ask people for introductions to others and to pass along messages of trusted connections. These become easy networking actions to take on LinkedIn.

The transfer of trust works both ways, too. If you make a poor connection, the trust you enjoy and your online reputation can be damaged very quickly. So you need to be a good filter of talents, as well as a good advocate.

We will be talking much more about this.

---

34 http://www.speedoftrust.com/

Advancing the networking thinking of the last 20 years

You can blame Kevin Bacon for being such an appealing guy, but the *Six Degrees of Kevin Bacon* sure cemented in the early Internet culture the idea that there are only a few degrees of lineal separation between each of us and everyone else in the world.

As the Bacon meme mushroomed out, many people spent long hours piling up astounding numbers of connections on the social and business networks. Some took pride in adding L.I.O.N to their LinkedIn profile title (LinkedIn Open Networker) taking all requests.

Quantity over quality.

Many still take pride in their far-flung connections. *"Wow, look at me!"* they seem to be shouting. But to what end?

Well, if you have 10,000 fairly loose connections in your network, you can bet that you will always have a contact for any given need. But how many of them will you know well enough, or have shared interests deep enough, to tap when in need?

On the other hand if you have 500 fairly tight connections that you know much better, share things, talk things over, recommend things, and generally attend to each other's interests . . . will this smaller network in fact be more valuable?

Now that social networking has matured, almost to an artform, there are plenty of studies on network sizing. Loose vs. Tight, Large vs. Small, etc. There are also plenty of arguments on this, with some saying you can't have too many contacts, others making the opposing case, and still others saying that weak connections can be a valuable asset that strong connections cannot be.

There is, in fact, good sense in each of these arguments. What's right for you will depend on your goals in networking, and your industry.

Nonetheless, a dominant theme has emerged, an intuitive theme. As the saying goes:

One good friend is better than 20 strangers in a street fight!

Quality usually trumps quantity, then. That makes online networking similar to offline, doesn't it? So what, then, is a reasonable number of connections to strive for on LinkedIn?

LinkedIn doesn't really release information on connections that members average. But a 2016 survey by Statista is considered an accurate measure (Fig. 4.2):[35]

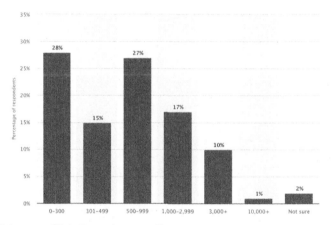

Fig. 4.2 Statista survey of LinkedIn member connections

We see that more than half of LinkedIn members have more than 500 connections (although one of LinkedIn's Blogs claims that every connection reflects an average of 400 new people you can get introduced to and begin to build relationships with[36]). Getting to the first 500 connections is the stiffest hurdle, because you don't yet enjoy network effects. Many of the 500 will be obtained one by one, or two by two . . . not 20 by 20. And LinkedIn freezes the reporting at 500+ on your public Profile page when this number is reached. So the immediate incentive to 'appear connected' is then satisfied.

How many connections do you and the people in your company have?

Enough to satisfy your business-building requirements?

If not, let's look at our best networking tactics...

---

35 http://www.statista.com/statistics/264097/number-of-1st-level-connections-of-linkedin-users/
36 https://blog.linkedin.com/2017/april/24/the-power-of-linkedins-500-million-community

The Secret of the New Networking

The secret of the new networking is that there is no secret. There is only attitude. Anyone can have it, if we work at it. We learned as much from the networking genius, Jan Vermeiren, who we've had the good fortune of working with for over a decade. In his book, *Let's Connect!*, Jan defines the ideal networking attitude as:

> "Sharing information in a reactive and proactive way
> without expecting anything immediately in return."

Let's dissect Jan's definition, because the sum of the parts is greater.

"Sharing..."

This clearly stipulates two or more parties. It's not a one-way street, but a multi-lane boulevard. The desired outcome is always a win-win situation in which all parties are satisfied. You need to be comfortable with giving help *and* making requests.

"...information..."

This refers to both general and specific information you have or business matters you understand. It's all valuable. And think about it; when you give it to others in an online setting, you still have it. You haven't lost anything, you've gained something.

"...in a reactive and proactive way..."

This suggests that you offer information or help when asked. But more, it means randomly sending people information they could use and thus connecting tangibly with them, without their asking. That is, being proactive without being spammy.

"...without expecting anything immediately in return."

This is *not* about giving your products away for free. This is about connecting with people in an open-ended way. By giving freely and not expecting anything in return, you may well receive much more than your initial 'investment.' You just don't necessarily know from whom or when it will come.

So putting Jan's definition back together again, we conclude...
- Networking is a long-term game involving at least two players.
- When you share something in an online setting, you actually still have it – so you don't lose a thing but instead gain something new.
- Failure to understand the networking *attitude* is the main reason people give up on LinkedIn. Focused only on themselves, they don't receive help from others and soon become frustrated with the lack of positive responses.

Quality over quantity, relationship over return. Let's jump to an advanced tactic first, because it's so interesting...

The scientific scaling of a network

Like any good science story, this one begins with the original Adam. Not the one who networked with Eve – mission accomplished at scale. But Adam Rifkin who did his doctorate at Caltech on scalable systems.

Mr. Rifkin's seminal idea involved relationship building. He figured out how to run up the size of his personal network without running up the time spent on it. As a result, he quietly built one of the most powerful networks in Silicon Valley and was named *Fortune's* best networker.[37]

How did he do it?

As he grew more successful in business, and his professional network grew in tandem, he faced the challenge that many successful people face.

He was overwhelmed by the requests on his time.

---

37 http://fortune.com/2011/02/09/fortunes-best-networker/

And then he had the insight, as reported by *Forbes* contributor Michael Simmons:[38]

> *"Most people fail to reach their network's potential because they subconsciously view their relationships within a hub-and-spoke paradigm. Like a bicycle wheel, they see themselves at the center and each relationship as a spoke. The problem with this paradigm is that each relationship you add increases the amount of stress on you until you're eventually overwhelmed. Adam's insight was to view others as part of a network connected to each other, not just him. In other words, he viewed his network as a community."*

To build this community, Mr. Rifkin understood that his entire network needed to be connected to one another. So he set a goal of arranging three introductions every day from December 2003 forward. If he has kept to his pace, he has, at the time of writing, introduced 15,000+ people to each other!

Mr. Rifkin viewed the short-term work involved in all of this as a small investment in his future happiness and success. His impressive model, summarized in Fig. 4.3, is one that anyone can follow. It requires no special skills or budget, just the original insight!

Fig. 4.3 From network building to community building

38 https://www.forbes.com/sites/michaelsimmons/2013/09/04/the-science-behind-how-super-connectors-scale-their-networks/#319039393470

Another insight was how Mr. Rifkin went about asking members of his community for help when he actually needed help.

He didn't.

Instead of calling in favors, or leaning on connections, he asked his connections if the could help other connections of his. By asking only that his connections help one another, he distributed goodwill across his community. As a result, the community continued to grow in strength and relevance to its members, with remarkably little involvement from Mr. Rifkin.

Today his LinkedIn page says that 76, 529+ people are following him. This is an amazing number for someone who is not a household name celebrity.

You could say that he was the first collaborative economy success – achieving his results by gathering around him a networked community, orchestrating the activities of his community at scale, and dramatically reducing the cost of doing business.

Mr. Rifkin's extreme methods won't appeal to everyone, but the basic principles can definitely be put to work to create a powerfully effective network.

REALLY Network Using LinkedIn

With 550+ million members, the people you need to meet in business are practically *guaranteed* to have some level of visibility on LinkedIn. The trouble is, of course, that before you can form a mutually beneficial relationship with them . . . you need to find them.

So we assume that you are a LinkedIn member and have browsed the network suggestions of people you may know. Now let's tackle more advanced connecting.

Starting with the end goal in mind

It's a common mistake for people who are searching for help on LinkedIn to look only at their own connections. Their first-level network. This limits them.

The genius of LinkedIn is how it can work in the networks of people you know. LinkedIn makes these unknown third-parties suddenly visible to you.

And the value of this? Let's answer that by walking through a search with the end goal in mind. These are then the steps you take:
1. Define the ideal people you need to connect with
2. Find these people using LinkedIn's suite of tools
3. See who they know who also happens to know you
4. Ask the person you know to make an introduction

With just a few degrees of separation, we are all second- or third-level connections with many millions of people. And in those millions, as often as not, you'll have someone in your network of connections who is also in the network of the person you need to connect with.

For example let's suppose you are looking for a job at Coca Cola in your country (or you are in the position to work with them as a supplier or partner).

What most people first do is ask themselves: "*Who do I know at Coca Cola?*"

When they can't think of anyone, they give up. Or they call the front desk at Coca Cola, ask for the HR Manager and get pigeonholed by a gatekeeper. Or the HR Manager says she is going to call back, but never does. Frustration!

Let's now reverse the process with the end-goal in mind:
• Define Coca-Cola's HR Manager as the person who can help you best
• Use LinkedIn to search "HR Manager" + "Coca Cola" + "Your Country"
• You get the name of "Exact Right Person" you want to meet
• You also get the connections you share with this exact right person

When you look at the mutual connections you may have, perhaps you discover that 'Exact Right Person' is connected with your neighbor, or cousin, or former partner!

You didn't know this because Coca Cola has not come up in your conversations with your close connections. They never mentioned anything because, perhaps, you didn't say you were interested in Coca Cola or they didn't put two and two together.

But after discovering the connection between 'Exact Right Person' and 'Neighbor A' in our example, you drop by to see 'Neighbor A' and find that she worked together with 'Exact Right Person' and is happy to fire-off an email to introduce you. As this serendipitous story ends, a few days later you are meeting with 'Exact Right Person' and talking about the Coca Cola contract.

Of course, it doesn't always happen so smooth and conveniently. But it happens. A lot. That's how LinkedIn graduated from being a resume-posting service to the Global Maître D of Business Introductions. Boom!

Commit to a daily routine (that pays networking dividends)

Our next networking tactic can ideally begin when you wipe the sleep from your eyes and log into LinkedIn in the morning. Right away, since it can take only a minute, post a *Status Update.* (*Homepage, near the top*)

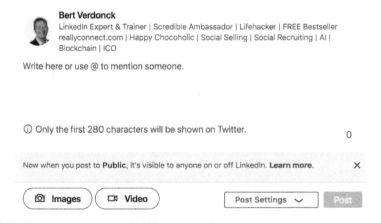

Fig. 4.4 Posting an update to constantly tickle your network

To post a Status Update (Fig. 4.4):

1. Go to your homepage top – there's a *Share an article, photo, video or idea* box and it's ready to go.
2. Drop into the text box and write a short message (15-25 words) of interest to your network. There are all kinds of things you can share:
   - Company press release announcing a new product launch
   - Interesting article or blogpost that deserves a wider audience
   - Upcoming webinar with a unique URL to take people to a sign-up page
   - Ask an open question to your network, and get help in solving a problem
   - Run your own survey about an interesting topic in your industry
   - Tell your network what jobs you have available if you're hiring
   - Or any other subject interest you may have that is:
     - Business-oriented
     - Useful to your network
     - Complementary to your brand
3. Add a URL and LinkedIn will automatically add the webpage.
4. To add a photo to your post, click the left button *Images* tab.
5. To add a video to your post, click on the second button *Video* tab.
6. Choose who you want to share the update with:
   - Public
   - Public + Twitter
   - Just Your Connections

   Done!

   Just by clicking the Comments tab and ticking the box *Allow comments on this post* you can keep the conversation going.

This daily routine of sharing *something valuable* cements one idea in people's minds:

You are knowledgeable and helpful;
and for that, you are valuable.

We skipped over 'the basics' to get into the advanced potential of networking. Now let's take a step back and cover...

The fastest way to build a valuable network

To benefit from the far-reaching power of LinkedIn, you need to build-up your first-degree network. The real power of the network is in the second degree, as we just saw in the Adam Rifkin and Coca Cola stories. But you get to those second-degree connections through your first-degree connections.

To build this network, you will be using free LinkedIn tools. You will be reconnecting with contacts you already have – to prime the pump. The KLT Factor already exists with these contacts, to a certain extent. They will be the foundation of your network.

Phase 1: Create the First Layer of Your LinkedIn Network

You first want to upload your existing contacts to your LinkedIn account. Here are the step-by-step instructions for importing your address book: https://www.linkedin.com/help/linkedin/answer/4214

As LinkedIn regularly changes this functionality we believe it is easier for you to follow this link and get it done.

How to compose a personal message to a contact:
- Go to his or her Profile.
- Click *Connect*.
- You can customize this invitation by clicking on *Add a note*.
- Write a personal message that references a shared interest or activity, so you are making it clear this person is important to you.
- Click *Send Invitation*.

Within minutes of completing these steps, you can expect people to begin accepting your invitations. Your network is beginning to grow,

Phase 2: Discover People You May Know

Every time you visit your *My Network* page, LinkedIn presents you a carousel showing thumbnail boxes of three people to interact with. These people...
- May be names in your contacts file that you haven't reached out to
- May be second or third-degree connections of potential value to you (though the third-degree is much tougher to connect to)

Remember to always add a personal note when inviting people. Click on their name or picture to go to their Profile and follow the steps of the previous paragraph.

"How does LinkedIn know that I know these people?"
"I don't know these people at all,
why is LinkedIn suggesting that I do?"

LinkedIn make these matches using 18 parameters on your Profile and your activities. Although the algorithm is a secret, it probably contains:
- Mutual connections
- LinkedIn Groups you both belong to
- Schools you both attended
- Companies you both worked for
- And so on.

Phase 3: Find colleagues and classmates

This next tool is a reminder, as we saw in Chapter 2, that it is important to complete your LinkedIn Profile in full – listing companies you've worked at, and schools you've attended, so LinkedIn's computers can make the connections for you as we show here.

Look for current colleagues:
- On your homepage type in the name of your company in the search box.
- Go to the Company Page.
- Click on the number of employees and find the ones you know.
- Send them a *personalized* invitation to connect.

In this way your network grows with your current colleagues.

While you most likely share fewer interests with former college classmates, they can be valuable additions to your network because of the diversity of reach they represent, and also because the memories are often so good!

The KLT Factor was (very) high when you where studying. By reconnecting you can pick it up (nearly) where you left it…

Look for former classmates:

1. In the search bar, type in the name of your university (or college or organization your studied at).
2. Go to their Company Page.
3. Click on the *See Alumni* button.
4. Adjust the *Start year* and *End year* of when you attended.
5. Scroll through the list of people and click on their name or picture to go to their profile.
6. Send them a *personalized* invitation.
7. Repeat these steps for every school/college/university you've attended.

In this way your network grows with past classmates.

This is how you build a network over time. It's a good idea to return to and repeat phases 1 and 3 on a regular basis, such as monthly. Phase 2 can be done each time you open up LinkedIn.

Phase 4: Connect with still others that you already know

Next to the people found in the first three phases, there are a fair number of others you can connect with. Simply use the search function on LinkedIn to find them. Then go to their *Profile* and send a personalized invitation.

Here is a list of additional people that are ideal to connect with:

- Family (they have business connections you may be unaware of!)
- Friends (a very high KLT Factor!)
- Clients/Customers
- Prospects
- Suppliers and other partners
- People you meet (at meetings, mixers, conferences…)
- Your role models, mentors, advisors and coaches (probably a smaller group, but most important).

The list can go on and on, producing a great depth and variety of potential connections as you build your network.

Do you know the most frequent mistake in network building?

You probably do!

The mistake is only working on the network when it's needed, such as when looking for a new job or needing more customers.

If you only work on your network when you need it, people will sense desperation. Most will be reluctant to connect, even less interested in making introductions for you.

It does take time to build any network worth having. So start building your network yesterday and continue through tomorrow. Then repeat.

Once you make it a habit, like checking your email in the morning or the ski report in winter, you will find your network expanding at a faster and faster clip.

Other LinkedIn members will hear about you, or see your name coming up in their 'top 3' carousel, and they will invite you to connect. And the larger your network grows, the more people want to connect with you.

Everyone loves a winner, right?!

Tapping your connections comfortably

You've probably heard this basic networking principle:

> "It is always better to be introduced than to introduce yourself."

So why not apply this principle on LinkedIn?

Some people get squeamish asking for introductions . . . until they discover how, when done right on the new LinkedIn interface, it becomes a relatively painless win-win-win activity.

How to request an Introduction:
- Go to the Profile of a someone in your network you know fairly well. Even if you haven't asked for an introduction before, it's okay!

- On his/her Profile you'll see the *See connections (500+)* or the actual number of connections between brackets (s)he has. Click on the number and you will be taken to a page of his/her connections. *(If (s) he doesn't share his/her network, this big number will appear in gray. Choose someone else instead)*
- Browse through his/her network or search by *All Filters* (e.g. name, company, title…)
- Select one or two people you would like to meet and who you believe would like to meet you – because of shared interests, goals, aspirations, etc.
- Call your connection to ask how well (s)he knows these people, and if (s)he knows them well enough to introduce you.
- Even better, do the introduction through a Magic Mail that creates a genuine win-win-win for all three parties involved (Detail on Magic Mail coming up)
  - You get a chance to meet someone new who may be of interest to you
  - Your first degree contact deepens his/her relationship with a trusted associate
  - The third party meets someone of value unexpectedly – a great feeling.

This is one of the 'treasured' tools on LinkedIn, yet only a handful of people take advantage of it. Be one of the few!

Why search when you can specify?

One of the best ways to track someone down (whether you know their name or not) is to use LinkedIn's Search.

You can find people based on their job title, company, school, location, degree of connection to you … you can also curate your searches based on their industry, former company, language, and volunteer interests.

Maybe you want to find other professionals in your field who live close by and have similar qualifications to you. Just fill out the keywords, industry, and location fields in the *All Filters* popup, and LinkedIn will show you all the members who meet those criteria. Now you've got a really valuable list of people to ask out for coffee.

To properly use *Linkedin's Search*, go to the top of the page, put your cursor in the search bar and click on *People* in the dropdown menu, before you start typing anything. Then click on the *All Filters* link and the box shown in Fig. 4.5 will slide onto the page.

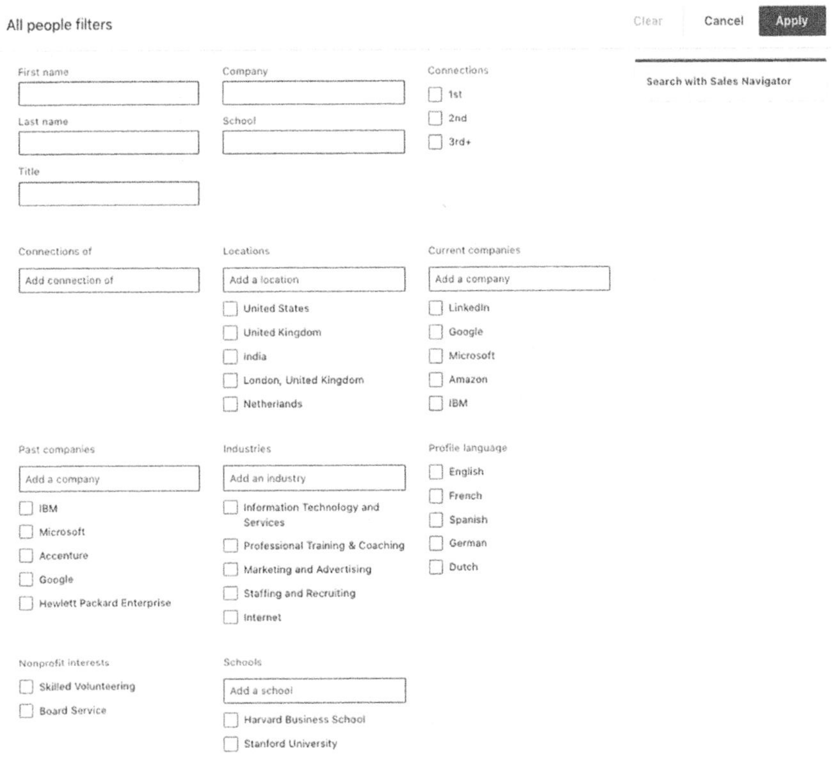

All people filters   Clear   Cancel   Apply

First name   Company   Connections   Search with Sales Navigator
                                             ☐ 1st

Last name   School   ☐ 2nd
                                             ☐ 3rd+

Title

Connections of   Locations   Current companies
Add connection of   Add a location   Add a company
                        ☐ United States   ☐ LinkedIn
                        ☐ United Kingdom   ☐ Google
                        ☐ India   ☐ Microsoft
                        ☐ London, United Kingdom   ☐ Amazon
                        ☐ Netherlands   ☐ IBM

Past companies   Industries   Profile language
Add a company   Add an industry   ☐ English
☐ IBM   ☐ Information Technology and   ☐ French
☐ Microsoft   Services   ☐ Spanish
☐ Accenture   ☐ Professional Training & Coaching   ☐ German
☐ Google   ☐ Marketing and Advertising   ☐ Dutch
☐ Hewlett Packard Enterprise   ☐ Staffing and Recruiting
                        ☐ Internet

Nonprofit interests   Schools
☐ Skilled Volunteering Add a school
☐ Board Service   ☐ Harvard Business School
                        ☐ Stanford University

Fig. 4.5 Why search randomly when you can specify precisely?

Using LinkedIn's *Search* or the Advanced Search as we sometimes call it, you can make REALLY specific searches. For example, maybe you'd like to see all the HR managers in the aerospace industry who went to your college and currently live within an hour's drive of you (you might!).

Simply fill out the *Title* field with "HR," the *Industry* field with "aerospace," the *School* field with your alma mater, and the *Location* field with your current zip code. Click *Apply*. A targeted list pops up of everyone on LinkedIn who meet your parameters.

95

To get the most out of *Advanced Search*, approach it methodically, step by step.

1. Start with one or two criteria. See how many results you are having.
2. Fine-tune further until you have less than 100 results. That's because with a free account you can only browse the first 100 results. Even with a premium account, digesting more than a 100 results can be a challenge.
3. As you fine-tune your search results, keep track of the parameters you are using. This keeps things orderly when you start conducting lots of searches, as you surely will!
4. You can search in any industry. So if you begin in Financial Services, for example, select everyone who interests you, save your search and make a note that you have ticked off one industry. Go on to another. Repeat.

We will return to this *Advanced Search* feature several times in this book, because it is one of LinkedIn's most valuable tools, saving many hours of search time and yielding many new connections that otherwise would not have been made.

Transform your reading into networking

Surprisingly few people use LinkedIn's publishing platform as a networking tool. So by using it to its fullest potential, you can effectively differentiate yourself and your company from your competitors.

How to use LinkedIn's publishing platform for networking:
On your homepage, go to the first article, right under the *Share an article, photo, video or idea* box. At the right, you will see three dots (…). Click on them and choose *Improve my feed* (or you could go directly: https://www.linkedin.com/feed/follow).

By default, you will be taken to a page with four sets of news sources:
- *Companies*
- *Influencers*
- *Topics*
- *People*

When you choose news sources from these sections, LinkedIn will add them to your LinkedIn Homepage feed. Shown in Fig. 4.6 is the first line of news sources from each of the four categories, to give you an idea of the breadth of the offering. You can click to follow or leave unfollowed to create your very own customized daily briefing.

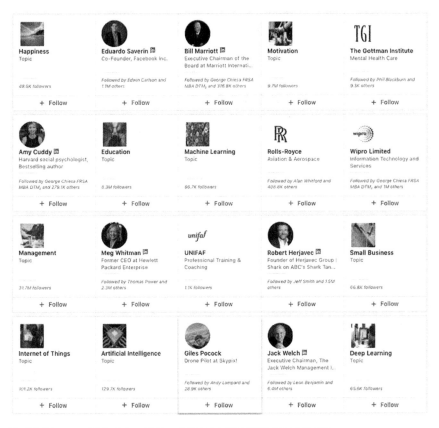

Fig. 4.6 Cutaways of LinkedIn's publishing platform's news/influencers categories

Let's say you run a small business. You could choose the *Entrepreneurship* category and see all of LinkedIn's curated articles under that heading.

The articles will be great, but focus on the authors and influencers!

These are some of the most knowledgeable, socially connected people in your field.

- Follow their career trajectories and current interests

- Reach out to them when you have ideas to share
- With patience these authors and influencers can become connections for:
  - Getting advice and mentorship
  - Forming partnerships
  - Finding new hires
  - Obtaining great publicity
- And much more in the networking opportunity pipeline...

Finding Subject Matter Experts When Needed

If you are working on a project and need information or expertise – whether either outside or inside your own organization – here is how LinkedIn can help:

1. Obtain expert answers to your questions (Chapter 5)
2. Identify the influencers with articles on Pulse (Chapter 5)
3. Receive introductions to experts (Chapter 4 below)
4. Discover the relationships between colleagues, experts, influencers and other contacts (Chapter 4 below)
5. Get notifications when people change jobs – this is a trigger to contact them and get introduced to their replacement (Chapter 6).

Use the "People Also Viewed" feature

LinkedIn has a crowdsourcing tool built right in – it is at once a clever prospecting tool and sociological study. It's the *People Also Viewed* feature, sitting in the right column of the profiles you've search for (if the feature is turned on).

As the name suggests, this is a list of people that others have searched for at about the same time they searched for the profile on your screen (as shown in Fig. 4.7). This becomes an affinity cohort, a group of people who all have *something* in common with each other.

Perhaps they all work at the same company, or in one industry.

More to the point, they may be the person you've been looking for, but couldn't find, because you didn't input the right parameters. Now you can see how you may be connected to this person, and how to go about building a tighter relationship.

Let's say you already know Lee Troxler of Scredible, and you want to build a tighter relationship with others in his company.

As you see in the Fig. 4.7 screenshot of Lee's LinkedIn Profile, others in Scredible are listed in the right column – because it's common for people to investigate several members of a team at once. You now have a list of people you can connect with.

With a free account, you can click on these thumbnail profiles and view their full Profiles if the people are two or three degrees removed from you.

With a premium account, you can click to see anyone's full Profile.

Fig. 4.7 In the right column LinkedIn show a list of people you can connect with

You have an option for using this *People Also Viewed* feature. You can choose to have it appear on your public Profile page, or not. It's your preference. Some members see this feature as a double-edged sword. Yes, you can use it to research prospects, but others can use it as well. We advise using it, and then if you'd prefer not to, then changing the setting.

In the next section, we talk about the best ways to connect...

Communicating With Your LinkedIn Network

For many years, LinkedIn's messaging was its Achilles heel with an old-time interface that looked enough like Hotmail to earn little but groans. Even LinkedIn CEO Jeff Weiner joked about the seeming glacial pace when he finally announced decent on-platform messaging:

"Welcome, LinkedIn, to the 21st century of communications."

Since September 2015 LinkedIn rebuilt its messaging from the ground up. Now it's REALLY efficient to have two-way conversations with your professional connections; as efficient as on any platform.

To send a message, simply click on the messaging bar at the bottom right corner or click on the Messaging icon in the top navigation. Choose the person you want to communicate with and send your message.

Managing your LinkedIn connections

As your network builds on LinkedIn, you will want to manage your network and keep it well organized so you can find people easily, access information on them just as easily, and steadily increase the value of your network to you, your company and the members in your network, as well.

So let's backtrack a bit, and review some management basics.

On your *Connections* page, you will see the names, professional headlines and photos of each of your contacts and connections.

To find people quicker, you can sort this file by:
- Recently added
- Last name
- First name

You can filter the results you see by using the specific search.

Removing connections you no longer want

You may want to remove a LinkedIn connection from time to time. Perhaps you are changing jobs or reorienting your career, and don't want to be associated with a certain industry anymore. Or you've had a bad experience that you would like to put at some remove.

Only this second reason is a good reason, in our experience, for removing a connection. In the other cases, you never know 'who knows who' and how they may be able to help you in some new situation.

Either way, if you choose to remove someone, they are not notified. (FYI: They may notice that you are no longer in their first-degree network when (1) they look at your Profile or (2) when you appear in search results.)

To remove a connection:
- Click on the top menu *My Network* and go to *Connections*
- On your *Connections* page, search for the person to remove and hover over their three dots next to the *Message* button.
- You see then *Remove connection.* Just click it and remove that person as a connection.

Once deleted, the individual will be hidden away in your *Contacts,* available should you want to re-invite them later.

Connecting with People Using the KLT Factor

Personalized connection requests

Once you build a list of people you want to connect with, you can begin actually connecting. Be sure that you use a *personalized* connection request. It's mind-boggling how many otherwise intelligent people do not take the time to send personalized invitations on LinkedIn. Instead they just use LinkedIn's boilerplate:

> "I'd like to add you to my professional network."

How inviting! The invitation might as well read...

I don't care enough about you to learn anything about you!

Or more apropos...

"I'm lazy."

Most LinkedIn members will ignore these lazy introductions, or report them to LinkedIn as spam. LinkedIn may then restrict the sender, blocking the ability to send connection requests in the future.

How to send connection requests
- Find the Profile of someone you want to connect with – click *Connect*.
- Personalize your request to connect by following these tips:
  - Include a salutation
  - Remind the recipient of how you know them
  - Reference something personal about them or their business
- Click *Send*

What if you don't know the person?

When sending an introduction, it's easy to add some words of familiarity. But if the person is not so well known, the task becomes fraught. Here's how to overcome:

Open up the individual's Profile and read it looking for something personal to mention. (You probably already did this, since you are reaching out to make a connection request.)
- Maybe the individual went to the same school as you
- Or lives in a city you once lived in
- Or has a similar hobby or a cause you both care about
- Or is a member of the same LinkedIn Group as you

These are all ways to use the KLT Factor to connect with someone. Another way is to bring up something not related to work, but interesting. This may come to the recipient as a surprise. And your invitation will StandOut. It will build a relationship in a personal context, which is more likely to leave a good first impression and even lodge in the recipient's memory.

They key thing: Letting the recipient know you are socially credible.

This time spent crafting a personalized connection request REALLY makes the difference between obtaining a great new connection with the potential for a growing network of opportunities, or being dismissed without a second thought.

In addition to *sending* connection requests, there is the *receiving*...

How to receive connection requests
- As the recipient of a connection request, you are not obligated to accept
- You have three options:
  - *Accept*
  - *Ignore*
  - Send them a *Message* without accepting the invitation.

Click on the *Manage all* link on your *My Network* page. A new conversation dialogue starts. Take it from there...

Paying to connect with 'InMail'

LinkedIn's internal email system is called InMail. These emails can be sent to anyone on LinkedIn, unless the member chooses to block them. They are only available to premium accounts.

Here are tips from our training sessions on getting results with InMail and the stats from the data we've collected:
- InMail is not for securing a meeting or selling something; it is for establishing rapport and starting a conversation. It should set the stage for what comes next. Relationship first, meeting second.
- LinkedIn data on InMail of interest:
  - Increase the odds by 12% if you send InMail on a Thursday morning between 9AM and 10AM
  - Don't send over the weekend (16% less results)
  - Having a connection in common improves the results (think second degree)
  - Having LinkedIn Groups in common improved the likelihood of response 21%
  - If you share a previous employer in common, you get a 27% increase
  - Your Company Page followers are 81% more likely to respond

- Some editorial and message crafting tips:
  - Choose a short and engaging subject line
  - Create a compelling touchpoint with a clear call-to-action
  - Always personalize the InMail by browsing their profile and picking topics you share, or can ask questions about, or that interest you
  - Talk in the language of your target audience. For a financial director, for example, use numbers, stats, graphics, savings, infographics, etc.

The best use of InMail is when you need to contact somebody, and cannot do it any other way. So if it comes down to InMail, approach it with all the preparation of a Suzanne Collins *Hunger Games* character, and *"may the odds be ever in your favor".*

This said, there is an even better tactic at hand...

What if you just can't get through?

Many of the people you want to connect with are busy already, or have overloaded inboxes. That's what comes with success. Your LinkedIn connection request or InMail, no matter how well-crafted and personalized, may get lost or ignored.

From a decade of informally surveying LinkedIn members, we've found that the success rate of these requests ranges from 10% to 30%. This is why in our own business, and in our trainings, we teach a tactic that we've found to double the acceptance rate – 20% to 60% success is common, and often higher.

This tactic is neither difficult nor easy to implement, but it does have to be executed precisely to spec in order to be effective...

The 'Magic Mail' that opens tightly shut doors

The Magic Mail is simple beauty–it is the best way to get introduced to someone you *want* to know by someone you *already* know.

It's an email that goes from someone in your first-degree network to someone in your second-degree network.

And it works because of the KLT Factor.

The more trust there is in a relationship, the more inclined someone will be to help you reach your objective. Earlier we referred to Stephen Covey's *The Speed of Trust* to explain how this mutual trust can accelerate the speed of goal accomplishment and, more importantly, how it can be transferred from one person to another. At its core, the idea is...

> If I trust you, and you trust another person, that person will usually trust me, as well.

This trust dynamic begins on LinkedIn and continues with the Magic Mail – creating the ultimate tool to transfer trust.

Here's how it works: Use LinkedIn as a research database to find the people you want to meet or be introduced to. Then actually do the introduction via Magic Mail—outside of LinkedIn.

If you use LinkedIn's messaging feature to try to meet someone, you are the one taking the initiative. That's okay. The person you want to reach will get the message via someone he or she trusts – which is good – but you clearly took the first step.

In contrast, when a mutual interested party introduces you with a Magic Mail, it is equally clear that the mutual party is invested in the outcome. That generates the mutual trust which is crucial for success.

See how in Fig. 4.8 the traditional networking pattern, and the method of introduction that most people use, are both dramatically improved by the Magic Mail approach.

In our experience, many people intuitively understand the value of the Magic Mail, but get nervous about asking a colleague to make the 'mutual introduction'. Our solution to this is the 'Magic Question':

When talking to your colleague about the introduction, be sure to ask: *"Would you be open to receiving a draft version of such a Magic Mail?"*

Most people say *"Yes!"*

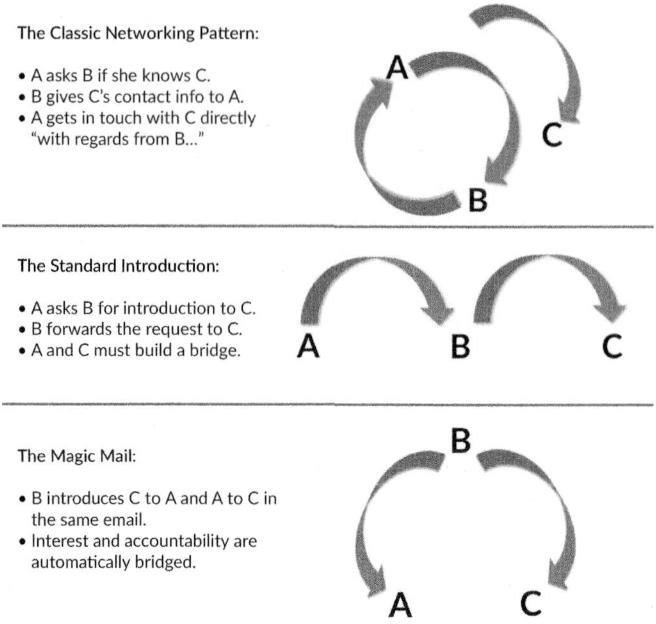

The Classic Networking Pattern:

- A asks B if she knows C.
- B gives C's contact info to A.
- A gets in touch with C directly "with regards from B..."

A

C

B

The Standard Introduction:

- A asks B for introduction to C.
- B forwards the request to C.
- A and C must build a bridge.

A   B   C

The Magic Mail:

- B introduces C to A and A to C in the same email.
- Interest and accountability are automatically bridged.

B

A   C

Fig. 4.8 'Magic Mail' dramatically improves introductions

So, when you draft a Magic Mail and email it as an attachment to the introducer, you facilitate. The only thing they have to do is copy/paste your draft, read it through and make any desired changes, then send it on. It all can be done in a couple minutes! Not a burden at all.

Let's look at a sample Magic Mail, then how best to send it.

Sample Magic Mail: John asks his friend Bert to introduce his friend Eric

From: Bert Verdonck
To: eric.rogers@CPAmazing.com
Cc: john.johnson@BigBangWebDesign.com
Subject: Introduction

Hi Eric,

I want to introduce you to John Johnson (cc'ed) who runs BigBangWebDesign. I've known John for a while; we actually worked together on the HoverShoes project. John might be perfect for helping with your new responsible website we talked about. He's great at meeting customer needs while staying within the budget and is really customer-focused. In fact, sometimes he'll suggest another solution or even another vendor if he thinks it's in the best interests of his customer. Can you get in touch with him and have a coffee together?

John,

Eric Rogers is my accountant and a personal friend. He's truly an 'amazing' accountant because he's more focused on people than on numbers. Eric is looking for a new website—and because of our joint experience, I thought you might be interested in working with him. Can you contact Eric?

Also, I understand you both are tennis buffs. Maybe you can combine this project with some time on the court!

Gentlemen, you now have each other's emails. I'll let you take it from here.

All the best,

Bert

Let's examine this sample Magic Mail with the idea that we are creating instructions to give to a mutual party as a guide in crafting a Magic Mail:

Header

From: The mutual party–the 'connector'
To: The person who may value hearing about your service
Cc: You, who supplies the service
Subject: "Introduction," making it quickly clear what this email concerns

Body

- First address the receiver, then address the supplier.
- Always give the reason for connecting them.
- Tell each party something about the other, and about your relationship with each. This creates common ground and trust, starting the relationship on a much higher level than any cold call.
- Mention the qualities you like about each person. This strengthens the relationship all around. Even if there is no future interaction between them, the email is worth the effort as a 'relationship builder' for all involved.
- Try to find commonalities beyond the professional. In this case, they share a passion for tennis. There is an instant bond which confers value even if it is not acted upon.
- Sometimes you can include other references and credentializers such as the supplier's client list, but this is not a 'hard sell' introduction, it is a 'social' introduction.
- You can also include both parties' phone numbers if that fits your style and your understanding of the parties. It depends, but they will at least have an email and that's a great beginning.
- Always conclude each introduction with a suggestion that they contact one other. This makes it easier to get them going: "*Bert thinks we should talk…*"
- Transaction complete–it's a win, win, win deal with all three parties valuing the interaction and the possibilities ahead!

For some, this sample Magic Mail might seem 'pushy.' It's true that this sample is ideal for people who already have fairly good relationships. There's little fear that bringing the parties together will prove anything but beneficial. But often the two parties won't know each other at all, and a different Magic Mail is then more useful.

Finally, it's worth repeating that Magic Mail can be a great relationship builder on its own, even if unprompted. This is true simply because it brings folks closer together in an online environment that begs for greater togetherness, less facelessness.

So, unprompted, consider taking your next spare moment to write a Magic Mail for two of your trusted colleagues who could both benefit from a mutual introduction.

Who knows what it might lead to!

Networking Tactics of the Superconnectors

We know from the experience of hundreds of networking training events over the years that if you make a solemn oath to yourself, a pledge to try these tactics one after another, you'll soon find that you've gained a few of the superhero powers of the superconnectors, and your bottom line will thank you.

And so at these training events, we often begin with a fun exercise on the whiteboard. For our purposes here, we'll skip the lead-up and just show the ending (Fig. 4.9)

COINCIDENCE OR NOT?

IF...

A B C D E F G H I J K L M N O P Q R S T U V W X Y Z

EQUALS...

1 2 3 4 5 6 7 8 9 10 11 12 13 14 15 16 17 18 19 20 21 22 23 24 25 26

THEN...

K+N+O+W+L+E+D+G+E

11+14+15+23+12+5+4+7+5 = 96%

H+A+R+D+W+O+R+K

8+1+18+4+23+15+18+11 = 98%

BOTH ARE IMPORTANT AND FALL JUST SHORT OF 100%

BUT...

A+T+T+I+T+U+D+E

1+20+20+9+20+21+4+5 = 100%

Fig. 4.9 A Bit Of Fun Math With The Networking Attitude

Adopt the attitude, if not the big flowing cape, of a superconnector

A good attitude can overcome bad weather, a poor hand of cards, even a lousy checkup at the doctor. Attitude is a skill – something you can learn. You can learn to think positively or negatively about whatever that's in front of you. Superconnectors have learned to think positively. Not Pollyannaish positive. Just positive.

Specifically, according to management professors Adam Kleinbaum and Robert Cross as quoted in the *Wall Street Journal*,[39] the winning attitudes to keep in mind at all times, on post-its on the monitor, are:

1. Outgoing: Extroverted and exuberant but also good self-monitors
2. Empathetic: Approachable and able to sympathize
3. Accessible: Fully present and welcoming
4. Energizing: Fellow employees feel invigorated by them
5. Optimistic: Doesn't focus on the faults, but on the remedies

Again, the only difficult thing about networking is committing to a 'networking attitude' that says:

> "I will dedicate real and meaningful time; I will always be connecting; I will systematize it so I stick with it."

Post this on a sign above the door if you must! Dedicate to spending real time with others, listening to their needs and passions, being available to them, and bringing value without regard for immediate gain. All in a systematic way, until it becomes a routine networking attitude. Success will follow.

This overarching attitude drives every networking tactic that follows...

Build your network around core values

People will *join* your network for a number of reasons – because you do business together, or perhaps you met at a conference, or you share common industry associations and interests. But they'll *stay* in your network, participate and share more often if there is a core value system that they genuinely believe in. These core values are the cement that first joins relative strangers, and allows for the building of camaraderie and ultimately enables far more fruitful connections.

Be certain in building your network, then, that you are driven by core values that are clearly communicated to all whom you encounter. You will then build up a network that you can believe in, as well.

---

39 Rachel Feintzeig, "Office 'Influencers' Are in High Demand", *The Wall Street Journal*, Feb. 12, 2014

Introduce people with shared interests

Amazing things can happen when you introduce two people, especially if each has the Networking Attitude. Santa Barbara-based bridge loan specialist, Daniel Corry, went ahead and introduced a walking buddy and an old business associate by email:

> *"Lee, meet Colin. Colin, meet Lee. Lee is the best marketer I know. Colin has an amazing algorithm in search of a market. You could have some fun making money together, or at least arguing politics because you're wholly opposed:):) Consider yourselves cheerfully introduced..."*

Daniel didn't know what would happen. He didn't ask to be cc'ed on future emails. He figured that if good things came from the introduction, that would be reward enough. So what happened?

Colin and Lee did keep the email stream alive, and then escalated it to regular Skype calls, then formed a company named Scredible.

Daniel did receive something in return – some stock options in the new company as a thank-you plus some investment analysis business sure to come.

All from bringing mutual friends together. Daniel didn't think twice about his own gain. He had two business friends he thought ought to chat. One thing led to another. He gave first and received a lot later. You always receive more than you give. It's the Give & Receive Principle that animates the Networking Attitude and brings success into view – whether right away or out on the horizon.

When planning a trip...

Keep LinkedIn in mind. Do a search for the city you're traveling to, and reach out to people there who are using LinkedIn.
- If you know them well enough, arrange a coffee.
- Or even better, lasso a third associate into the coffee so you reconnect with two people and they both appreciate connecting with a local talent.

- If you don't know them, but would like to, send a link to your Profile and tell them you'd like to meet when you're in their city.

In this way you're building a solid offline network through LinkedIn.

Add LinkedIn to your email, blog, website

Include a link to your LinkedIn Profile on your email, blog and website as a subtle encouragement to view your Profile. It works – people see the link (aka badge) on your email and feel that it credentializes you, and will sometimes click it to see what you have been up to. It's worth doing! Go to your Profile, then click on the Edit public profile & URL link, then scroll down and find the Public Profile Badge. Click on the Create a badge button to get started.

Get back in touch

If you figure, for the sake of illustration, that you've met an average of two new people every business day of your adult life (100s at the conferences; zero some days) and say you're 40 now, then you've met more than 10,000 people!

And how many are you still in contact with?

Maybe 1%, 2%, or even 5% . . . which would mean 100-500 people from your past?

Some of these people were once important in your life. They were meaningful connections. But are they so much water under the bridge now? What's to stop you from reaching out and saying hello again?

Especially since LinkedIn makes it so easy.

> "Hey, it was great knowing you long ago. What are you up to? Here's what I'm doing. Let's keep in touch again, okay?"

You may be surprised at how welcome this 'reach across time' can be. Or what it could lead to! Remember that your KLT Factor was high before; all you need is a little first step to pick up where you left off…

Bring something to the table

Ivan Misner, founder of BNI calls it "Givers Gain". We call it "Give & Receive". Whatever you might like to call it, it's the stuff of the new online networking artform that supports and enables all the strategies and ideas that follow.

In four steps, you bring something of value to the table…
1. Decide who you want to meet and get to know better
2. Spend time researching their business
3. Come up with at least 10 ideas that could help them
4. Just give those ideas to them, no strings attached

Then what? You might soon be knotting the thick rope of friendship. At the least, you will have learned something new about your contacts line of work. And at best, you will have made a valuable new relationship developing.

> In our training sessions, we teach up to 50 networking tactics of the superconnectors. To know more about this, get in touch and we'd be happy to share a few with you.

Takeaways

- Your LinkedIn network can be a high-value currency with the KLT Factor
- Keep focused on the quality of connections, more than the quantity
- Reach out daily to cold contacts and turn them into warm connections
- Work with connections to earn referrals to their connections of value
- When someone visits your Profile, try to find ways to bring them value
- When you find a professional with a shared interest, be sure to connect.

EMPLOYER BRANDING IN THE DIGITAL AGE

5

SUMMARY: To optimize and ultimately monetize an employer brand, the personal and professional brand of every employee must align with the corporate brand on LinkedIn so that it resonates consistent and true with online communities, driving customer acquisition and retention, helping to source and attract top talent.

Why Spend Large on Marketing, Little on LinkedIn?

Since at least 2012, major enterprises across all industries have spent heavily on marketing, according to Gartner:[40]

- Average of 12% of total revenue is spent on marketing
- Successful companies spend much more – IBM and Microsoft, as examples, spend between 21% and 23% respectively each year, or 50% more than on R&D. They understand that it's nice to have the best technology, but it's essential to have the best marketing.
- Social business leaders spend even greater percentages on marketing, with LinkedIn at 35%, Twitter at 44%, and Salesforce.com at 53%.[41]

Though the importance of the marketing spend is well known, companies allot remarkably little to *digital* marketing (software as service, agency services for website, search, content, social and mobile marketing, and associated salaries).

This digital spend averages just 2.5% of revenue across industries, or about a quarter of the marketing total.

Why so little?

With consumers completing 75% of the buying decision online and 67%

40 Gartner's 2015 report https://www.gartner.com/doc/2984821/cmo-spend-survey
41 https://vtldesign.com/inbound-marketing/content-marketing-strategy/percent-of-revenue-spent-on-marketing-sales/

of B2B buyers evaluating a company through online channels prior to ever speaking to a sales rep, [42] why aren't companies allotting a greater percentage of their marketing spend to digital?

The usual response is that digital is new, unproven, hard to measure. All true, to an extent. But we believe the lopsided spending ratios have another, perhaps even larger, cause: biases built into the system, biases that form a three-legged table to support the needs of powerful constituencies and longstanding customs:

- Ad Agency Model. Advertising agencies rely on big expensive TV buys that are relatively simple to manage and pay handsome commissions. Agencies don't want to sacrifice their commissions, so they continue to produce self-reverential studies affirming the ROI of big ad spends, taking care to note the brand-building power and extensive reach of TV (for which there is ample evidence). And company executives are generally happy to play along, partly because...

- Digital is Difficult. When social media took off, it was largely written off by established business leaders as a wastrel's pursuit. It looked so . . . light and fluffy. And it was. But something happened on the way to the online forum. It graduated from fad to focus practically overnight. It suddenly had to be taken seriously. And everyone who once wrote it off as marketing-lite now saw that it is, in fact, enormously complex. Not at all easy to figure out. Much easier to fall back into the familiar pattern of...

- Big Screen Envy. Everyone likes to see their brand on the big TV screen, for all the ego stroking and bragging rights it confers. And since it is always a challenge to prove the precise ROI of any advertising spend, it's comforting for executives to reassure themselves that even if nobody is watching their ads, at least they are making it up in brand exposure.

Right.

Recently, we have seen the legs pulled out from this table of biases.

We've seen it from industry-disrupting startups that are billion dollar babies (unicorns, in the vernacular) without spending more than a

---

42 https://hbr.org/2015/03/making-the-consensus-sale AND https://business.linkedin.com/content/dam/business/sales-solutions/global/en_US/c/pdfs/idc-wp-247829.pdf and https://www.business2community.com/b2b-marketing/b2b-buyers-search-tech-solutions-01909793

rounding error on traditional marketing.

These companies with names like Airbnb, RelayRides, TaskRabbit, Liquid, Zaarly, LendingClub and yes, Uber, are digital natives, leading the way to the marketing format of a new generation.

We are in league with these digital natives, believing that companies will be forced by hard ROI considerations to abandon their old biases and commit a much greater ratio of marketing money to social marketing solutions . . . with LinkedIn gaining the lion's share of the spend across platforms.

So let's drill down on how top marketers are spending on digital strategies.

Top three digital marketing expenditures

Marketing leaders believe the bulk of their digital spend *should go* to their corporate websites, social networks, and digital advertising, as per the same Gartner study (Fig. 5.1).[43]

In confirming, LinkedIn's surveys show that the annual cost of a bad

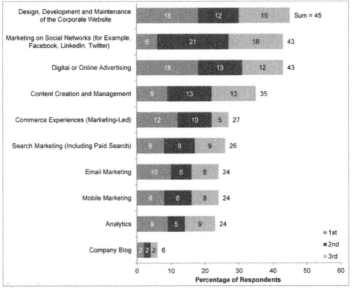

Fig. 5.1 Gartner study of top digital marketing preferences

---

43 https://www.gartner.com/smarterwithgartner/gartner-cmo-spend-survey-2016-2017-infographic

employer brand in the UK is $5.9m and in the US $7.6m. Nearly 7 in 10 said a strong employer brand is a top priority.[44] This figure increases as company size increases, with 78% of companies with 10,000+ employees prioritizing the active building and nurturing of an employer brand online.

The four top reasons CEOs are prioritizing employer branding are summarized in Fig. 5.2:

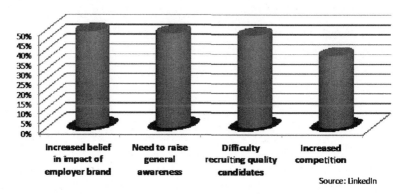

Fig. 5.2 Why CEOs are increasing the spend on employer branding

Let's review an employer branding program that addresses these pain points, beginning with...

Aligning Personal, Professional, and Corporate Social Brands

As individuals, we tend to be most acutely aware of our personal and professional brands when we are seeking employment.

Similarly, as companies, we are keenly focused on our brand positioning statements at the time of origin and in the occasional offsites.

But as time goes by, both individuals and companies get caught up in the day-to-day of business. Often forgotten, or backburnered, is the brand – valuable as we know it to be. This can lead to confusion among consumers

---

44 https://business.linkedin.com/talent-solutions/blog/employer-brand/2016/research-shows-exactly-how-much-having-a-bad-employer-brand-will-cost-you

in the marketplace and, ultimately, to a longer-term loss of momentum and financial viability.

Yet in today's social marketplace with online networks playing outsized roles in our daily activities and everyone finding a place in those networks, organizations must have a consistency of message and purpose coming from *anyone* who might possibly raise their social voice for the organization.

By anyone, we mean *everyone* in the organization. Yes, you read it right: everyone!

This idea is becoming the new normal in business, and there are five pieces of a socially credible business:

1. Everyone's unique talents are surfaced. Few among us are ever taught to think in terms of what makes us unique in business, what makes us StandOut. Yet gaining a working understanding of each individual's core qualities, skillsets, and character traits is the essential first step in elevating the overall organization's social credibility and value in the marketplace.

2. Everyone has a role to play. The entire organization must know how they fit into the company's brand idea, its primary differentiator, the key social communities it serves, and the customer experience. And each has a scripted role and responsibility in the execution of every social business initiative.

3. Change is embraced. Little of the old workplace remains – organization charts are being flattened, walls are coming down (even Citigroup's new New York office is wall-free), job titles are going away, and individuals have their own plays to execute. So performance reviews also include an assessment of the individual's social branding, to ensure that it is authentic and credible.

4. Time is prized. As the terabytes come faster, the *ways in which the hours are spent* and *who they are spent with* become key factors of success. Everyone must be mindful of the social relationships they are creating, and how those relationships reflect on the organization.

5. Opportunity seizing is swift. In everything, there is now an urgency and a swiftness. An entrepreneurial spirit is the thing. It allows organizations to stay nimble and course correct in a time of massive disruption. It also allows individuals at every level of the organization to better develop their capabilities and make a significant impact in the workplace.

These are the first principles of alignment, the ideals that drive the creation of a socially credible corporate brand that aligns with the personal and professional brands of each and every employee (and visa versa, importantly).

These principles are operationalized on the LinkedIn platform, as we'll see.

Socially credible footprints – for all!

Just about everyone in the company – not just public-facing employees – require a socially credible footprint for the reasons shown in Fig. 5.3:

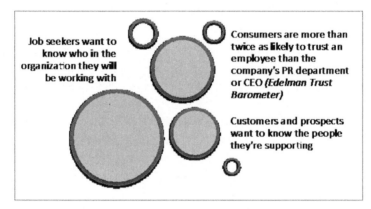

Fig. 5.3 Why ever employee needs a socially credible foodprint

Employees' personal presence and visibility online is now – as often for better as for worse – seen as an extension of the company. This idea has been summarized adeptly by Mark Burgess, a fascinating TEDx Speaker and author of The Social Employee in which he and wife Cheryl Burgess talk about the social revolution:

> *"With the transparency and opportunity for personal connections that social media offers, pushing fabricated, unauthentic sales pitches doesn't work anymore. Instead, we are witnessing the rise of the social employee, who creates a win/win proposition by leveraging their personal brands to build trust and increase the digital 'surface area' of the brands for which they work."*[45]

---

45 Source: https://www.youtube.com/watch?v=FZUlp0ybaec&feature=youtu.be

Employees are already company spokespersons, actually

Since most employees are conversing on the social networks, they are effectively acting as spokespersons for the company – whether positive, neutral, or negative.

So the challenge is to empower these employees to share their knowledge *simply,* in an *engaging* way, and feel *rewarded* for it.

- SIMPLE – Everyone's busy and it has to be fast and efficient
- ENGAGING – They won't continue if they're not seeing an impact
- REWARDING – They have to know what's in it for them

Having employees sharing about the company on social networks, numbers-wise, makes sense. There are a lot more employees than folks in Marketing, of course, and the average employee can have 10x more connections than the company has followers (LinkedIn).[46]When this is done correctly, employees usually feel a greater sense of belonging and the entire team advances together toward shared strategic goals.

From a job seeker's perspective: who doesn't want to belong to such a team? Right!

CASE STUDY: Why every manager needs a first-rate LinkedIn Profile

The "less is more" advice we got from a telecom client...

A telecom company (a leader in their country) asked us to present a LinkedIn workshop for their IT managers. They wanted only one thing:

"Attractive LinkedIn Profiles for all our managers."

That was it. They didn't want to learn any strategies for attracting new customers, or aligning employees with the company brand, or partnership building. We wondered why, naturally, and were told: "These are managers from our IT department. They don't have to find new customers, employees, partners or investors. They need to have excellent LinkedIn

---

46 https://business.linkedin.com/talent-solutions/blog/employer-brand/2016/7-stats-that-prove-your-employees-are-your-secret-recruiting-weapon

Profiles because potential employees check out their LinkedIn Profiles before even considering applying for a job with us."

So here was a customer, telling us it's critical to have an engaging LinkedIn Profile as a manager in order to attract the most qualified new employees.

To ensure that your managers' LinkedIn Profiles are optimized for recruiting purposes, here are some tips to give them:

- Craft a summary of your job description with interesting details – people like to work in an interesting environment with an inspired manager.
- Share a specific role you held in the past – this might be the actual job the other person is seeking.
- List all the jobs you held in the past – this shows your career path that other people might be interested in following, even emulating.
- Link to the job site of your company in the *Websites* field of your LinkedIn Profile and to the Company Page, where they can also find the job vacancies at your company.
- Use SlideShare and YouTube to...
  - Upload presentations you have given that reveal projects of yours that might appeal to potential employees (check compliance and confidentiality issues before uploading).
  - Upload rich media job openings – especially if you are trying to attract visually motivated applicants.
  - Showcase team activities – this might also be beneficial for your visibility *within* your own organization.
  - Showcase Testimonials – the people in your organization are the people that others want to hear from, and in an authentic format.

These actions are part of a passive strategy. To get more aggressive in attracting new team members, there are advanced tools for use in more active and finally proactive strategies. More on these ahead.

Why the CEO needs the best LinkedIn Profile of all

Having an attractive LinkedIn Profile for CEOs, C-level executives and spokespeople is essential for two letters: PR

When CEOs and top execs are mentioned in the media, a link to their

LinkedIn Profile is often included. When people click on that link and see an incomplete or dull Profile, they could assume that the company itself is also dull when the truth is no doubt different.

Only 30% of Fortune 500 company CEOs and 75% of all CEOs have a LinkedIn Profile[47], much less one that is optimized to tell the company's story.

There are lots of reasons given by CEOs for not having a Profile, or for having a boring one. Some of those reasons made sense five years ago, when LinkedIn was still little more than a resume-posting service to many. But...

> "LinkedIn is rapidly becoming the outsourced HR and Sales and Marketing platform for most of the world."

This has ripple effects across the commercial world. If the CEO of an innovative company is not on LinkedIn, many in the media and across the marketplace may well conclude that the company...
- Really isn't innovative at all – so fewer media stories
- May not be worth working for – so fewer job candidates
- Doesn't understand the marketplace – so fewer business opportunities.

To get current and relevant on LinkedIn, and send the right PR message to all of the company's constituencies, it's critical to build up your executives' Profiles with:
1. SlideShare presentations that spotlight the company's expertise
2. YouTube clip of the CEO sharing the company's vision, values, and culture
3. Videos with insights to show the world what the company excels at
4. Regular updates on the Profile linking to new blogposts and articles.

Don't fall into the trap of making the CEO's LinkedIn Profile a commercial pitch for the company.

Sure, it's the CEO we're talking about here. Ego is always an issue. But there is nothing to be gained from heaping praise or trumpeting industry awards that mean little to your customers. The Profile is a place instead to show both the professional and 'human' sides of the CEO. A chance for

---

47 http://www.adweek.com/digital/report-61-of-fortune-500-ceos-have-no-social-media-presence/

the CEO to share helpful information, as well, to set the tone for the entire organization.

And bottom line, the CEO should look good on LinkedIn for one simple reason:

People do business with people they want to do business with – that is, people they know, like, and trust (KLT Factor).

Okay, for a second reason, as well:

Of the 178 million searches conducted on LinkedIn every day, 25 million of those are viewings of LinkedIn Profiles. What is your company missing if your CEO's Profile is not among them?

Or looking at it differently, would you want to work for a company where the CEO doesn't have a profile, or worse, has a weak one? Most people wouldn't!

For CEOs holding out, in fear of being stalked

All the best arguments for a CEO to create an attractive and valuable LinkedIn Profile mean nothing if the CEO had a bad experience with troublemakers, or fears it might happen. Which is why LinkedIn continues to improve its protections and allows you to limit the number of invitations, messages, and emails that get through.

To set privacy options (Detailed in Chapter 2):
- Hover over your photo on the Me -button and dropdown to Settings & Privacy, and click.
- You will be asked to login again (a security aid)
- Click the Communications tab
- Click Who can send you invitations and choose the most applicable setting.
- Also click on Messages from members and partners
- Make the right selection from the options available. The stricter ones are most likely the best for a CEO.

The downside of this approach is that it restricts networking options. But it might help to persuade a recalcitrant top manager to have a LinkedIn

Profile. No pesky salesperson can stalk them while the organization enjoys the marketing, PR, and recruitment benefits of having a LinkedIn Profile.

LinkedIn becomes the tool for aligning the three brands

We have seen how aligning the personal and professional brands of your employees with your corporate brand can be accretive to the organization. Now let's look at execution...

Creating a Consistent Brand Message That Resonates in the Marketplace (The Model Profile)

To lift online visibility and social credibility, your organization first needs to look its professional best online and communicate the value you offer to your marketplace. Then, when you do reach out to people, you will be well-positioned to engage efficiently and productively.

For companies that do not have a strong online footprint, a good first step is to create what's known as a Model Profile. This is the first LinkedIn profile you will professionally craft, and ideally for one of your executives. It becomes the model, or template if you will, to guide the rest of the team in creating their own Profiles which are both individualized and still aligned with the corporate's Profile.

When we assist with this process, these are the five steps we take, and they will work for you, as well, if the process is managed in-house:

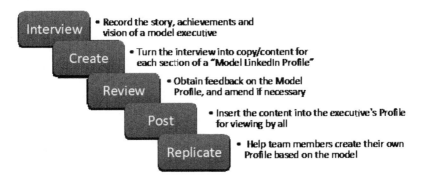

Fig. 5.4 The Model Profile: Creating a Consistent Brand Message that Resonates in the Marketplace

Keep in mind that a company cannot force an employee to complete a LinkedIn Profile to a set of specifications. Their Profiles are their own property, and do not belong to the company.

Instead, you want to invite them to create a Profile that highlights the best of their personal and professional skills so they align with the company's brand messaging.

This is an exercise that any good employee will welcome.

Indeed, in our training courses, many participants don't even know where to start and are relieved to be offered a model to work from.

Additionally we provide a LinkedIn Profile makeover service. You can find more details about this on https://www.how-to-really-use-linkedin.com.

As with the crafting of an individual LinkedIn profile, (as we did in Chapter 3), we begin with the all-important question:

Do the team's LinkedIn Profiles pass the six-second test?

With over 90% of recruiters relying on LinkedIn to find out more about potential candidates (according to data from the Society of Human Resource Management), from our research we've seen that searchers decide in the first six seconds of scanning whether a LinkedIn Profile is worth a closer look.[48] So in six seconds...

- What do customers and prospects see in your brand?
- Why would a job seeker pick your company?
- How do know you are coming come across credibly?

It begins with the first impression. From the very beginning, what is every employee doing to grab viewers and implore them to stay longer than six seconds, read deeper into their Profile, and want to learn more about the company, even engage with it?

This is the top-line objective.

---

48 http://time.com/money/5077954/linkedin-profile-tips-resume/

The remainder of the profile should be crafted just as we laid-out in Chapter 3 to execute on this objective.

Then with the individual team Profiles in order, the next step is...

Building a High-Value Company Page on LinkedIn

LinkedIn has taken steps to make it easier for your company to present your wares to the public, and to build relationships with customers – *all for free.*

Whether you have a basic Company Page in place on LinkedIn, or could use some help in optimizing one, here are the steps to take.

> <u>NOTE</u>: We're assuming you have a Company Page. If not, begin one: https://www.linkedin.com/help/linkedin/answer/710?lang=en.

To optimize your LinkedIn Company page:
- Go to your Company Page and click the *Edit* tab
- You will be taken to the *Overview* page.

Company Page

Go ahead and complete all the perfunctory data fields. They are straightforward.

We have created a LinkedIn Company Page checklist for you. Just go to on https://www.how-to-really-use-linkedin.com/company

Tip: Do some people find the name of your organization difficult to spell correctly? Just like with your personal name, be sure to insert some alternative spellings in the description here!

Challenge for International Companies

International companies face an additional challenge: Whether to have one Company page for all countries, or a separate one for each country?

> Advantage of a single Company Page worldwide: The identity of the company is clear. This simplifies communication with co-workers, customers, suppliers, partners, potential new employees, etc.

> Disadvantage: It's harder to appeal to different visitors. Someone who wants to work for the German branch of an American company, for example, might not find appropriate Job Posts. Lots of issues surface, such as:
> - How to handle different products designed for different countries?
> - Which products should be featured, and which set aside by country?

One solution is to create two Company Pages: one for the international parent company and one for the local organization.

This becomes especially critical if you use LinkedIn's Recruiting Solutions (Chapter 7) and all your employees are linked to the same Company page(s). But recruiting is often best done on a localized, country-by-country basis. So it is often better to create two Company Pages.

> Tip: If you use two Company Pages, be sure to integrate them using the *Affiliated Companies* function on your Company Page. It is easy to setup, but the Admin from the main office and the local country both need to agree on settings.

Use our LinkedIn Company Page Checklist to get the full breadth of information you need for fully optimizing your Company Page to drive social business. Let's just add some guidance from LinkedIn:

Always be optimizing your Company Page

Seven Tips from LinkedIn

> 1. Make it easy for the right people to find your Company Page by adding SEO terms in the description and 'Specialties' sections.

2. Keep your Company Page fresh with rich cover or 'hero' images that reflect your company's accomplishments, events, and offerings.

3. Studies show that a strong employer brand can cut cost per hire by over 50%. Use rich media (like video) on your Careers Page to showcase yours[49].

4. For business lines or initiatives with unique messaging and audience segments, create a dedicated LinkedIn Showcase Page (coming up).

5. Tie all of your LinkedIn communities together by using Featured Groups on your Company Page to list the Groups you manage or participate in.

6. Every *Like, Comment,* and *Share* increases your reach – prompt your followers to take action on your updates by asking thoughtful questions.

7. Get insight into what's working and what's not by using Company Page Analytics to test frequency, topics, and formats.

For more on Company pages, see LinkedIn's FAQ

And here are our five additional tips

1. Keep the cover images compatible with your employer brand visuals. Job seekers might have spotted them already elsewhere and this gives them a visual confirmation that they have arrived at the right place.

2. Make sure your job openings are available on your *Career Page*.

3. Get in touch with your followers. These are people who have raised their hand to say that they are interested in your organization.

4. For international companies, create your Company Page in multiple languages and be sure to speak the language of your target audience.

5. Target your Company Page updates. You can set targeting parameters for Company size, Industry, Function, Seniority, Geography, and Language preference.

Tailor Company Page posts to your community's needs/interests

With your Company Page up and shining brightly, you want to plan out a schedule of updates and posts that will be seen as interesting and helpful

---

49 https://business.linkedin.com/talent-solutions/blog/employer-brand/2016/7-stats-that-prove-your-employees-are-your-secret-recruiting-weapon

by your community (*yes, community, not audience – we are building communities*).

As always, be sure to post content that is of genuine interest within your industry. You want content that demonstrates your thought leadership in your specialty.

High-quality content is the most important element in building thought leadership.

The aim is to engage meaningfully with your communities – so helpful tips, industry advice and resources make ideal post material.

Always be careful about posting anything too salesy. Your company's Showcase Pages, which we'll discuss shortly, are the proper places for sales pitches.

Fig. 5.6 is the Company Page of Barclays, a client of ours. While Barclays is a financial services powerhouse, they present a welcoming face to the business world by consistently posting articles on a range of interesting subjects. The top post, as we write, is about responsible investing and the United Nations. Previous post topics were protecting your accounts from cybercriminals, and a bank-sponsored expedition to Mt. Everest – both of interest to the bank's clients, advice that might be passed on to peers, or shared across the networks for maximum brand exposure.

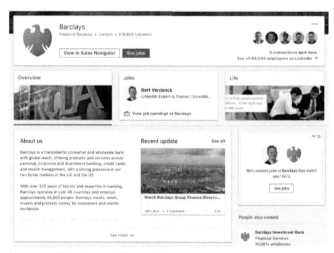

Fig. 5.6 Barclays – powerful social credibility on LinkedIn

Choose the best times to post

Your Company Page doesn't need to be as active as your team's individual Profile pages. You don't want to overload your followers' feeds with too many updates on your company – unless a lot is truly happening! It's generally ideal to post one update a day at the most, one update a week at the least.

There are reams of data on the best hours for posting. And plenty of disagreement, which is natural since every industry has its unique rhythms and flow. And every so often, the so-called 'best' hour to post shifts and the gurus scurry to explain why. As of this writing, we are finding it best to post:
1. Tuesday, Wednesday, or Thursday
2. Early in the morning between 7-8 am (in your major market)
3. Or end of day between 5-6 pm

FWIW, the website optimization experts AddThis analyzed the activity of 14 million members to determine, in all seriousness, that posts done on Tuesday between 10-11 am get the most clicks and shares on LinkedIn.[50] Maybe.

Save time by scheduling your updates in advance using one of the social tools such as Scredible, Hootsuite, or Buffer. But always take caution: If you are scheduling posts in advance, a sudden news event could impact how your post is received, so never set it and forget it. When posting, always be tracking what's in the scheduling cue.

Connect your employees to the Company Page

Make it easy for employees to follow your Company Page:
- Ask them to click the *Follow* button
- Provide them with a set of links to use (taking the reader back to your Company Page)

We'll talk about promoting your Company page below.

---

50 https://simplymeasured.com/blog/best-time-to-post-on-linkedin/#sm.0000uuk43uzq2fkv11kl5re862l81

Use LinkedIn's 'Follow' button everywhere

Embed LinkedIn *Follow* buttons in all the places that you touch your communities:
- Your website
- Your corporate blog
- Your corporate jobsite
- Corporate email communications
- Employee email signatures and LinkedIn Profiles.

LinkedIn has a number of other plugins you can drop into your website, available: https://developer.linkedin.com/plugins. Each of these can add incremental increases in response, and since they take just minutes to add, it makes sense to add them:
1. Share
2. Follow Company
3. Member Profile
4. Company Profile
5. Company Insider
6. Jobs You Might Be Interested In
7. Alumni Tool
8. LinkedIn AutoFill

With the Company Page completed, we move onto the Careers Page...

Attracting Top Talent with LinkedIn's Careers Page

The Life Page (previously called Careers Page) augments a LinkedIn Company page and is a premium service. It sits tabbed behind the Company Page and is ideal for running social recruiting campaigns that target specific pools of talent.

On a Career Page you can...
- Speak directly to prospective employees about specific job opportunities.
- Share the warmth of personality and culture of your company.
- Give candidates a genuine feel for their 'fit' in your organization, among your employees, and within your culture.
- Strategically engage candidates by giving them information about

apropos employees, company news or your industry leadership.
- See a dashboard of analytics on the success of your recruiting campaigns.

NOTES:

We do not sell LinkedIn Talent Solutions, that's what they do! So we are not giving a sales pitch on upgrading to a paid Career Page, but instead laying out the benefits as we see them. Also, having a paid Career Page alone is not going to cut it. It should be part of a larger set of tools to attract talent (as we'll discuss).

There are different levels of Career Pages worth discussing with a LinkedIn representative. If you don't know your area representative, ping us and we'd be happy to introduce you.

Top-line value of a Careers page

- Your content can be automatically adapted to candidates, based on their Profiles. Depending which type of Career Page you have selected, you can have multiple version, such as:
  - Engineering jobs
  - Sales coordinators
  - Project managers.
- Since your Company Page Admin can do targeted company updates, these can be aligned with your targeted Career Pages.
- Job seekers will see jobs tailored to their backgrounds.
- With multiple-page versions, you can target individual candidates.
- Recruiter Profiles connect candidates directly with your company.
- Detailed analytics show you who is engaging with your brand.

Key elements on your Careers page

- Your Header Image. LinkedIn lets you use a different header here, and you should. Choose a photo or image that specifically relates to your company culture and hiring efforts and reinforces your brand positioning with prospective employees.
- Your Posts. *Your Company Page posts auto-populate here, but* you also have the ability to post separately. *Focus on* roles that you are trying to fill, team-building activities, employee testimonials, and company

perks *that tell the 'human side' of your company.*

- **Your Openings.** Your available openings auto-populate on the right side bar if you use LinkedIn Talent Solutions to post your openings. Make the most of this benefit by keeping your openings up-to-date.
- **Visual Appeal.** Use bold and lively visuals to imprint your brand, and compelling copy that grabs the reader. Use video clips and custom modules to bring your culture to life (include also your other social media like Facebook, Twitter, etc.). You can also run your own custom ads with a branded look.

For a sampling of well-executed Career Pages, visit some of our clients:[51]

- RBS
- Deloitte
- Travis Perkins
- Fluor

Using LinkedIn's Showcase Pages for...Selling!

We speak so much about the changes in sales processes brought about by social business ascendancy. But on LinkedIn's Showcase Pages, a harder sell is still in vogue. This is the place to "showcase" your Company and products and to be as commercial as you like.

You can create up to 10 Showcase Pages on LinkedIn – each with a different area of focus so you can build a relationship with segmented followers.

A Showcase Page can be used for:

- Brand or sub-brand
- Product
- Service
- Business unit
- Company initiative (e.g., a product launch)

So instead of having everyone following your Company Page, you can be building up a dedicated group of followers for each brand, product, service, unit, or initiative.

---

51 https://www.linkedin.com/company/royal-bank-of-scotland/careers?trk=top_nav_careers
https://www.linkedin.com/company/travis-perkins/careers?trk=top_nav_careers
https://www.linkedin.com/company/fluor/careers?trk=top_nav_careers

EXAMPLE: Let's use Microsoft. You may be interested in their suite of Office products, but not necessarily their other products. If every Microsoft product was under one roof, you might not follow. There's too much, given your particular interests. But with a single Microsoft Office Showcase Page, you are happy to follow.

This is why Showcase Pages are popular with larger companies on LinkedIn. And when you hit your maximum of 10 pages, and they are working so well for you that you would like more, LinkedIn is happy to give you more. Just ask!

Your Showcase Pages appear in a list on your Company Page, making them easy for viewers to find and visit.

For an excellent example of a Showcase Page, see another of our clients, BNP Paribas, in Fig. 5.7.

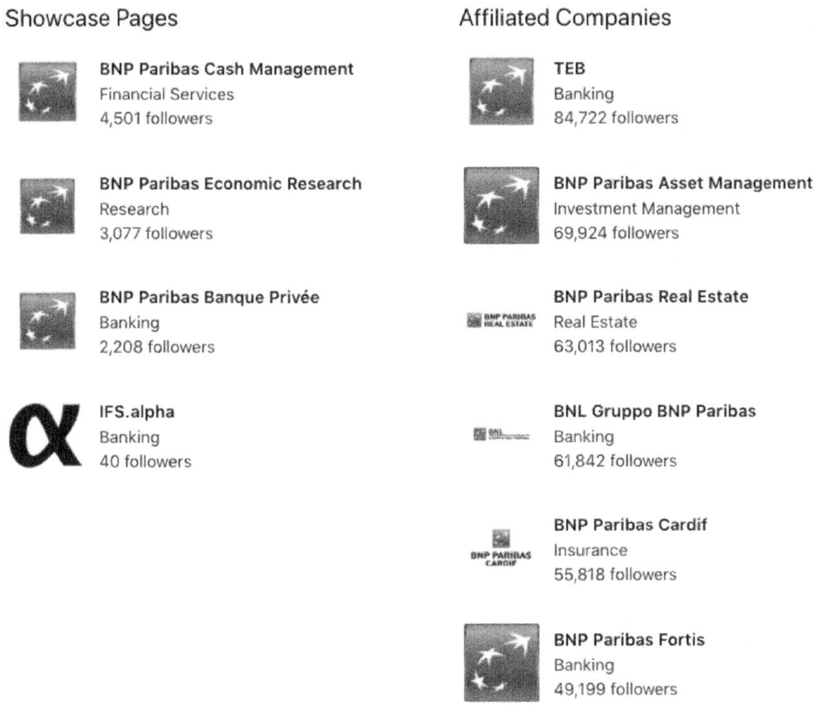

Showcase Pages

BNP Paribas Cash Management
Financial Services
4,501 followers

BNP Paribas Economic Research
Research
3,077 followers

BNP Paribas Banque Privée
Banking
2,208 followers

IFS.alpha
Banking
40 followers

Affiliated Companies

TEB
Banking
84,722 followers

BNP Paribas Asset Management
Investment Management
69,924 followers

BNP Paribas Real Estate
Real Estate
63,013 followers

BNL Gruppo BNP Paribas
Banking
61,842 followers

BNP Paribas Cardif
Insurance
55,818 followers

BNP Paribas Fortis
Banking
49,199 followers

Fig. 5.7. BNP Paribas' best practice LinkedIn Showcase Pages

A top benefit of Showcase Pages – SEO

Showcase pages have their own URL, and for good reason. You can use these pages to claim keyword space in LinkedIn's search results.

For example, Dell is a top company that will always enjoy a high search ranking, but they want to make sure they are found in LinkedIn searches for their services, security products, and cloud products. So they use a URL on their Showcase Pages that includes common search terms, increasing the odds that they come up high in search results:

> https://www.linkedin.com/company/dellservices
> https://www.linkedin.com/company/dell-security
> https://www.linkedin.com/company/dell-cloud

Build your Showcase Pages, and then promote them to followers, encouraging people to interact with these pages in the ways we've discussed. The higher the level of engagement with your pages, the higher your search results will be on LinkedIn and, in turn, Google.

Turning Employees Into Social Champions for the Organization

At least since the Bronze Age it has been common knowledge that a personalized message from a trusted source in the strongest message. Yet in recent years as business adopted new technologies to reach extended audiences, the *personal* was often sacrificed on the altar of *scale*. Now it seems that business is re-learning this timeless wisdom anew in the digital age, and discovering that personalized messages sent out across the social networks *from employees* are the most trusted messages of all.

This is based in a truism that we've revisited often, that consumers trust employees much more than the company PR or the CEO (https://www.edelman.com/trust-barometer).

But trust is only a piece of an interesting puzzle...
- It turns out that if you have 100 employees, you have the potential to reach 63,400 people on their social networks (*Pew Research Center*)
- What's more, 90% of an employee's social audience is usually new to

the brand, so in this example 57,000+ of your employees' connections will likely be new *(based on Dell findings)*[52]

We'll return to break down these numbers, for they are vital to the case we're making. But we know that any quibble will be not with the numbers themselves but with the path to execution – the nitty-gritty of "doing" it. And so, let's get straight to the point:

There is only one way to bring employees into a campaign that transforms them into social champions for the organization. And that is to show them all the rewards that will come. Show them how they can:
1. Look brilliant online with a more professional profile
2. Become better known as experts in their specialty
3. Build their social credibility on the networks of their peers
4. Find similar talents like themselves to build-up the team
5. Relax more when understaffed situations are resolved quicker
6. Contribute to a social environment that is customer-welcoming
7. Learn entirely new things through these new social connections.

These are handsome rewards that any employee can value, handsome enough to open their minds to the how-to portion of it all.

As for the company, the rewards are potentially just as sweet. The precursor study on this dates to 2006. It was done by the enormously talented Fred Reichheld (Bain Fellow, author and speaker on employee loyalty, creator of the Net Promoter System). His study on the power of brand advocacy was published in the *Harvard Business Review*, and found:

A 12% increase in brand advocacy, on average,
generates a 2x increase in revenue growth rate . . .
and conversely a 2% reduction in negative word-of-mouth
boosts sales growth by 1%.[53]

These are audacious numbers! They suggest that when someone talks favorably about a brand, and passes along positive word-of-mouth messages about the brand, it can have an exponential impact on the bottom line. Boost brand advocacy 12%, double revenue.

---

52 http://www.targetmarketingmag.com/article/why-you-should-trust-your-employees-with-social-media/1
53 Fred Reichheld, The Ultimate Question: Driving Good Profits and True Growth, Harvard Business School Press, 2006
    ... http://www.marketingprofs.com/opinions/2015/26782/why-social-media-marketers-and-brand-managers-should-care-about-employee-advocacy

These are the findings from Mr. Reichheld's studies of top-performing companies.

This is why the most successful social businesses today are tapping the shoulders of their biggest potential champions – their own employees...

- Educating employees on the company's employer value proposition.
- Offering the right incentives to promote the company across social channels.
- Turning them into social tools – leaving people feeling better about the company after every interaction.

Yet many companies remain hesitant

Despite the evidence on the potential of employee social activation, a majority of companies globally are somehow afraid of it and even draw a line before anything with the word 'social' in the title.

These companies maintain that any employee involvement in the social networks exposes the company to risks that must be avoided, whatever the opportunity costs. They point to all the usual examples of social media misuse on the job, and the social black eyes that result.

And indeed, a June 2015 survey done by Scredible of 1,000 professionals found that nearly half (47%) of UK professionals believe there is just "*too much useless content on social media*". A significant proportion (38%) believe that social media is "*a distraction that should be banned at work*".

This exposes a stark contrast between UK and US professionals who view social business more favorably. Some 61% of Americans recognise that social media will be important for their careers in five years' time, compared with only 39% of Brits.

For those who worry about social media and see the light at the far end of a tunnel as a train bearing down, they are perhaps more accurately looking at a mirror that is reflecting the headlights of the train coming from behind, driven by 'more with it' competitors about to overtake them because they remain stuck in indecision.

These competitors know that employees who are properly trained and motivated can become powerful social advocates that directly impact the bottom line.

Indeed they can become a powerful brand-selling engine that drives revenues to match or even exceed those driven by Sales & Marketing.

Yes, even exceed!

As summarized so well by Jennifer Jones Newbill, Director of Global Employment Brand at Dell:[54]

> "If you help brand your people,
> they will help brand your company."

Let's look at the path to social championship...

Case studies of 'employee champions' piling up

Companies such as Cisco, Citrix, Dell, Adobe and IBM were early onto the path – they saw the writing on the social wall.

They saw the concept of the network economy gaining genuine purchase among consumers in the late 2000s, moving beyond fanboy blogs to critical mass.

They saw the 'tried and true' pipeline-marketing model losing its oomph.

We call the old business models **Pipeliners** because they rely on methods that were once efficient for moving corporate messaging through the pipeline to target audiences. But with the rise of social business, an entirely new model of **Networkers** is steadily gaining strength and displacing the old marketing.

In Fig. 5.8 you'll see a continuum that organizations find themselves on whether they like it or not – moving from the old Pipeline Companies through four progressive phases in the development toward becoming Network Companies.

---

54 https://business.linkedin.com/content/dam/business/talent-solutions/global/en_us/c/pdfs/li-employee-activation-ebook.pdf

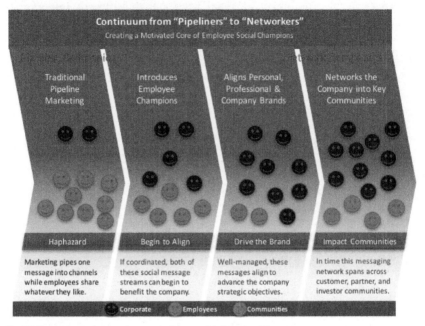

Fig. 5.8 The path a company takes to employee social championship

The continuum begins with...

HAPHAZARD: Marketing sends one message, employees send another

A majority of companies still approach the new economy haphazardly.

Their marketing department sends out advertising messages across channels, including the social channels, trying to maximize their spend.

Meanwhile, the employees are holding conversations in public about the company – some are understandably positive, others not so much. But without coordination, the company is vulnerable to missteps and loose lips.

What's more, the company's brand message can be seen as disjointed or confused. This is because employees are speaking their minds, and consumers trust the employees' personal messages much more than the company's marketing messages. So whatever employees happen to be saying plays an oversized role in the public imagination.

BEGINS TO ALIGN: If coordinated, both of these message streams benefit the company

When the company begins to coordinate the efforts of Sales & Marketing and employees with the introduction of employee champions, the company moves to a more mature stage of the continuum with coordinated message streams that reinforce each other and benefit the company.

At this stage, the marketing message is much more consistent and the company's employer brand in the marketplace crisps and gains clarity.

IMPACTS THE BRAND: With increasing management, these messages align to advance the company's strategic objectives

Over the course of the year, as employees come to recognize the value of aligning their personal and professional brands with the company's brand, the company moves much closer to enjoying a single powerful message in the marketplace, advancing its strategic objectives.

INFLUENCES THE COMMUNITY: Over time, these messages are networked across new communities for new opportunities

A company reaches full maturity as a Networker when its fully aligned messaging spills out across its network of customer and partner organizations, actually influencing those third-party organizations and building a community of champion advocates.

How to manage the transition from Pipeliner to Networker

This transition from Pipeliner to Networker is not an all-or-nothing proposition. That's why it's on a continuum. It's the process of moving from the old model to the new, along the path that is ideal for your organization, bringing new opportunities onto the company radar.

It certainly makes sense for the organization to continue with on-going marketing initiatives as scheduled, at least for the near-term. The transition can occur side-by-side with regular business operations if properly managed.

Here are the management guidelines we develop in our training:

- **C-Level Leadership.** Like any business initiative, a social champion program requires genuine buy-in and backing from the highest levels to ensure acceptance across the corporate culture, and cement the idea in everyone's minds that the program is a top priority.
- **Clear-cut Objectives.** Not only must the program's objectives be set out in clear terms, they must align with the company's strategic vision so that results can be measured to management's satisfaction.
- **Companywide Training.** Before unleashing your team on the social networks, they must be adequately trained in the fundamentals and also understand the company's vision, policies and governance so they can maximize their activities.
- **Content Sharing.** There must be content developed by the marketing department and by the employees themselves to share; using an App such as Scredible to automate this process is highly recommended.
- **Monitoring and Measuring.** From the outset, systems must be in place to monitor the program and measure it against KPIs that matter so that the ROI of the program can be calculated and regular course corrections can be made.

Social champions can be found throughout the company

It just makes sense that the people best suited to champion the company already work for the company, and often feel underappreciated in a social context.

We're reminded of back when the Sydney Opera House was being constructed in 1960. One day the workers heard the most unlikely sound ever for a construction site. It was a beautiful voice, somewhere on the jobsite. One by one, they put down their tools and went in search of the voice. It turned out to be the American performer Paul Robeson, just singing away to nobody in particular. When he finished, the workers asked him what he was doing. He told them that a beautiful cathedral was being created; and in time the architects would be honored, the foreman would be there at the grand opening, but there would be no moment of appreciation for the people who actually built the thing, and he wanted to thank them in advance.[55]

---

55   http://www.sydneyoperahouse.com/about/house_history/1959_1965.aspx

Mr. Robeson's approach bears witness today. It's the approach that an employee champion program takes. It recognizes the great contribution that can be made by every member of the team when they are recognized for the valuable role they play.

It can also be an outsized role.

In one study, researchers found that the average LinkedIn Company page reaches 2% of its followers while Facebook claims that users reach 16% of their fans. These numbers have a lot of play in them[56]. But they do illustrate one way employees might reach an eight times larger and presumably broader audience than the Marketing Department, allowing the brand message to radiate out to new communities.[57]

What's more, we know that the public trusts what ordinary employees say twice as often as what the Marketing team says. So the case for transforming the company's employees into social champions continues to gain strength.

Of course, it's not just a matter of throwing a switch.

Employees won't share business-related content because they are told to. They will share because "the opera singer came out for them". They need to be shown why, and then how. They need to understand the value of their contribution.

Activating Employees – the Six Steps

In Fig. 5.9 we see more of our top-line management guidelines which can be used to model this program:

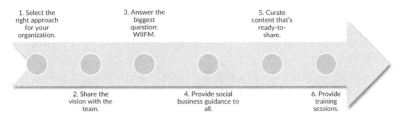

1. Select the right approach for your organization.
2. Share the vision with the team.
3. Answer the biggest question: WIIFM.
4. Provide social business guidance to all.
5. Curate content that's ready-to-share.
6. Provide training sessions.

Fig. 5.9 Activating Employees – the Six Steps to Social Championship

56 https://www.linkedin.com/pulse/death-social-media-organic-reach-best-resource-sparking-david-gabriel/
57 http://www.ignitesocialmedia.com/facebook-marketing/facebook-brand-pages-suffer-44-decline-reach-since-december-1/

1. Choose your approach

Before asking employees to participate, take a step back to identify the right people to work with you. There are two approaches that work, and one will surely work better in your organization:

- Cast a wide net. This is a *top-down* approach that is championed and driven by five to eight people ideally from Social Media, Corporate Communications, and Marketing.
- Start small and scale. This *bottom-up* approach brings in *anyone* in the organization who is a big believer in social business and a natural-born leader, even if they're not currently recognized as such.

Often the bottom-up approach is more successful because employees can be naturally suspicious of 'the latest directive from on high.' But as Eva Löwenberg, a customer success manager at LinkedIn, says:[58]

"If they see their peers participating, they'll be more compelled to follow suit and your initiatives can grow organically and authentically."

2. Share the vision

Make it clear in aspirational terms what vision you have and how every employee is claiming a real stake in the company's future by sharing a consistent message on their social networks – a message that attracts new followers, turns them into prospects, and ultimately into customers.

3. Answer the biggest question: WIIFM

Every good employee will want to help, but they still need to be told how they benefit in crystal clear terms. *"What's in it for me?"* The old WIIFM. It's a valid question and easily answered, as we've discussed:

- Increased social exposure drives leads and increases sales, leading to greater company stability and the potential for higher bonuses or profit sharing.
- Enhanced visibility on LinkedIn elevates their industry profile and improves their reputations, in turn advancing their careers.
- Pressures that an understaffed work group feel are released because HR is able to fill job vacancies faster and with better-fit candidates.

---

58 http://www.slideshare.net/EvaLwenberg/linkedin-employee-activation-playbook

Answering these questions is not a one-time event. On an on-going basis the employees must be reminded of the value of the Social Champion program with inspiring communications and events, including:

- Employee competitions with meaningful rewards
- Gamified so people are ranked by the media they earn
- Fun and splashy videos posted on team pages
- Break room posters and similar collateral
- Team meetings spotlighting the top sharers.

All of these help raise awareness and speed adoption of the program.

4. Provide social business guidelines

Employees will need to know what content is and isn't appropriate for sharing. The guidelines should not be difficult, as they can mirror the guidelines and governance in place for your social media and corporate communications teams.

5. Curate content that's ready-to-share

Be sure to create a storehouse of relevant content that employees can easily tap into and share, knowing it is approved by Legal.

A little exploration will reveal what is best shared. Take some time to understand which social channels employees are using most comfortably. Tailor content to bring value to the social ecosystems your employees naturally gravitate to.

Send regular emails to the team suggesting blogpost ideas, LinkedIn *Status Update* ideas, and Tweet ideas they can copy and post. These shares will look more personal and credible if employees are allowed to edit them into their own voice.

Even better than email, use the social media tools that allow you to constantly and unobtrusively remind employees to post and re-post company content.

If you have a company intranet like Slack, post the content there. Set it up so employees can login to see content they find interesting and can share instantly on channels the company has preselected.

Also show employees how to use LinkedIn *Elevate*, a mobile App that makes it easy for employees to instantly share articles on LinkedIn and Twitter. (See Chapter 8)

6. Provide training sessions

Many employees will take naturally to sharing, because they are doing it already. Others will feel much more comfortable, especially since the sharing is on behalf of the company, if they first receive basic training.

Companies like Adobe and Dell have created certificated programs and we have training designed for companies in most industries.

For our most recent and more detailed case studies
of employees social activation,
visit https://how-to-really-use-linkedin.com

Now with these six steps ticked off, you can be up and running.

Assuming that your team's LinkedIn Profiles are up to snuff (*they are, or will be soon, right?!*) ask your employees to begin sharing the content that you are creating for the social business channels. (More on content creation ahead)

Measuring your social champion campaign

The best way to measure the effectiveness of employee social sharing is to make sure that hashtags are attached to every communication. Every hashtagged post, tweet or photo can be tracked and measured for impact.

Here are some great examples of company social champion campaigns, with the hashtag they use to measure their success across Twitter, Facebook, Pinterest, Instagram, Vine, Tumblr, and LinkedIn:

Adobe	#AdobeLife
Dell	#iwork4dell
LinkedIn	#LinkedInLife
HP	#lifeatHP
Lululemon	#joblove

NPR	#nprlife
Salesforce.com	#dreamjob
Target	#targetvolunteers
Zappos	#insidezappos

The most common KPIs used to measure a campaign:

- Participants – when the focus is adoption, measure new and total participants on a weekly or monthly basis.
- Reach – when the focus is total influence, measure the number of people who see the employees' sharing (using social media tools, or tracking employee follower increases)
- Posts – when the focus is volume of activity, measure the company's hashtag (using social media tools)

One last thing:
It's common for employees to leap into this program and start sharing aggressively and impressively, only to soon lose interest as other pressing tasks take priority.

But this Social Champion program is not a run and gun endeavor. It takes time to develop it, as with any program worth developing. It's critical that you and the 'leader' of this program keep it alive, week after week, actively monitoring and managing it.

We place reminder alerts in Slack and on our team's calendars, to help imprint and ingrain the activities so that, before long usually, everyone has a routine in place with a developing core of social champions that are becoming known in the industry and beyond.

Conclusion

An Employee Social Champion Plan empowers employees to share their knowledge simply (*everyone's busy – it has to be easy*) in an engaging way (*they won't continue if they don't see impact*) and feel valued for it (*they know what's in it for them*). With this plan effectively implemented, the opening numbers come into focus:

- Every 100 employees who participate could reach 63,400 people on their social networks;
- 90% of this audience will probably be new to the brand, resulting in

57,000+ new connections in this example;

- Setting a goal of a 12% increase in brand advocacy could generate a 100% boost in revenue for the company.

Any company that is not leveraging employees to amplify the social brand is missing an exponential opportunity.

Publishing on LinkedIn to Radiate Expertise

When LinkedIn announced an all-new Pulse publishing platform in February 2014, the goal was to become the largest publishing platform on the Internet. And they may yet succeed in this ambitious vision. Lately LinkedIn seems to have dropped the 'Pulse' brand, but keeps the functionality of blogging or writing long articles alive.

Looking back over the timeline of LinkedIn's business model development, we see:

2002	Launch a network for finding jobs and opportunities.
2008	Fold in business knowledge to help members perform better at work.
2012	Give access to hand-picked influencers who publish world-class information worth paying attention to and learning from.
2015	All members can become influencers and build their own base of followers based on the merit of their writing and engagement.
2018	Pulse is completely integrated into LinkedIn. The name Pulse and all its links are discontinued.

Essentially, LinkedIn is now offering the biggest reward of all in exchange for publishing outstanding original content. They are offering every member the opportunity to build a potentially large community of fans and followers and to become an *Influencer.*

After a decade of encouraging its members to be *connecting*, the emphasis is shifting to *following*.

A convenient 'write an article' button as part of your *status update* on your homepage makes it easy for anyone from job seekers, customers, prospects, partners, to competitors no doubt, to follow you without the higher-bar of having to connect with you.

How to publish brilliantly on LinkedIn

Get Oriented

Go to your homepage and click on *Write an article.* And the screen like Fig. 5.10 appears.

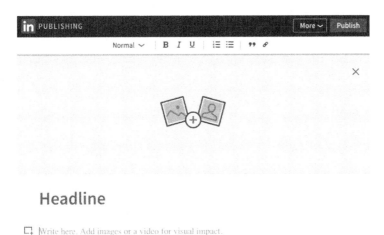

Fig. 5.10 Overview of how to write an article on LinkedIn

Start Writing

You will see a blank page with instructions for beginning.
- Write about your specific area of expertise
- Don't try to cover too much; a great post goes "a mile deep and an inch wide"
- Express an opinion if you like, mixing passion with reasoned analysis
- Write in your speaking voice – it's most authentic

Focus on Title

Spend the most time with the Title. If it's not eye-catching, people who are moving fast across the Internet won't be slowed down to read your great words below.

There is general agreement among social business experts that the best-performing titles are 'how to' and 'lists of' titles, and the worst-performing are 'question' titles. In other words, an article titled *How to Disappear from the IRS* and *18 Ways to Disappear from the IRS* are both going to perform much better than *Can You Disappear From The IRS?*

Specificity Works

Use specifics, numbers, examples, verifiable statistics; the more precise the writing, the higher the readership in this medium.

There are no limits on word count, but posts in the 1,000-word range are best received. They are long enough to make a case, but not so long that they eat into a reader's busy day.

Visuals Essential

Include rich media with a simple click on the chain-icon. By adding rich media, you lend credence to your insights and can increase your readership substantially.

Jeff Bullas writes that articles with images get 94% more views over those without an image[59].

Neatness Counts

Be sure to have a colleague edit or at least proofread your post. We all need a second set of eyes, and LinkedIn is not a forum for sloppy writing.

When to Post

On average, the best day to post, in terms of historical readership cumes, is Thursday followed by Sunday. The worst days are Monday (catching up after the weekend) and Friday (thinking about the weekend). Please check with your target audience. It changes per region, language, etc.

Keep Posting

Return to publish whenever you have valuable thoughts to share. You are building your social credibility with each article you publish, strengthening your professional brand and in turn your company's brand.

---

59   http://www.jeffbullas.com/6-powerful-reasons-why-you-should-include-images-in-your-marketing-infographic/

Ideally publish at least once a week and develop a reputation for consistently good posts. This can be a hefty schedule, and so coordination with and assistance from the Marketing Department is generally useful.

Cross Promote

When you post, make note of it with a *Status Update* on your personal and Company LinkedIn pages. Be sure to include a link to your article in your update.

Tweet about your articles, which you can do right on the LinkedIn platform.

Also post to your Facebook page if the material is softer and appropriate for your Facebook audience.

Sharing on bookmarking sites like reddit (www.reddit.com) is also good for generating traffic.

Alert your network that you've written something important or valuable on LinkedIn, in case they miss it in their news feed. Send a message through LinkedIn to key readers you want to reach, letting them know, as well.

Also share with any LinkedIn Groups that are appropriate. Just be certain that the article is not overly promotional. You want the Group moderator to approve the article for sharing in the Group because it brings value to the Group.

How to get your posts featured on several channels

As we discussed earlier, when you post an *ordinary* article, the LinkedIn machinery will notify your entire network and include it in the email digest sent to members on a schedule they determine in their Settings (Daily, Weekly, None).

Fig 5.11 shows a typical email digest of LinkedIn updates, and for fun, we selected one that highlights the hard-driving spirit of many professionals regarding the relationship between salary and happiness ☺.

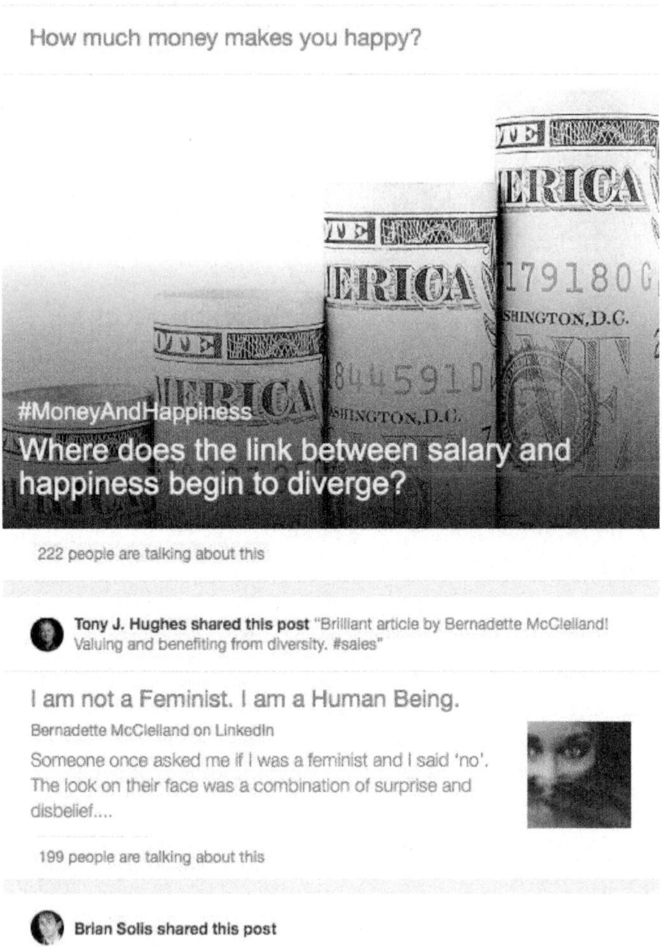

How much money makes you happy?

#MoneyAndHappiness
Where does the link between salary and happiness begin to diverge?

222 people are talking about this

Tony J. Hughes **shared this post** "Brilliant article by Bernadette McClelland! Valuing and benefiting from diversity. #sales"

I am not a Feminist. I am a Human Being.

Bernadette McClelland on LinkedIn

Someone once asked me if I was a feminist and I said 'no'. The look on their face was a combination of surprise and disbelief....

199 people are talking about this

Brian Solis **shared this post**

Fig. 5.11 Your article can reach wider audiences with email distribution

Now when you post an *extraordinary* article that gains a lot of attention, the folks at LinkedIn will be watching as well. They could make a decision – either a human one or algorithmic – to feature your article on the home pages of millions of members who are likely to find it relevant in their professional lives.

A perfect example of this comes from one of our clients, Tom Stevenson, founder of The Twenties London. His post to LinkedIn was so impressive, LinkedIn shared it widely and as a result he earnt 178,776 views, 3,624 likes, and 315 comments as shown in Fig. 5.12. In his own words:

"I was looking to increase my exposure to my target market, and during the LinkedIn Social Selling training, Bert recommended writing an article and becoming a publisher on LinkedIn. I did this, and within weeks I had another problem: One of my articles went viral and hit 100k views and hundreds of comments. I then needed their advice to turn that traction into business!"

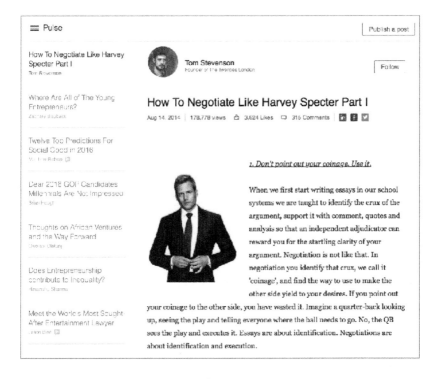

Fig. 5.12 Results of an extraordinary post – the author found himself swamped with queries and requests for work

So when you plan to post, plan to spend extra time creating an extraordinary post. Great things can happen!

Four common posting mistakes to avoid

- Rehashing common knowledge. In the online forums there is way too much cutting-and-pasting of others' work, and quickly churned-out chaff meant to pass for erudition online. These kinds of efforts come across, well, like a dead skunk in the road. So those who take the

time to properly frame an important issue, and provide an actionable solution, will StandOut brilliantly.
- Confusing thought leadership with a sales pitch. The former leads to the latter, not the other way around.
- Targeting the post to an uncaring audience. Always speak to the top-of-mind concerns of your company's core communities.
- Wandering astray from your core competency. Readers will know at once if the poster is a genuine authority on the subject, so stay within competency.

Avoid these mistakes, craft extraordinary posts on LinkedIn, and you will enjoy the deepest and potentially broadest reach across the LinkedIn universe.

Driving blogpost readership with Status Updates

The *Status Updates* on LinkedIn are an underappreciated tool. When used properly, these updates can drive serious traffic to the company blog. Let's see how.

As we've discussed, you use the *Status Update* to announce important developments that are of interest to your connections, such as a new job opening or a blogpost you just wrote. So try this:

Write up your thoughts offline and then email the piece to a selection of co-workers, asking them to use it in a *Status Update* on their own pages, and to Tweet it, as well.

Every organization has employees who feel underutilized and wish someone would tap them this way. These are the natural social leaders in the organization, people who think of themselves as social bandleaders, who secretly play Guitar Hero at home or frequent karaoke bars because they want to belt it out, musically, yes, but also in writing. These people would welcome the opportunity to contribute their thoughts on LinkedIn on a regular basis.

These people just need to be identified, and let loose with a goal in mind.

Engagement power of your employees

Let's see how much more engagement is possible when employees are drawn into the company's blogpost promotion efforts. To do this, we make three assumptions:

1. You have a team of 500 employees.
2. Each employee averages 100 LinkedIn connections (this is a good working average based on LinkedIn stats, though this number will quintuple to 500+ when your employees have applied the strategies in this book).
3. The Company Profile has built up a following of 1,000 on LinkedIn.

See how powerful the employees' engagement can be in driving readership of the company's blogposts. Instead of having 1,100 potential readers, as per our example in Fig. 5.13, the company can expect to have 51,000 readers.

Engagement Power of the 2nd Degree		
	You alone post a status update	Your team of 500 each posts a status update
Personal Connections	100	50,000
Company Connections	1,000	1,000
Total Potential Readers	**1,100**	**51,000**

Fig. 5.13 Tapping your employees voices to drive blogpost readership

This exercise demonstrates the power of leverage, of course. But serious leverage with minimal work – a genuine Archimedean effort with the potential readership of the company's blogposts ratcheting up nearly 50x because your entire team has been involved in the activity.

All your team has to do is link to the company blog when setting up their profile, and the reach of your blogposts levers up to impressive numbers. So be sure to:

1. Ask your team to mention company blogposts in their *Status Updates*.
2. Ask people who have a Twitter account to mention it there, as well.
3. Also ask (a select group of) people to post it as a Discussion in the Groups they belong to when the blogpost is relevant to the discussions there.

Levering up potential readership

By adding Twitter shares and LinkedIn Group shares to the activities of your team, you lever potential readership even higher. Let's continue our assumptions about the team of 500 and stipulate that your team of 500 has become socially active because you've created an environment where they are excited and rewarded for their activity.

The math on this excitement works out as follows:

> 500 post a LinkedIn Status Update x 100 connections
> = 50,000 potential views
> 500 share via Twitter x 100 followers
> = 50,000 potential views
> 500 insert into a LinkedIn Group x 500 Members
> = 250,000 potential views

Result: A total of 350,000 potential views. Even if only 15% of the potential viewers actually read it, which is reasonable across the three platforms, then your blogpost still nets 52,500 readers. That's a mighty number for any company!

Plus this hypothetical blogpost of ours will rank higher in the Google search listings. That's because Google registers the traffic being send to your blog's webpage. As a result, even more people will discover your blogpost when making a general web search.

Excellent exposure for a few minutes' work optimizing your LinkedIn *Status Update*!

Using LinkedIn Groups to REALLY Get Known

LinkedIn Groups are communities that members have formed around topics of interest, mostly, but also around industries, professions, brands, you name it – there are more than two million Groups on LinkedIn. There certainly is at least one with your name on it. ☺

Groups are an important way for individuals to find their industry's latest news and sharpest minds, and for companies to cultivate a community of customers and prospects. At no cost beyond the time that you commit, you can find yourself in the company of people you want to get to know, and be known by.

Companies use LinkedIn Groups most often for:
- Customer service
- User experience
- Cause advocacy.

Additional reasons why LinkedIn Groups are so important:
- Give and receive help in Discussions
- Share experiences with peers
- Discover potential employees
- Stay top-of-mind with current/potential customers/employees
- Discover people with the same interests
- Prepare for events
- Follow up after events
- Increase your KLT Factor
- Share interesting information.

With so many Groups around the world, there is almost always a Group in your areas of interest.

How to find LinkedIn Groups

1. **Through the Profile of your target audience.** Scroll down and have a look at the Groups your targets belong to. Join them! It is all about being present where your target audience is. You become visible on their radar, which is a great way to start a relationship.
2. *Go to the Groups Directory.* You will find about 2,500 Groups listed here. Just browse through them and join the one that appeals to you.
3. *Discover Groups.* This is a suggestion tool provided by LinkedIn – it works similarly to the *People You May Know* feature. Here is the direct link: https://www.linkedin.com/groups/discover. Browse through the suggestions for Groups that appeal to you, and join.
4. Search for Groups. LinkedIn does not make it easy for you. Start with typing in a search term in the search box. On the results page, choose the *More*-button and then opt for Groups. Now you will get the results for the LinkedIn Groups.

To find your current Groups:
- On the navigation top menu, hover over *Work*, dropdown to click *Groups*
- You will go to the Groups main page
- You will see Today's Highlights, a personalized selection of conversations from your groups.

Groups are great, as we said, for finding and having conversations with target audiences. But you don't necessarily have to join Groups only in your area of business. You can also join Groups that have interesting members, or intriguing discussions, or fascinating idea discovery, or for anything that grabs you.

For all the good of open-entry LinkedIn Groups, there were problems growing in them for years. Too many Groups were infested with self-serving spam artists that muddled the conversations and detracted from the central purpose of the Groups. So in October 2015, LinkedIn struck back. And rather decisively.

All Groups are now "private"

The privacy settings are now simpler on Groups. They are now wholly private, and come in one of two kinds (full detail):
- Standard Group. Findable in search; members can request to join or be invited by any existing member.
- Unlisted Group. Not findable in search; membership requires an invite from a manager.

This means that conversations going on in the Groups remain private to the Group. This turns these discussions into learning and networking delights, not a spammer's delight. Only Group members can see the conversations. Content is no longer indexed by search engines. Says Minal Mehta, LinkedIn's product lead for Groups:

> "We want you to be professional when you're having conversations. Groups is such a valuable part of LinkedIn. When it works and when I engage, what I get is amazing."

Some more Groups changes...

- You can now @mention someone to tag them to a post if they are a member of the Group. Just click their name from the dropdown menu to mention them in a conversation. This lets you draw them in.
- A new tab dedicated to job discussions should make it easier for companies to hire talent within Groups, and to have conversations with professionals who are looking for jobs.
- You will receive fewer emails. LinkedIn will digest the best content from all of your Groups into one weekly or daily email, your choice.
- You can send only 15 messages per month to other members in a Group you belong to. At the start of a new month, your allotment renews. This applies to members, and Group owners, as well.
- Only Group members can post, erecting a barrier to non-member spammers who previously could post in an open Group.
- When you post your comments in a Group discussion, the post is accepted automatically right away, though the Moderator can still remove a post if it does not meet the Group standards. Also, Group members can still flag posts as inappropriate.
- Group members can now post images along with comments – LinkedIn is keeping pace with the video-motivated marketplace.

The point of Groups is to deepen your relationships. If you meet someone in a Group that you want to know better, you can still send a connection request or Magic Mail (Chapter 4). When they accept, you have made a first-degree connection, and can then email on LinkedIn as often as you both would like.

How to maximize your time spent in Groups

Fair to say that everyone is 'busy' and not in need of additions to the To Do list. So by keeping clear on the highest and best use of Groups, you use your time wisely. Here's how:
- Pose questions in the Groups discussions if you need information – members tend to be accommodating and interested in answering questions.
- See the Profiles of other members to gain direct access to people who are not in your first- or second-degree networks.
- Directly contact members up to 15 times a month. Some members are

not open to being contacted, and disable that option in their settings. However, the standard setting is for members to directly contact one another.

- Post articles to **raise visibility**. Again, no sales pitch. But it is accepted etiquette to end a post with a 'signature link' to your website or blog.

- Answer questions in the discussions to **demonstrate expertise**. Just make certain to provide valuable answers, and not to make a sales pitch.

- When answering questions, you can add an ending tag of one or two lines about your company. This is also accepted etiquette, and helps build reputation.

- Bring other people into a discussion. This could be suggesting a colleague as an expert. Or even ask one of your customers to answer a question and name you as the solution. People believe existing customers far more than you trying to sell yourself.

Of all the LinkedIn networking tools available to you, these Groups may offer the greatest leg up in your networking. But why limit yourself to *joining* a Group?

How to start a LinkedIn Group as if time matters to you

Imagine being asked to be a speaker at a popular event held specifically for professionals in your industry. You'd agree immediately, right?

Or maybe you're a service provider and receive an invitation to talk at a conference where every attendee is a potential customer. Saying *Yes!* is a no-brainer.

Fact is, LinkedIn Groups give you these same opportunities—only online.

Joining a number of Groups is great, but why not start your own?

As the owners of your own Group you can accomplish three things:
1. Create a valuable experience for others (step #1 in effective networking)
2. Increase your company's visibility
3. Access an audience you might never have found

These are all valuable objectives, right? Running your own Group is, as you might expect, a time-intensive experience that only bears fruit over time, and only with a serious dedication and tireless execution. So it is not for everybody.

And with two million plus Groups now in existence, it's not like the world needs another one! But look back over the three things you can accomplish above, and think about them as we review the lessons we've learned from creating dozens of successful Groups over the years.

First off, while having your own Group can cement existing relationships and build new ones, there's no greater waste of time than to use your Group to promote your company. That it doesn't work is only the start. This killjoy approach will often backfire and cause great harm to the brand and a wary eye from LinkedIn's censors.

> Promoting your company in Groups is not the best way
> to promote your company in Groups.

The best way to promote your company in Groups is to organize your Group around a topic or theme that interests you enough to want to be helpful and enter into conversations with others who are also interested in the topic or theme.

So the first principle of LinkedIn Groups is: Be helpful...
- Post interesting and relevant links
- Post and answer questions
- Ask experts to weigh in on discussions and share their responses
- Invite relevant contacts to join the Group.

These are the organic ways to share your interests non-intrusively so that Group members grow to respect you, trust you, and yes, do business with you.

As the Group owner, you will also be the Manager and Moderator, or need to appoint these two positions. Having an active Moderator is essential to keep the discussions lively, professional and non-promotional (which will continue to happen though to a much lesser extent than before).

Grow your LinkedIn Group's membership

Here is how to grow a Group to a size where it becomes valuable:

First familiarize yourself with the all the LinkedIn Group Rules: www.linkedin.com/help/linkedin/answer/6?lang=en.

Next decide which kind of Group you want to have. Again, the two types:
- Standard Group. Findable in search; members can request to join or be invited by any existing member.
- Unlisted Group. Not findable in search; membership requires an invite from a manager.

Then invite friends and colleagues from your organization by email. If you have an *Unlisted Group* and don't want to approve each person on your list manually, you can pre-approve them all (via the *Manage* tab).
Build the size of your network using the tactics in Chapter 4 so you have a steadily increasing number of people to invite.

Invite your own first-degree network to join the Group.

Use the following strategies to find potential members:
- Use the search to set the criteria for targeting the precise audience you desire.
- Browse in the networks of your connections for people who have Profiles of a similar look and feel to your Group members.
- Look at "Viewers of This Profile also viewed" to find peers.
- Look for Companies to invite: If you focus on a specific industry in a specific country, this should provide you with some names.
- Create alerts: Once you have defined your target audience, you can save your searches and be notified of new potential members.

Use Magic Mail to contact high-value associates of your associates who would logically be interested in joining the group.

Spread the word about your group as follows:
- Share an update
  - Write a brief sharing message, and use the @mention to make sure certain people see the message
  - Check the box to post your message to Twitter, as well
  - Choose to share with the Public, or just with your Connections
- Post to other LinkedIn Groups

- Choose other Groups who could benefit from your message
- Give a title to your message – keyword rich is recommended
- Write a brief sharing message
  NOTES:
  1. Not all Group Managers will be happy with you promoting your Group in theirs. Some may label you a spammer. So instead of inviting people in other Groups to join yours, announce a free event or webinar and give them valuable information. Then if they want to join you, they can and everyone is happy.
  2. Always check a Group's rules before posting.
- Send to individuals you know
  - Enter the name(s)
  - A message title is pre-populated – use as is, or change to your own
  - A message is also pre-populated – use as is, or write your own

Invite others with *Send Invitations* inside the *Manage* section of Groups:
- You can invite your LinkedIn connections, or anyone whose email address you have (you can even upload a list).
- You can allow other members to use this option as well or disable it depending on your goals for the Group. If you want to keep the Group under control, it is better to disable it.

Create a Welcome message that invites members to invite others they know. As a Manager you will create a welcome message for all who join. In your message you can kindly ask the new members to invite someone else they think will also enjoy the Group.

As you spend more time with each of these Group-building strategies, you will begin to see the snowball effect taking hold.

That's because LinkedIn members will be seeing in their Network Updates and in emails that their connections are joining your Group. These alerts will arouse interest, because who doesn't want to be part of something popular?!

The more members in your Group, the higher it will rank in the search results of the Groups directory. That should attract extra attention, and members, as well.

Make sure new members are aware of your Group's rules. Some managers point them out in the invitation, others merely mention them.

How to stimulate interaction between Group members

Having members in your Group is one thing, having activity is completely different. Many Groups start out enthusiastically, but die a silent death after a few months.

But with a consistent discipline of stimulating interaction, you can grow an impressive Group, as follows:

☑ Post interesting articles. Make a list of 25 or so topics that support the theme and target audience of the Group. Then either write or have someone write articles on these topics for periodic posting. The key factor is that the content is of genuine interest to the members.

☑ Post your questions in the discussions. In addition to your 25 topics for articles, make a list of questions that might stimulate discussions. Add relevant news that is important to members, and ask them to comment.

☑ Post a review of a past event. Encourage members who attended the event to add their opinion or share the ideas they found enlightening. Members who couldn't attend might also want to share an opinion via this channel.

☑ Announce a future event. If your Group organizes or sponsors an event, announce it and ask who else is joining. Without overpromoting, you might want to add something extra, like a one-to-one with you or with the speakers.

☑ Ask a guest to contribute an article. This becomes most interesting when you secure a well-known expert who is not generally or easily accessible. Good conversations are sparked because members feel special and enjoy the access and interaction.

☑ Ask members to respond to questions. Certain members will have expertise on a subject, but did not see a question that was asked in a discussion. Prompting the member to respond is a win-win. Remember, this is easily done with the @mention function.

☑ Send teases to a few members. Tell them about discussions they may be missing that are of interest. They may have set their notifications to *Weekly Digest* and miss out on timely topics. (Do this only when the discussion topic is REALLY interesting to them:)

☑ Post the name of the expert. If a Group member may know of a solution to a problem or an issue that's common to the Group, post their name as the go-to expert. Public praise is always appreciated.

☑ Avoid clutter in the Discussions. When members post messages that are outside of established rules, don't hesitate to explain that the Discussions are not the place for such messages. This is expected and appreciated by other members. Removing undesirable messages in favor of the germane will keep the largest number of members happy.

☑ Help connect members. When you meet someone (online or off) who might be interesting to another member, connect the two via Magic Mail. This will create a happy community of members who remain active over time.

☑ Send a personalized reminder. You can send up to 15 emails to members each month, so you cannot be wasteful. But if there is a high-value member who is not contributing, send an email to rekindle their interest with an interesting or worthwhile message personalized to them.

☑ Feature an interesting Discussion. Select a discussion as 'Manager's Choice' and the title of that discussion will be highlighted at the top of the Group's homepage.

☑ If possible, organize events. The full power of networking can be found in the combination of online and offline. If you have the time and the resources (and your Group is located around a specific geographic area), consider organizing a local event so members can meet each other.

☑ Involve people in leadership roles. You can have up to 10 Managers. When people have an official role, they feel more involved and will contribute more. So you can divide all of these strategies between up to ten people if you like – decreasing your workload and increasing your leverage.

Why some organizations shy away from LinkedIn Groups

Some companies remain nervous about starting a Group because they don't have a critical mass of people to participate. They worry that if the Group is seen as unpopular, it will create a negative spiral leading to fewer visits and a PR black-eye.

But the facts and experience of LinkedIn argue otherwise:

> *"There are nearly two million groups on LinkedIn and since members can join up to 100 groups . . . safe to say, there is no larger event going on anywhere in the world right now!"*

People are on LinkedIn to connect – not to post cat memes or rant about politics. They want to build their network. They want to join Groups that look interesting. And yours can be – you need simply to commit a few hours a week to it. You can even take existing content and post it into discussions of the group. So no extra production time is required.

Often a group will even nominate their own Moderator, helping with the workload.

Bottom line: Having your own LinkedIn Group can generate interest in paid memberships and in attending events. Just go about it right.

Outsourcing LinkedIn Groups: Maximizing ROI

After the last section, you can see the potential of these online gathering grounds, but also the time and resource commitment. At this stage, it is not uncommon to outsource the project to experienced Social Business Architects who have:
- Built and operated highly successful LinkedIn Groups
- Using a proven methodology for achieving the Group's goals.

When clients approach us on this subject, we outline our own experiences with Groups to offer decision-making guidance. Here is an example project we completed for one of Europe's premier equipment leasing companies:

LinkedIn Group – A Project Outline

1. PURPOSE
   a. Statement of goals
   b. Define ROI requirement
   c. Set KPIs
2. TIMING
   a. When to launch
   b. Establish audience and required reach
   c. Milestones of membership
3. STRUCTURE
   a. Branding
   b. Primary platforms
   c. Platforms to monitor and link with
   d. Workflow and process flow
4. MANAGEMENT
   a. Ownership
   b. Management authority levels
   c. Moderation styles
   d. Membership
   e Member acquisition
   f. Members policy
5. DISCUSSION THREADS
   a. Editorial calendar
   b. Encouraging advocates

Choosing a Model for the Group

Whatever the goals for the Group, it should be built to achieve critical mass as swiftly as possible. This is not an absolute number, but the point at which the number of comments and discussions from members exceeds the number from the Manager/Moderator or 'official contributors'. That is, the outsiders care about the Group as much as the insiders. That's critical mass.

Here are some sample models for Groups as created by us and our partners:
- The Business Technology Forum (for Oracle) was created for a broad, international base of senior managers in medium-sized companies. The subject matter is current, but not urgent. The Group reached critical mass at 12,000 members after 15 months. It is now at 40,000+.

- By contrast, Gas: Fuel of the Future? (for Norwegian energy company Statoil) was created to urgently gather the views of specific groups of people in the UK relating to the public policy debate. It reached its critical mass of 1,000 within 10 weeks. It was a short-term campaign, handed over to the client after three months.
- A group like Software as a Service has 70,000+ members and is intended to be the active go-to forum for SaaS that it is.
- The UK China Business Forum has less than 1,000 members, which is perfect, since it exists solely to drive entries to their Annual Awards Events.

Attracting Members to the Group

A membership acquisition campaign focuses on identifying LinkedIn members who will be naturally interested in the sponsoring company's target industry.

The messaging will be friendly and succinct, emphasizing the calibre of the Group and the number of industry leaders who are/will be members.

The conversion rate is expected to start at 10% and grow over a year to 20%.

Moderating the Group

Assuming the company's goal is to project impressive thought leadership to industry professionals, the type of Group should be *Unlisted* in which only the invited may join.

Similarly, all members may post in the Group but the (outsourced) Moderator reviews all discussions and submissions to verify that they are suitable for the Group.

Lively Group Interaction

Member interaction is critical. Visits to the Group are far more frequent if members can be confident of reading lively, interesting discussions. But a small percentage of members actually contribute, as in any milieu. So the outsourced Moderator sparks excitement with a steady stream of unique content, influencer leveraging, and proven strategies for motivating people to seek the 'reward' of interaction.

Finding Your Champions

It's the Moderator's job to find champions and advocates who will advance the discussions with an ear to the brand, and to recruit those champions into the Group. This can be time-consuming and thus a budget item, but it is worth the investment.

Any LinkedIn member can become a champion in the Group – the key is identifying the legitimate ones...

- Catch the jumpers. Your most rabid champions will jump out at you. They are constantly sharing, liking and commenting on posts. They need to be shown that they are valued members of a social community. For instance, ask them to invite a friend – the biggest fans will consider that an honor.
- Use an @mention tool. A clever way of finding new champions is to identify big contributors in Groups similar to yours, and tell them what's going on in your Group. Tools such as Mention help you find them by tracking on the keywords being used in communities with similar interests. With the premium version of Mention, you can track the locations of your potential champions.

The more energy spent showing potential champions how valuable they are, the stronger your community will become and your investment will be returned.

Setting KPIs

In setting-up the Group, the key performance indicators are established. These are meant to align with the strategic objectives of the organization so that ROI an be assessed. The three most common KPIs we see:

- Deliver operational cost-savings for the company
- Identify new opportunities and changing customer needs
- Increase online engagement with the company's brand.

There you have an overview of how to outsource LinkedIn Group management and on-going operations.

And with this, you have three ways of approaching these LinkedIn Groups:

1. Join a handful of Groups to learn, network, and increase your influence (max. three!).

2. Create and manage your own Group to spread your influence even wider.

3. Outsource Group management to an experienced social business expert.

Measuring Your Employer Social Branding by KPIs That Matter

As online networks go, LinkedIn was a laggard in generating performance metrics for its members in the initial years.

Then LinkedIn went 'enterprise' and began providing detailed analytics that include demographic data on readers, with breakdowns by industry, job title, location, and traffic source.

LinkedIn members can now publish on the platform, target posts more effectively, and measure efforts using key datapoints:

- Who's reading and engaging with your posts?
- Are you reaching the right audience?
- Which posts are resonating with readers?

One of the early evaluations of LinkedIn's new publishing metrics was the social selling expert David Petheric. His review:[60]

- *I can see the audience I am reaching by industry, location and even job title, and see if it aligns with who I am trying to reach*
- *I can see where traffic is being driven from, and see where I can try to stimulate more traffic*
- *I can see patterns of visit behavior, and act to share further when traffic starts to tail off*
- *I can engage with and thank the people who have read, liked, commented on or shared my work easily*

Employer Branding – Soft KPIs

There are rather soft metrics that are valuable early in any campaign to transition the team over to active use of LinkedIn. These are not metrics

---

60 http://blog.linkedin.com/2015/05/07/new-analytics-for-publishing-on-linkedin

that you can easily attach an ROI figure to, but they are critical measures of usage and engagement that are essential for social business success. These soft KPIS are:

- Number of LinkedIn Profiles completed companywide
- Number of LinkedIn connections made individually and companywide
- Number of views of Profiles (measured over a 90-day period)
- Number of "Recent Activity" updates (over a two-week period)

Hard KPIs

Other activities on LinkedIn can be measured very accurately to determine the return on your investment in LinkedIn. These hard KPIs can be tracked initially using LinkedIn's analytics and then analyzed by the company:

- Number of InMails sent
- Number of emails sent
- Number of appointments generated
- Number of proposals created
- Number of sales/deals
- Revenue generated.

Strategic KPIs

There are larger-scale initiatives that are mission critical – the very success of the organization rides on their successful execution. These are the strategic initiatives, and they are not easily measured by any tool, including LinkedIn, though LinkedIn advances these strategic KPIs very directly:

- Product development and support
- New business development
- Strategic business referrals
- Professional development
- Joint ventures and partnerships.

These are the three areas of KPIs that we discuss with clients in order to fashion the ideal social business strategy. With a set of KPIs agreed upon and shared with every member of the participating team, all will know:

- What they will be held accountable for
- How they will be measured
- When they will report on their results.

So in wrapping, these are the topics to discuss at the start of any initiative:

- Which of the three sets of KPIs are most relevant to capture?
- What are the overall quantifiable targets for this campaign?
- What will the success of this campaign look like?

We run an in-depth workshop on creating meaningful KPIs which are ideal for selected organizations. Get in touch if you want to know more!

NOW MISSION CRITICAL: SOCIAL SELLING

6

SUMMARY: Organizations that evolve beyond the comforting reliance of running up numbers of online connections, followers, and recommendations . . . and learn to leverage social business strategies as part of an integrated social business plan . . . are seeing significant improvements at every stage of the new sales funnel.

The Sales Process Is Evolving – Radically

It is often said now, because it is startlingly true, that a selling process that endured for centuries has been completely upended by today's social technologies.

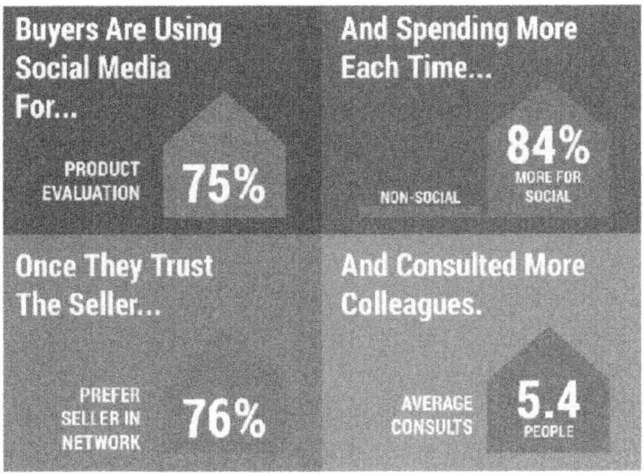

Buyers Are Using Social Media For...	And Spending More Each Time...
PRODUCT EVALUATION 75%	84% MORE FOR SOCIAL NON-SOCIAL
Once They Trust The Seller...	And Consulted More Colleagues.
PREFER SELLER IN NETWORK 76%	AVERAGE CONSULTS 5.4 PEOPLE

Fig. 6.1 The Internet truly has changed the way we buy

In Fig. 6.1 we see a 4-square chart summarizing a 2014 IDC study that summarizes how very different the new social selling math:[61]

1. Three in four business buyers now use social media to evaluate a product before buying, often never setting foot in a store or warehouse.

---

61 https://business.linkedin.com/content/dam/business/sales-solutions/global/en_US/c/pdfs/idc-wp-247829.pdf

2. These social buyers spend almost twice as much per purchase than their non-social peers. They have larger budgets, more discretionary purchasing power, and can actually be identified with greater accuracy (*as we will see*).

3. Of these social buyers, three-quarters prefer a vendor that has been recommended by someone in their network over a vendor they don't know.

4. They will consult with an average of 5+ friends or colleagues in their network before finally buying. And they will sift through an avalanche of reviews and recommendations from formal online sources and their own social networks before making choices.

In short, buying decisions are being made at an early stage when people are looking for answers online. Your company either has a big presence in this early-stage decision-making, or you cede that space to the competition.

This upending of buying behavior has thrown marketing departments for a loop globally even as it has reshaped the old sales funnel (with its waterfall of Attention, Interest and Desire leading to Action – remember *AIDA?*).

The New Social Business Selling Funnel

In today's world of social business, the traditional sales funnel has been turned into something more closely resembling an hourglass or even a nuclear power reactor – both of which are apt metaphors for the new process since timing has become critical and the opportunities explosive if capitalized on properly.

The new social business selling funnel, with the highest-priority sales activities summarized at each level, can be seen in Fig. 6.2. Here is the rationale behind it:

- Exposure. The sales process begins when the prospect is exposed to a product/service and becomes aware of it. This is similar to the old funnel in which *Attention* was the first goal, except that getting intention amidst the terabyte distractions is extremely difficult and the marketer focuses instead on gaining exposure and basic awareness as a first step.

- Discovery. The sales process continues as the prospect begins doing online research and talking with friends or colleagues about the

The New Social Business Selling Funnel

EXPOSURE	
Social Media Sharing	Targeted Advertising
Online Publishing	Earned Media

DISCOVERY	
Online Publishing	Demo Requests
Webinars	Downloads

RELATIONSHIP	
Sales Qualifications	Online Publishing
Follow-up Calls	Personalized Emails

CONVERSION	
Online Publishing	Nurturing Emails
Special Events	Social Media Sharing

RETENTION	
Follow-up Calls	Online Demos
Appointments	Social Media Sharing

ADVOCACY	
Online Publishing	LinkedIn Groups
Employee Champions	Social Media Sharing

Fig. 6.2 The New Social Business Selling Funnel

product/service. During this period the company must be listening to and engaging with the prospect, learning about interests and desires. Through the insights gained, the social divide between your products/services and your prospects can be bridged.

- Relationship. Now the prospect begins sharing personal or business information as part of a relationship-building process. The sharing helps the prospect make a subjective evaluation about the suitability of the company. During this period, the company provides helpful content that's relevant to the prospect's needs – making it clear this is a real two-way relationship.

- Conversion. With success at this stage, the prospect becomes a customer. But with the costs of customer acquisition, the sales process cannot stop. The company must enter a new phase of the selling funnel.

- Retention. The customer must be retained through a continuing series of social conversations that continue to reinforce and imprint the company's social credibility and the value of the company's products to the customer on his or her path.
- Advocacy. Lastly the goal is to turn the customer into an advocate – willing and even eager to tell the company's story across the social business channels and spread a positive message as widely as possible. Shy of this, the customer's potential to the organization has not been fully realized (monetized).

For companies that understand this new selling paradigm, the future is looking very bright indeed! There are more markets than ever across the globe for most every product or product extension. And these products move fastest off the proverbial shelf when the organization's social selling strategies are driving audience engagement, making them mission critical. This is the main reason LinkedIn has gained such popularity with social selling professionals. LinkedIn offers a highly credible platform for engaging in this social business activity at each level.

LinkedIn is the socially credible selling platform for...

- Accessing social buyers
- Earning their trust
- Eventually turning them into customers
- Strengthening the relationship over time
- Staying ahead of the competition.

Let's look at the LinkedIn social selling tools available to you...

How many social selling tactics are you using?

Fig. 6.3 Assess how effectively your company is using social selling tactics

Key Social Selling Tactics	Using This LinkedIn Tool	1 is not using, 10 is maximizing, where are you?
Be among the first to know about trends breaking in your industry	LinkedIn Articles, Groups and Influencer Program	
Identify the right contacts in a customer or prospect business	Find their Profile on LinkedIn	
Discover relationships between customers, prospects and other contacts	See the connections in their Profiles	
Manage the relationships between colleagues in your company (to avoid having multiple salespeople calling the same prospect, unawares)	See the connections in their Profiles	
Be notified when someone changes jobs to get introduced to the replacement or to follow your contact to a new company	Network Updates, Notifications	
Receive referrals to prospects, or to other departments in current customers, and engage with warm introductions	Use Introductions tool (which is improved with our Magic Mail tactic) and Groups	
Discover information about prospects to make conversations easier	Read their personal and company Profiles, and LinkedIn Sales Navigator	
Maintain on-going relationships with customers by demonstrating expertise in forums they frequent	Discussions in Groups	
Be visible on the network so you are top of mind when prospects go into purchase mode	Publish Status Updates and articles on LinkedIn regularly	
Obtain endorsements from colleagues and clients and make them visible to prospects	LinkedIn controls recommendations process for high perceived credibility	
TOTAL (Add score for 10 measures)		

Fig. 6.3 Assess how effectively your company is using social selling tactics

How did you do? From our experience training 65,000+ professionals on LinkedIn since 2004, we've found that for every 100 people the scores look something like this:

81-100	51-80	0-50
Leaders	Average	Laggards
Exceeds sales quotas consistently	Leaving business on table, need to optimize	In trouble, and in need of a serious game plan

Is your sales team using the LinkedIn platform and other critical social business tools to maximize your effectiveness at each stage of the new social selling funnel?

Let's look at the five steps to take to unfold a winning social selling strategy...

Identifying Your Target Audience and Their Needs

In handcounts taken at our training sessions, we've found that fewer than 50% of salespeople have used or know about the more advanced *Search filters* or the 'Advanced Search' as most of us call it. This is the selling equivalent of fishing in a big ocean with a single line – no nets, no sonar. Sure, it's a pastime, but it's *Old Man and the Sea*. All the more so, because *Advanced Search* is free to use on LinkedIn (up to a point, handling most needs).

Advanced Search: Shortest route to hottest prospects

Whether you have a free or paid account, you will see an entire page of search filters to help you narrow your search down to results that fit your requirements exactly. The more filters you complete, the more refined your results.

To open *Advanced Search*, click the *Advanced* button next to the right of the top search bar. A window will slide in, similar to Fig. 6.4. Here's an orientation...

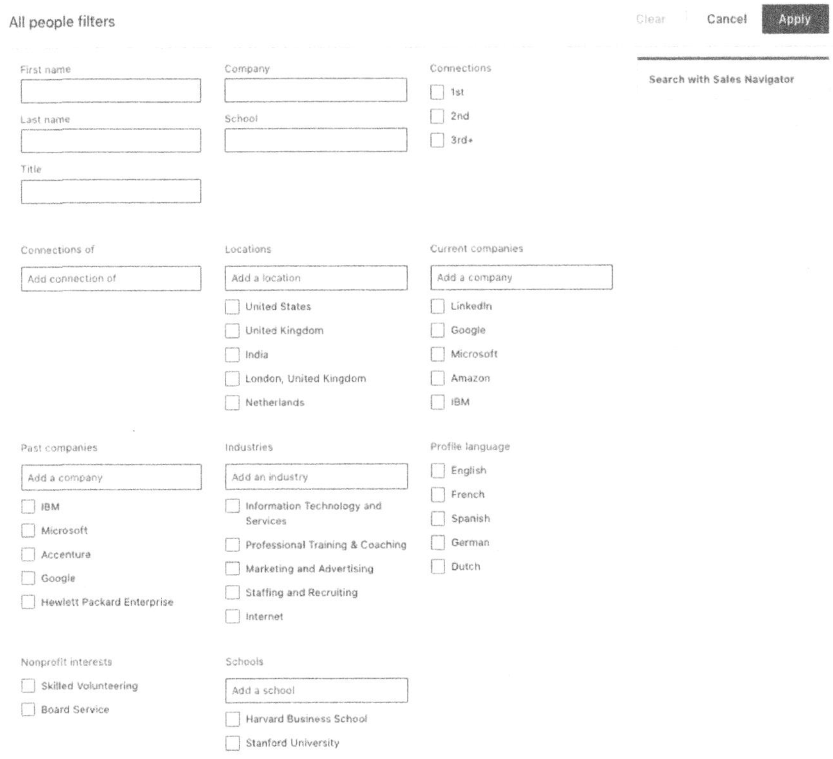

All people filters

Clear   Cancel   Apply

First name	Company	Connections
		[ ] 1st
Last name	School	[ ] 2nd
		[ ] 3rd+
Title		

Search with Sales Navigator

Connections of
Add connection of

Locations
Add a location
[ ] United States
[ ] United Kingdom
[ ] India
[ ] London, United Kingdom
[ ] Netherlands

Current companies
Add a company
[ ] LinkedIn
[ ] Google
[ ] Microsoft
[ ] Amazon
[ ] IBM

Past companies
Add a company
[ ] IBM
[ ] Microsoft
[ ] Accenture
[ ] Google
[ ] Hewlett Packard Enterprise

Industries
Add an industry
[ ] Information Technology and Services
[ ] Professional Training & Coaching
[ ] Marketing and Advertising
[ ] Staffing and Recruiting
[ ] Internet

Profile language
[ ] English
[ ] French
[ ] Spanish
[ ] German
[ ] Dutch

Nonprofit interests
[ ] Skilled Volunteering
[ ] Board Service

Schools
Add a school
[ ] Harvard Business School
[ ] Stanford University

Fig. 6.4 Essential social selling tool – all filters in the search or 'Advanced Search'

TOP LEVEL FILTERS

First Name and Last Name:
  Be sure to try different spellings if you're not sure (e.g., Cindy and Cindi)

Title:
  You can choose people who currently hold a position, or who once held the position, or both (which is LinkedIn's default). This search is based on the function that members input in their Experience (e.g. Operations Director).

Company:
  You can search for people who currently work at a company. Make sure you are using the appropriate spelling (e.g., PriceWaterhouseCoopers will give you different results than PwC).

School:

Members who list a school(s) on their Profile will come up in these results.

Connections:

Search all LinkedIn members, or limit your search to people you already have a relationship with, such as first-, second-, or third-degree connections. The greatest benefit will come from your first- and second-degree connections because you can more directly contact them via LinkedIn.

MIDDLE LEVEL FILTERS

Connections of:

Here you can specifically search for connections of someone in your first-degree connections (on the condition he/she has opened up their network with you).

Locations:

If you want to narrow your search to a specific city or country, such as Los Angeles or Luxembourg, click and add your specific location.

NOTES:
1. Some people fill out their home address, while others use their professional address. There is no way to know which one they have used (if it differs).
2. In some countries, there are areas which are improperly indexed, e.g., the province of Limburg in Belgium falls partly under the province of Liège.

Current Companies:

You can search for people who currently work at these companies. Make sure you are using the appropriate spelling or just select from the suggested companies.

LOWER LEVEL FILTERS

Past Company:

If you are only interested in people who worked at a particular company at one point in their past, enter it here. This is handy when you are remembering people you met ages ago. You know they were working at a particular company at the time, but no longer.

Industries:
Choose a specific industry or set of industries to focus on – LinkedIn allows you to select from 150+ industries.

Profile Language:
You can filter for people who have created their profile in a certain language. However, be careful when applying this filter because you might miss (a lot of) people who have not changed their default *Language* on their Profiles. (e.g. Dutch as default language, but they filled it out in English, because they don't know you can have your profile in multiple languages.)

Non-Profit Interests:
If you are looking for people interested in charitable Board or volunteer work, check these items.

Schools:
You may notice that this is a second *School* filter. Next to the free text field, this time there is a predefined list of schools, colleges, and universities – it's handy if you know the exact school you are looking for.

Putting Advanced Search to work

Let's look at how our sales manager uses *Advanced Search* to locate high-value prospects for our own social business training services.

In this example, we aim to ultimately get on the phone with the right decision makers at financial services firms in the New York area that have employees who can benefit from our social business training and technologies.

So to begin, we open the *Advanced Search* window and apply five broad filters, knowing that we can (and probably will) adjust the filters as we build a list of prospects (*as shown in Fig. 6.5*):
1. Keywords: employee training
2. Title: Human Resources

3. Location: Greater New York City area
4. Relationship: We tick all boxes from first to third connections to begin
5. Industry: Banking

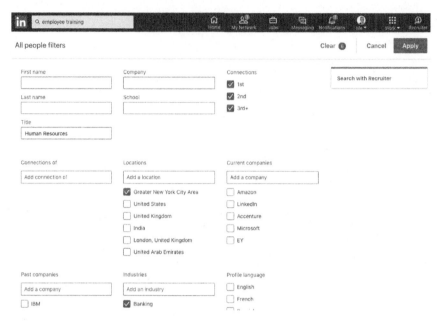

Fig. 6.5 Applying the first search filters

With this broadly targeted search, we identify 120 prospects that meet our target profile, with a cutaway of the results page shown in Fig. 6.6:

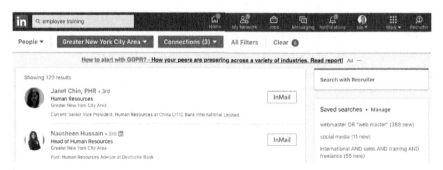

Fig. 6.6 Cutaway of results page

This is an excellent start. We will review these results in full, and adjust the parameters a couple times before deciding on a final list. As we do, we will save our searches and instruct LinkedIn to keep them in *Saved Searches* so that we can (as explained in the next step below) begin reaching out to them.

We have enough information to conduct a first-rate search. But we also know that with a premium account we can put even more filters to work, giving us more information to work with. In Fig. 6.7 you can see an overview of the filters available with LinkedIn Sales Navigator:

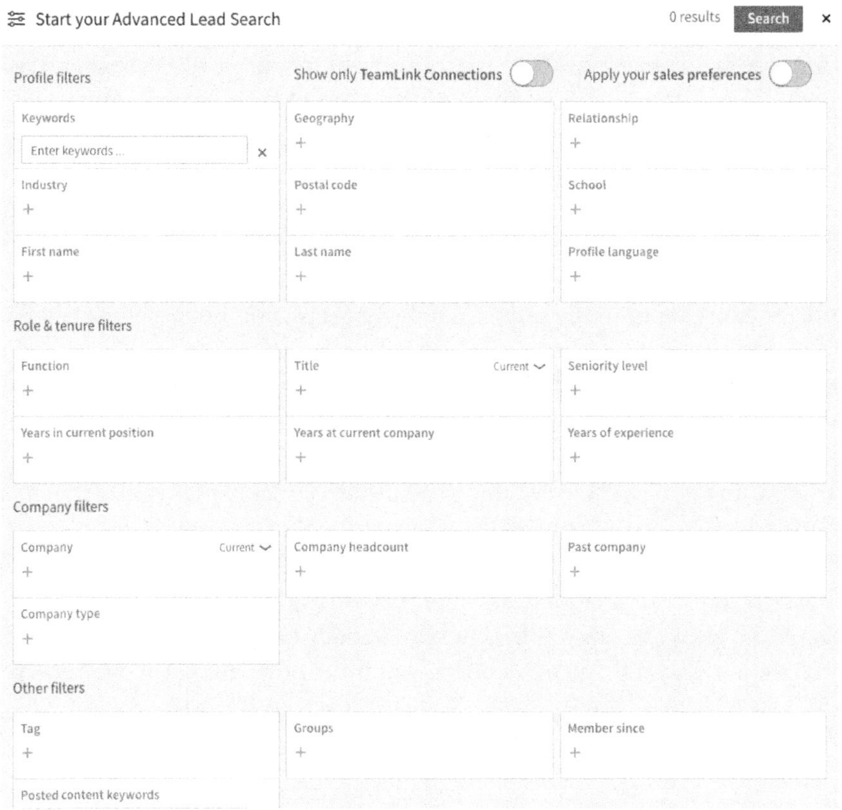

Fig. 6.7 List of search filters with LinkedIn Sales Navigator

Rekindling old relationships to drive new results

Most of us don't spend a lot of (productive) time thinking about our old relationships that date back decades. Even if we are good at keeping old relationships alive, we don't often see how they could play out across our current business activities.

But some academics set out to study the discounted present value of those old relationships. In their paper, *Dormant Ties: The Value of Reconnecting*, professors Daniel Levin, Jorge Walter, and Keith Murnighan demonstrated rather empirically that by rekindling those old relationships you can boost your social selling strategy measurably.[62]

The professors asked a group of their Executive MBA students to get back in touch with people they had not spoken to for a long time (e.g., drifted apart due to job relocations, changing interests, time demands) and to ask those old contacts to help with an important work project. Then the students were asked to make the same requests of their current contacts.

The outcome was surprising to many.

The long-lost cohort provided much more valuable and useful information than the current cohort. More creative ideas. More hands-on help with the project. More input to the problem-solving aspects of the project.

Some of the old contacts didn't pan out at all, of course, especially when the two parties had parted on poor terms. But interestingly, over the passage of time many of those old connections had grown in their own careers and skillsets, and as a result, were able to bring a fresh set of ideas and interests to the table "for an old friend". Once again, the KLT Factor!

Amongst our old relationships, we tend to have the best feelings for people we went to school with. Our alma mater can in fact be an excellent prospecting ground. And LinkedIn's Alumni feature makes it easy (even fun):

How to search for college contacts

- Type into the search bar the school you want to target.
  E.g. If we search for UCLA (Fig. 6.8), we see the number of alumni, the number of followers, the number of employees, 'About us', People also viewed, etc.

---

62 Daniel Z. Levin, Jorge Walter, J. Keith Murnighan, *Dormant Ties: The Value of Reconnecting*; Organization Science, 22(4): 923–939, 2011, http://papers.ssrn.com/sol3/papers.cfm?abstract_id=1625543

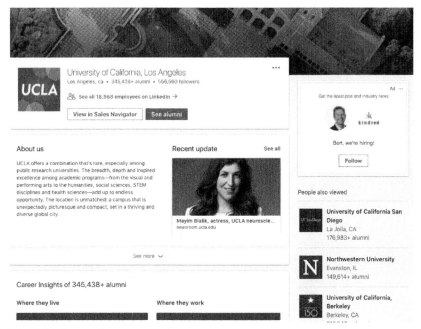

Fig. 6.8 UCLA Company Page

- We begin at UCLA's main page, then choose the *See all career insights*.
- We then can see all of the school's alumni (345,438 of them) that are on LinkedIn (Fig. 6.9).
- LinkedIn gives us a number of ways to filter through these results to find who we are looking for. The filters include:
  - Where they live
  - Where they work
  - What they do
  - What they studied
  - When they graduated
  - What they are skilled at
  - How we are connected with them.
- We select our filters, and LinkedIn outputs thumbnail Profiles on members who meet our criteria. We can then message any first-degree connection or send a personalized connection request to anyone on the list.

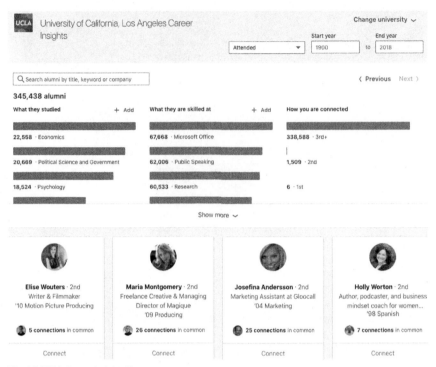

Fig. 6.9 UCLA Career Insights Page

We can conduct a similar search using *Advanced Search*, but it is easier (and frankly more fun when researching your alma mater) to use this Universities feature. Plus there is an added bonus:

A backdoor 'age' search

LinkedIn's *Advanced Search* doesn't give you a way to search by age, which would be useful if you sell products or services to a selected demographic.[63] But by using the alumni search, you can filter by graduation dates. In so doing, you can extrapolate to age. It's not a perfect science, since people attend college at different ages, of course. But it's close to perfect!

---

63 Prohibited by law in a lot of countries to search for job candidates based on age, sex, etc. E.g. The European Union (http://ec.europa.eu/justice/discrimination/law/index_en.htm)

Leveraging the relationships between your contacts

In Chapter 4 we talked about building a valuable business network with a 4-phase strategy based on having a strong first-degree network on LinkedIn:
1. Create the First Layer of Your LinkedIn Network
2. Discover People You May Know
3. Find colleagues and classmates
4. Connect with still others that you already know.

These phases are worth reviewing from time to time, as they are crucial to every success that follows. But what if you REALLY need to meet someone and are still unable to gain an introduction through your network, no matter how many ways you peel the onion?

You can still use existing relationships on LinkedIn to find a targeted prospect.

How to follow one member to reach another:
- Follow someone who your target prospect is connected to.
- Study that individual you are following, to learn more about your prospect.
- Use this information to leverage your second-degree connection into a warm first-degree prospect.

Tracking when connections leave their jobs

Also in Chapter 4 we talked about the best ways to keep track of your connections when they move to a new department or company.

When connections do move, you'll immediately want to establish a relationship with those who step into the position.

You'll also want to reconnect with your connections in their new jobs to determine if your products and services are as valuable in the new situation.

Saving your searches

Any time you search for someone on LinkedIn, you can save your search for future use. You'll find the *Create a search alert* button at the top right of the search results window.

When you save searches, you can later re-run the same search, saving time and allowing you to easily target people with the same tight criteria used the first time.

This Saved Search feature puts LinkedIn on autopilot for you. LinkedIn not only saves the search for you, but re-runs it automatically and sends you the list of people who were not part of the previous list.

How to save a search:
- On the top right of your search results page, click *Create a search alert*.
- Choose how often you'd like to receive emails with new results (e.g. Weekly).
- Tick the box that you want to be notified via Email.
- Confirm with *Save*.

Fig. 6.10 is a sample of a saved search.

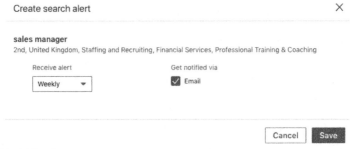

Fig. 6.10 Saved Search

This is worth a drill-down. Let's say you netted 42 results in a search you did today. And you would manually re-run the search next week, to see what's new, and you might have 44 results then. You would have to manually search through that list of 44 again to discover the two new arrivals. But instead LinkedIn saves you the trouble of doing that by sending you an email with the links to just those two Profiles. And LinkedIn continues to do that each week, as shown in the table below, giving you just the new names:

Today	Week 1	Week 2	Week 3	Week 4	Week 5
42	2	1	3	2	3

Considering that this runs on autopilot, those who say they don't have enough time for LinkedIn clearly don't know how to REALLY use it. With a free account, you get three saved searches. With premium accounts, even more...

Listening and Learning Before Engaging

Earlier we talked at length about the outsized role social media plays in purchasing decisions. Let's now break those figures down, and with the help of a Dell and Social Business Engine study on B2B buying, see how to best listen and engage in the early stages of social selling.[64]

Specific uses of social media play in B2B pre-purchase research	
Asked for suggestions and recommendations from other users	22%
Connected directly with potential vendors	22%
Connected with individual thought leaders to ask for their opinions	23%
Did not use social media for this purpose	28%
Browsed existing discussions to learn more about the product	57%

From this breakdown, we see that the top priority of a salesperson at this level is to get involved in the Group discussions that are going on, especially on LinkedIn. Much less important but still critical activity is communicating with the learning from actual customers, vendors, and thought leaders. These activities begin with...

Applying focused and relevant intelligence

LinkedIn is an excellent source of business intelligence, giving you knowledge about companies and people you can use to enhance your sales and business development. Just using LinkedIn, you can:

---

64 http://socialbusinessengine.com/socialselling/dell.pdf

- Do all of your research and be fully prepared to shine in sales calls
- Know who in your network is also in the network of a sales prospect
- Find out who has viewed your profile recently, indicating some level of interest
- See how you are connected to individuals within companies and industries
- Always have the latest news stories that involve or matter to prospects
- Find and leverage the influencers in your clients' industries
- Follow and join LinkedIn Group discussions that industry leaders are having
- Put questions to industry experts, and learn from them
- Figure out your clients' challenges and pain points, to better deliver solutions
- And much more!

Let's look closer...

Researching Prospects

Before calling on prospects, you want to research them to gain relevant information, insights into their needs and desires, and fun facts about them. All of this can be done by looking at their LinkedIn Profile, Company Page, and Website as well as social media sites where you will find things you have in common, such as:

1. Who they are connected to
2. Who they are following
3. What they've posted in their latest *Status Updates*
4. Which Groups they belong to, and participate in
5. Which organizations they value.

Having gained all this information, use it to start a sales conversation off on a friendly footing. For example, maybe your prospect went to the same school you did, or knows some of the same people you do, or worked in a nearby company at one point. These are conversation starter logs, pulling you out of the cold of preliminary uncertainty and placing you into the warm hearth of familiarity. Invaluable!

Spend nine minutes a day tending to prospects:

- **Latest updates made.** LinkedIn hand-delivers the latest updates on all of your connections on your homepage. You can *Like, Comment* or *Skip* onto the next update, and easily keep on top of all these connections (especially those that are prospects). Or check out their profiles manually and find out their most recent activities on LinkedIn.

- Groups belonged to. Consider joining the same Groups that your prospects have joined, and join in the discussions to show your shared interests (For a review of Groups, see Chapter 4)
- Social network visits. Which networks are your prospects following, and what are they talking about? This is another chance to join in with comments, share content that is relevant, and get to know your prospects better.
- Conference participation. If your prospects are attending a conference, or better, speaking or playing a role in the conference, be sure to contact them and congratulate them. It makes sense, right? You are further building your relationship. Same goes for any articles they publish, or important projects they are working on. Both can be tracked through LinkedIn – so show your appreciation!

QUICK CASE: These strategies were put to work and some results shared in a LinkedIn webinar by Muhammed Gündüz, a sales executive at enterprise software company Unit4 in 2016.

In two weeks, using LinkedIn tools, he identified 17 prospects and sent them InMail invitations. For his efforts, Mr. Gündüz netted 15 high-quality connections and one opportunity. With such encouraging initial success, he then sent out 35 vertical-specific InMails and this time he netted three leads and one opportunity.

Impressive! When we inquired further about his successes, Mr. Gündüz promptly replied and shared good information, further extending his own thought leadership as a mini-case within a case:

"LinkedIn is no longer an online CV, it is much more a powerful customer relationship management (CRM) system which every salesperson should use. Here are a few more tips on how to be successful:
- *generate traffic to your profile by sharing knowledge,*
- *make your profile so that you come over as an advisor,*
- *make sure visitors can download media or easily go to your company webpage,*

- *if they download from website or request information make sure you are the one to call.*

Researching companies on LinkedIn

By virtue of having the world's largest database on companies, LinkedIn offers a treasure trove of information on companies of interest to you. Some say this LinkedIn database is as useful as the leading Hoovers database. LinkedIn is certainly a powerful complement to Hoovers, with a focus on 'people' instead of 'financials' and therefore better suited for finding the right individuals within companies.

To search for companies on LinkedIn:
- In the search box start typing in the Company name to see all the results LinkedIn brings up and click on the right one.
- When you arrive on a Company Page, you will find plenty of information that is useful in narrowing your search for prospects. This database includes:
  - Status updates from companies that you follow
  - Company employees who have LinkedIn accounts
  - All the company employees who are in your network
  - Company job postings – more to be found on the Careers Page
  - Company pages that other searchers are looking at
  - Background information about the company.
- All of this valuable intel can be used to devise a strategy for approaching hot prospects with information they will value right at hand, more swiftly advancing the relationship.

Following your target companies

When you follow a Company on LinkedIn, you are notified when:
1. New job opportunities open up
2. The Company changes its Profile and shares updates

When could this be of value to you?
- *If you are in sales or purchasing*, you definitely want to know if your contact changes positions or departs the company. You can call right away and ask to be introduced to the person who is taking over their

previous job, so you can continue a good relationship within the company.

- *If you are in sales and it was not possible to do business with a company* because you did not 'click' with the purchaser, you might have a new chance when that person has a new replacement.
- *If you are looking for a new job,* you can be informed when your favorite organizations post a job.
- *If the company launches a new product or service,* or announces their annual report or an interview with the chairman in the press – any update may be interesting to you. When you call your contact soon after this, you show that you care by being up-to-date with the company's goings-on.

How to follow a company and receive notifications:
- Go to the top search bar and type the company name – you will see a dropdown menu with choices. Select the ones most useful to you.
- You will be taken to the Company Page and will find a yellow *Follow* button in the upper right – click.

How to stop following a company and stop receiving its updates:
- Click the *Following* tab near the top of the Company page and it will switch back to default yellow – you are no longer following.

Following companies is a key part of any selling, not just social selling. And it is so easy with LinkedIn's help to keep track of all the goings on in your target set of companies so you are advancing your relationship inside and outside of these companies, practically on autopilot.

Tracking on Twitter

Another very effective way to keep track of prospects' activity is on Twitter. You can make a private Twitter list with all of their names. This way, in a single viewing, you can see and keep track of what's most important to them. (Detail in Chapter 10)

Maximizing Industry Conferences

Most conferences now take advantage of Twitter #hashtags, making it easy and convenient to follow the proceedings by entering the hashtag in Twitter search.

Even better are the conference apps such as Double Dutch, which is used at LinkedIn's Talent Connect conference and most of the top conferences. This app makes it easy to connect and communicate with conference speakers and attendees – not only during the conference, but also for long afterwards.

Networking strategy for using conference apps:
1. Download the conference app.
2. Look up all the speakers, conference organizers and people you will meet.
3. Invite the speakers that interest you to connect on LinkedIn.
4. Follow the speakers on Twitter *before* the conference; some will follow you in return right away.
5. Make a point of meeting these standout people at the conference – when you hear their presentations you will feel as if you already know them.
6. Since you started the relationship before the conference, when you do meet it is not as strangers. That could be the difference between hearing a great speaker, and making a great connection.

Trumping Competitors

It's equally important to use LinkedIn and other social business tools to track on your competitors, to help you prevail.

Find out who's connecting to your competitors, and what LinkedIn Groups they are active in so that you can gain insights into the approaches they're taking.

Use these insights to hone and craft your own sales strategies. The better you know the key product positioning and messaging of your competitors, the better you can clearly differentiate your own product presentations.

Also it is common when several companies are competing for an account for one competitor to talk about the other, and to do it *inaccurately*. By tracking on competitors' activities, it's much easier to address any wrong impressions created by an overzealous competitor.

Aberdeen Group's 2013 study of social selling success

Business strategists at the Aberdeen Group have conducted perhaps the most significant study of social selling. In 2013, they released their findings on the effectiveness of social selling strategies used by sales professionals in 182 organizations worldwide. [65]

The findings surprised and shocked more than one executive suite. As Fig. 6.11 shows, the socially enabled sales professionals outperformed *and by significant margins* on the KPIs that drop most clearly to the bottom line. The performance improvements far outweighed the cost of investing in the social selling strategies.

PERFORMANCE IMPROVEMENT
- Total team attainment quota: 77% better
- Customer renewal rates: 13% better
- Sales forecast accuracy: 78% better
- % reps hitting quota: 83% better

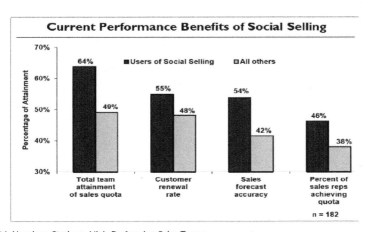

Fig. 6.11 Aberdeen Study on High-Performing Sales Teams

An analysis such as Aberdeen's is never done in a vacuum, of course, and other factors contribute. Certainly a sales team that was highly competent and outperforming prior to the advent of social selling strategies is going to be among the first to adopt the new strategies, and benefit the most. But these numbers tell a strong story, nonetheless.

65 Aberdeen Group "Social Selling Impact" Slideshare February 2013, https://contently.com/strategist/2013/04/17/the-powerful-force-of-social-sales-infographic

Aberdeen's strategists summed up the outperformance, as follows:

> *"Providing reps with mobile access to the social media sites and user-generated content drives increasing amounts of business conversation. Few would doubt the value of a face-to-face prospecting or customer service meeting in which the rep is immediately up-to-date on industry news, trigger events, or other information that can impact the sale or reorder."*[66]

Aberdeen next pinpointed the social selling strategies that are proving most effective – from *Best in Class* (top 20%), and *Industry Average* (middle 50%), to *Laggard* (bottom 30%). The rate of adoption of these top-performing social selling strategies between the leaders and the laggards is significant across the board, as shown in Fig. 6.12:

Fig. 6.12 Aberdeen Study on Social Selling Strategy Adoption

Net takeaway: Leading companies are 30% to 60% more likely than others in their industry to be using these top five social selling strategies:

1. Expand lead generation activities to social media marketing
2. Educate sales staff on use of external social media tools
3. Support customer acquisition/service with social platform enabling real-time customer communication
4. Educate sales staff on use of internal social media tools
5. Track prospect/customer sentiment to predict most affected messaging.

---

66 Aberdeen Group "Social Selling Impact" Slideshare February 2013, https://contently.com/strategist/2013/04/17/the-powerful-force-of-social-sales-infographic/

Pushing accountability to the edge

Each of these strategies is, at its core, an exercise in pushing sales accountability to the edge of the social business and into the hands of the salespeople who are closest to, and most knowledgeable about, the company's customers and prospects.

To accomplish this push to the edge, leading companies are:
- Developing internal policies and governance procedures for managing employees' work-related social business profiles.
- Helping salespeople build their own communities and act in those communities as *bona fide* spokespersons.
- Using relationships built-up by their salespeople to keep in closer touch with customer needs.

This push to the edge makes perfect sense for the combined reason that (1) people are more likeable than corporations and (2) new social selling tools put all the sales development tools needed into the hands of those more likeable representatives of the corporation.

It's a simple truism that humans are more interesting than corporations. So in social business, having a LinkedIn Company Page is a baseline necessity but great advantages can come from pushing sales activity to the edge of the company through individual employees.

Local salespeople will invariably know the 'latest thinking' of customers better than the marketing people back at HQ – especially when the company offices are far away or globally distributed.

These local salespeople can be empowered to build social relationships within their sales territories – to the benefit of the company. What better way to:
- Keep a finger on the pulse of local customer service concerns
- Swiftly devise better and needed solutions when needed
- Strengthen the company's brand in your customers' lives?

John McGee, President of the sales optimization software company OptifiNow, gave an excellent example of this local/edge focus attention making a sizeable difference:[67]

---

[67] http://www.targetmarketingmag.com/article/why-you-should-trust-your-employees-with-social-media/1

"For example, an insurance company with agents and representatives scattered across the country can use social media to reach new customers and increase services for current customers. If a hail storm occurs in Kansas, wildfires rage in Colorado and heavy rains flood South Carolina, the company can post messages about filing claims and the importance of having proper home owner's policies, but the messaging will include sweeping generalities.

To increase the effectiveness of social media in a situation like this, representatives of the insurance company should be posting messages saturated with local news. A local representative will know what neighborhoods were hardest hit, how long the clean up is expected to take and where people who need assistance can go for help. Social media posts can be crafted and tailored to fit a local audience, making customers feel like the company knows them and their struggles and is the best option for providing a solution."

An insurer responding to a disaster situation is a pat example, admittedly. But for almost every company today, reaching customers through the salespeople who are closest to them is a solid strategy.

Salespeople need to have access to a database of ready-to-go, current, relevant, legal-approved messaging that they can post to their social accounts.

This idea of 'pushing to the edge' has been out there for two decades now. But many companies have been slow to adopt. Some fear the loss of control, or the potential 'black eye' when the salespeople start overpromising! Others dread the operational aspects: actually executing on a strategy that has as many moving parts as the company has employees.

But the case studies are piling up proving the value of social at the edge, and the technology is maturing to make everything easier...

Tracking employees' social output

Most CRM systems now allow companies to easily manage and track social selling campaigns as part of the larger marketing plan.

Enterprise sales leaders, such as Salesforce.com, plumb their own Chatter product to track and analyze their employees across the social networks. They are continually analyzing the data on:

- Numbers of followers employees have
- How often employees post relevant content
- The responses those posts receive.

Based on these stats, employees are ranked internally and promoted or rewarded accordingly.

For some companies, linking an employee's social activity to their compensation may be a step too far. But more and more leading companies are creating this very linkage – because it delivers, bottom line.

LinkedIn has a similar product, called Elevate[68].

These leading companies are not stopping with their sales teams...

Enabling not just the sales team, but the entire team

Aligning employees' personal brands with the corporate brand is one thing, asking them to "sell for you" is quite another . . . right?

Not necessarily. In a marketplace where paid ads are mostly ignored or blocked, where cold calls, blanket emails, and other in-your-face techniques don't produce the engagement that employee champions get on social networks, why shouldn't every public-facing employee in your organization become an unofficial sales rep?

The most effective – that is, socially credible – messaging today is the custom and personal messaging that comes from a trusted source. Such as the entire workforce outside of the C-suite and marketing department!

---

68 https://business.linkedin.com/elevate

Let's break this down, revisiting studies shown earlier in the book...

- The widely respected Edelman Trust Barometer again found in 2015 that consumers are twice as likely to trust an employee over the company CEO, PR agency, or Marketing Department.[69] The 2018 study confirms that the voices of authority are regaining credibility.[70]
- Those trusted employees have an average of 634 people in their social networks that can be influenced, according to the Pew Research Center.[71]
- A Dell study found that 90% of an employee's social audience is typically new to the brand.[72] So doing the math...

Each employee brings a potential of
570 new connections to the company

Now let's add the hard financial metrics we detailed earlier from Bain's customer loyalty expert Fred Reichheld: A 12% increase in brand advocacy, on average, generates a 2x increase in revenue growth rate plus boosted market share.[73] And we can see clearly that enabling the social selling potential of the entire organization can be a powerful proposition.

The key to success at this, as shown in Chapter 4 on employee activation, is to demonstrate the rewards of social selling, to show employees how, as a result of participating, they:

- Become better known as experts in their specialty
- Also build their own social credibility on the networks
- Find other talented people like themselves to join the team
- Learn new things through their expanding social connections
- Help customers solve their problems, advancing the company.

And it can all happen naturally, adding very little to their workloads. Here's how.

69 http://www.edelman.com/insights/intellectual-property/2015-edelman-trust-barometer/
70 http://cms.edelman.com/sites/default/files/2018-02/2018_Edelman_Trust_Barometer_Global_Report_FEB.pdf
71 http://www.targetmarketingmag.com/article/why-you-should-trust-your-employees-with-social-media/1
72 http://www.targetmarketingmag.com/article/why-you-should-trust-your-employees-with-social-media/1
73 http://www.marketingprofs.com/opinions/2015/26782/why-social-media-marketers-and-brand-managers-should-care-about-employee-advocacy

Providing Helpful Content Relevant To Your Audience

Publishing and sharing content is the #1 most valuable social business activity. This applies to every employee from the sales team across to Operations and on up to the CEO's office. It's the single biggest lever on lead generation.

And so the first question for every social sharing company is: What to write about?

Well, we know that prospects don't generally wake up in the morning caring about your products, whatever they may be. They wake up wanting solutions to their problems, whatever those may be.

So the content you create, in an effort to drive people to landing pages and generate leads, should be immediately helpful to them and in a clear problem-solving way.

That's first. Then the problem-solving has to happen often...

According to a study by Kipp Bodnar and Jeffrey L. Cohen in their book, *The B2B Social Media Book: Become a Marketing Superstar by Generating Leads,* the half-life of a social media link is only three hours. That's a very short life!

A link's half-life has probably shrunk considerably since their book was published.

So all the effort you put into creating an outstanding article to post . . . could have an impact on the marketplace or with your target audience for only a couple hours. After that, you have to regenerate interest all over again.

That's why an often-used content marketing strategy is known as the 10:4:1. Many best-in-class organizations use this rule (or say they do). It's a way to achieve a healthy balance between 'being helpful' and 'promoting yourself.' It works like this:

For every 15 posts you do in social media, 10 should be OPC (other people's content), four should be helpful blogposts, and one should be an offer with a link to a landing page. In greater detail:

- Post 10 links to third-party articles – These posts should provide valuable information to your prospects that helps position you as socially credible. Share links to relevant content found in trade journals, business publications and newsletters in your customers' areas of interest. Be sure to give attribution to the original author. LinkedIn makes the finding and sharing of articles routine, as do Apps like Scredible and Hootsuite. (More in Chapter 10)
- Post four links to your blogposts – Be sure to highlight the relevant content that is useful to your prospects. Ask your readers to share your blog with others, including the now common tag, *"Please RT!" (Please Retweet!)*
- Post one link to a landing page – Let your prospects know how your products solve their business problems. Send them to a dedicated page on your website that provides problem-solving information and a call to action:
  - Request an eBook or whitepaper
  - Complete a registration form
  - Attend a webinar
  - Download a sales brochure
  - Watch a video

These calls to action, along with the earlier helpful information you've shared with your prospects, will create patterns of interaction and social credibility over time.

By connecting with prospects on a safe, helpful, two-way street, then growing to like and trust one another over time, just as in the old offline world, strong ties are created, and on that basis a lasting commercial relationship can blossom.

Maintaining visibility and relevance with a Company Page

Having a properly architected Company Page demonstrates your relevance in the digital flow, especially important to Millennial customers. In addition, it gives you a chance to add a human element to your brand. People are much more likely to buy from you when they feel personally connected to your company. (How-to covered in Chapter 5)

Seeking recommendations from colleagues and clients

To build your likeability and trustworthiness, actively encourage your co-workers and customers to post recommendations on your LinkedIn Profile. Buyers who are doing their background research on you will view these recommendations as an external validation that you and your products are worthwhile. (For a review, see Chapter 4.)

Having Proven Social Credibility, Present Value

With your target audiences well identified, your listening operation up and running daily, and your content being distributed frequently across the networks, you are ready to reach out from a position of social authority and fill your pipeline with qualified prospects on a consistent, on-going basis. There are 'proactive' strategies to take at this stage – to accelerate the pace of opportunities being realized. Let's look at the strategies...

Identifying all the decision makers in an enterprise sale

The days of a single decision-maker are over (and have been for awhile). In 2014 the analysts Marco Nink and Dr. John H. Fleming of Gallup published *B2B Companies: Do You Know Who Your Customer Is?* They found that a majority of selling organizations do not know who their *actual* customers are!

In Gallup's study of German companies (Fig. 6.13), between three and 34 people make the bulk (86%) of the major buying decisions in mid-market companies and enterprises. That's a lot of 'buyers' potentially.

Four different levels of buyers are commonly involved in the sale:
- Buyers – purchasing agents who review product proposals and set contract terms
- Influencers – often informal advisers who influence the decision-making
- Decision-Makers – senior management, authorized signatories, policymakers
- End users – the ultimate buyer who actually uses the product and interacts with the supplier.

Each of these buyers must be satisfied, each on their own conditions, for a clean sale.

SIZE OF THE BUYING CENTER

A study in Germany found that groups of from two to 20 people make 86% of the procurement decisions at large corporations and medium-sized enterprises.

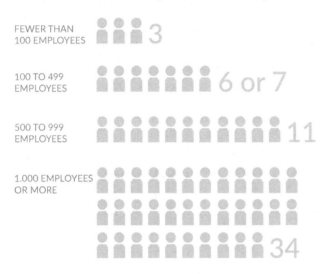

FEWER THAN
100 EMPLOYEES 3

100 TO 499
EMPLOYEES 6 or 7

500 TO 999
EMPLOYEES 11

1,000 EMPLOYEES
OR MORE

34

Source: Spiege-Verlag (E.d.) (1982). Der Entscheidungsprozess bei Investitionsgütern: Beschaffung, Entscheidungskompetenzen, Informationsverhalten. Hamburg: Spiegel-Dokumentation

GALLUP

Fig. 6.13 Gallup finds multiple decision-makers in buying situations in today's enterprises

Importantly, these buyers do not separate 'feelings' from 'fact' when it comes to making buying decisions. A small majority (54%) said that they would kill a deal if they had a 'bad feeling' about it, even if the salesperson has made a solid fact-based case for purchasing.

Increasingly then, the buying decision hangs on the company's social credibility. Being able to demonstrate a crisp, clear value proposition is still vital to completing a transaction. But more often than not, customers require that the transaction be done with a trusting partner.

Did you know that according to CEB (now Gartner) an average of 6.8 people are involved in each B2B purchase decision, up from 5.4 in 2015[74]?

Using LinkedIn to locate and satisfy the four buyer levels

Often your sales team will be targeting the account of a company, but does not have current names of all four buying levels. Here's a solution:

First use data from past deals to figure out titles that are most likely used, such as:
- Buyers: VP Purchasing, Procurement Manager, Operations Director
- Influencers: Consultant, Advisor, Mentor (this is a tougher one)
- Decision-Makers: CEO, CFO, COO, CMO, HR Director
- End-Users: Account Coordinator, Sales Director, Executive Assistant, Manager, Assistant Manager, Supervisor, Foreman, Staff

Working with these titles and additional ones that may be appropriate to the target company, next use *Advanced Search* to find the actual names of Buyers, Influencers, Decision-Makers, and End-Users at the company:
- Enter the *Title* options one after another until there is a hit
- Enter *Company* and *Location* if relevant
- Under *Relationship*, select first, second, and Group.

This process will winnow down to a list of potential buyers' LinkedIn Profiles, with a lot of useful information right at hand.

Now review any LinkedIn connections between the sales team and the potential buyers. Look for anything of relevance, or things in common, and based on that information request a referral or introduction.

LinkedIn offers the ideal point of entry. The chance of getting an appointment with the right person in the company incrementally increases as each of the four buyer levels is brought into the prospecting loop.

---

74 https://www.cebglobal.com/ceb-careers-blog/highlights-from-the-2016-ceb-sales-and-marketing-summit/

Set up your Social Centre

Identifying your target audience is one of the key elements for a successful social selling campaign. You should have one place and one place only where you are mapping out all your buyers, influencers and decision-makers. We call it the Social Centre, as this is the central place from which you will conquer the world, or at least your target audience.

Here are the five steps to get your Social Centre up and running:
1. Map out ALL your buyers, influencers and DMUs:
   Who are they? Names, titles, etc. Use the Advanced Search!
2. Where do you currently keep them? Are they in your CRM? Decide on which platform you are going to manage this. A CRM should be the right place, but an Excel could work to get you started if you don't have a proper CRM yet.
3. Are you following your leads on LinkedIn? If not, start by following them. This way you are at least receiving their updates.
4. How are you connected to them on LinkedIn? Is there anyone in your direct network, like colleagues who are already connected. Dive into that second degree! Who are the people in the first degree that you have in common.
5. Are any of them on Twitter? Follow them here too! Even better, set up your private Twitter lists, as explained in chapter 10.

As long as you don't have a map (of your target audience), it's like not knowing where to go. So, do yourself a favor and start with mapping them all out. Yes, we know, it takes a bit of time…but once you have this map, it will save you a lot of time, as you now know who to focus on. A lot of noise and timewasters won't have the chance to distract you.

Mentioning prospects and their companies in posts

Social selling is more of a farming operation than a hunting party. You want to be regularly tending to your connections, constantly cultivating the relationship.

A simple way to do this: Mention your prospects in your LinkedIn *Status Updates*, in ways that are relevant to them (Fig. 6.14).

Bert Verdonck
LinkedIn Expert & Trainer | Scredible Ambassador | Lifehacker | FREE Bestseller reallyconnect.com | Happy Chocoholic | Social Selling | Social Recruiting | AI | Blockchain | ICO

Did you know that Canon is recognised as the 4th most reputable company globally in the Global Rep Track 2018? Congratulations Shane Burchett, Robert Pickles and Debbie Brown!

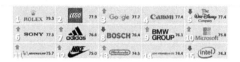

Fig. 6.14 Using @mentions to build stronger relationship

To do this, just type @ followed by their name and when LinkedIn's autocomplete dropdown shows their name, click on it. They will be added as a named link within your update. And when you hit *Share*, they will receive a notification.

Be certain, of course, to only mention your prospects when your post could be of genuine value to them, and not a useless interruption.

This little effort might not seem like it moves mountains, but a steady drip of these notifications over time, as in tending a field, nurtures the relationship and can yield real value over time. Importantly, it shows that you value them. And when the time comes to make a purchasing decision in your product category, you will be more favorably considered.

Building credibility in Group discussions

Establishing your credentials as an open, up-to-date, supportive – that is, socially credible – individual becomes more and more important as more and more of our business hours are spent in online activities and forums.

LinkedIn Groups (Chapter 5) help you establish this 'cred'. Not only do they help you fulfill top-funnel marketing needs by building-up positive awareness of your company's solutions, but they also allow you to reach prospects in the lower funnel who are aware of your solutions but need to see supporting layers of value.

Sharing thought leadership through publishing articles

LinkedIn (Chapter 4) is the publishing platform that allows you to brand yourself as both the subject matter expert and the go-to person in your industry. There is no better way to gain credence in the eyes of your prospects than to be sharing insights that have an impact in their lives.

You can post articles on LinkedIn that your prospects care about, trends in the industry or even fascinations about your company. By staying relevant and top of mind, you can over time come to be seen a prominent thinker, influential commentator, and valuable ally to the people in your industry and beyond.

Obtaining client and vendor referrals

Of all of the referral introductions you could receive, none is more powerful than a referral from a current or past client. This speaks volumes.

So use LinkedIn to identify which of your current/past clients are connected meaningfully to your prospects, and ask for introductions. It's the most powerful business development tactic of all.

Next in impact are referrals you get from your vendors. By finding out the names of vendors that you and your prospects share, you can approach those vendors and ask for mutual introductions.

This works best when your vendor is likely to receive more business from both you and your prospect as a result of this introduction. So look for these kinds of mutually beneficial connections.

Making return calls productively

The phone call is becoming something of a relic, but it's still essential for advancing deals of substance. So it's wise to give prospects the option of either "returning your call" or alternatively "scheduling a call". Often the latter works better.

To better ensure that you get quality phone time with prospects, simply send them a link to a call scheduler, such as TimeTrade. It's an easy way to get onto both of your calendars, at their convenience, to move the deal forward.

Using LinkedIn's InMail

LinkedIn's internal email system is known as InMail. These are emails you can compose and send to any LinkedIn member, unless the member has blocked them. They are available only to premium account holders.

InMail open rates can fluctuate greatly, as with any email, but typically deliver between 10% and 50% opens depending on:

- Quality of the email message
- Nature of the product or service
- Familiarity of the recipient

There is only one rule in InMails: Don't sell!

Sales pitches invariably fail to recoup your investment while damaging the connection for any future business. The main questions that recipients of InMail ask, in deciding whether or not to open it, are:

1. Who is this?
2. Why are they sending me a message?
3. What are they selling?
4. How long is this going to take?

To head these questions off at the pass, make sure that your InMail does at least one of two things:

- Makes a legitimate professional offer of interest to the recipient – as in wanting to buy from them, consult with them, hire them.
- Offers the recipient some information of value and request an opportunity to continue the conversation.

Consider the InMail a tactic of last resort when you absolutely have to make contact but all the other connection strategies we've discussed in these pages don't pan out!

These are the top strategies for filling your pipeline with qualified prospects on a consistent on-going basis. Now let's briefly review...

Big Fat Fails: What not to do in social selling

These are the seven most embarrassing and costly mistakes B2B salespeople make far too often on LinkedIn – practically guaranteeing that live prospects become inactive leads.

#1: Ask for an appointment on the first approach

Like in dating, first you flirt. It's just natural. You get to know one another, find common interests, offer to help with something. If you hit the recipient with a business offer, expect the recipient to hit DELETE. Or maybe swipe left in a future version of LinkedIn...

#2: Using LinkedIn to send an introductory message

While LinkedIn is an incredible resource for finding the right person, sending a message to someone you don't know is rarely effective. (We've talked at length about Getting Introductions and Magic Mail, so you know this already, right?!)

#3: Having an incomplete or outdated LinkedIn Profile

Having an unattended, years old, or sloppy Profile is like showing up to a formal meeting with a stained suit and no shoes. (Sure, some techies can pull it off, but most cannot.)

#4: Sending the standard LinkedIn connection request

When you ask someone to connect with you on LinkedIn, you are prompted to indicate how you know this person and you can then fire off the request. If you do this, you will be saying one of these things to your recipient, *"I'm lazy"* . . . *"You don't matter enough to me to compose a brief note"* . . . *"I'm a spammer"*.

#5: Copy, paste, and blast a sucky email

Most of the prospecting emails that land in our inbox start by talking about the seller's company, product or service. Most of these are ignored, and they can also trigger LinkedIn's spam filters, which will knock the sender off the platform.

#6: Old-fashioned follow-up

Back in the day, salespeople called prospects every few months to 'check in.' But now prospects can find whatever they want with a few mouse clicks. So if salespeople aren't distributing the information that prospects are looking for, they aren't earning the right to follow-up.

#7: Not intuiting when a sales pitch is welcome

It's disastrous to a business when the sales team misses the cues from prospects that say they want a connection, an outreach call, or a sales pitch. Listening closely for the 'tells' is crucial. Some tested tells:
- "I'm looking for..."
- "I'm trying to find..."
- "Our company needs..."

Sales teams should have a library of the keyword phrases that suggest someone wants to make a decision about a product in your industry. For example:
1. "What is the industry leading [your product]"
2. "How does [your product] compare to [competitor product]"
3. "What are the reviews for [product category]"

By monitoring these specific phrases across the social business channels, you can be alerted to conversations that are going on, and can join in – offering information that helps prospects make decisions and eases them through your sales funnel.

Measuring Your Social Selling By KPIs That Matter

In our work with organizations, we find that there are many ways of computing ROI, but three KPIs are universally most valued across organizations:
- Shortening Sales Cycle
- Reducing Touchpoints
- Increasing Revenue

If these are the measures that you value, as well, then you can use the following matrix to assess and measure the most relevant social selling KPIs.

Social Selling KPIs

Priority	High-level Metrics	% Sales Team	% Entire Company
1	Fully bought in to social business as a concept, and adopting social selling strategies.		
2	Has a professionally crafted LinkedIn and Twitter Profile that is also SEO optimized.		
3	Increasing reach, engagement and amplification measures at target pace (e.g., 5% per month)		
	Operational Metrics		
4	Profile Management • Number of completed Profiles • Number of connections • Number of Profile views (per quarter) • Number of *Status Updates* (per quarter)		
5	Outreach • Number of emails sent • Number of InMails sent • Number of appointments generated • Number of proposals created		
6	Social Selling Index Score *(see below)*		
7	Use of Sales Navigator • *Daily logins* • *Saved leads* • *Saved accounts* • *Searches performed* • *Profiles viewed*		

Fig. 6.15 Social Selling KPIs

Measuring is crucial. But ultimately, success will come from integrating these KPIs into the company's current reporting mechanisms. Then the salespeople and the larger organization will know:
- What they are being held accountable to
- Why they are being measured the way they are
- How to better advance the company's overall strategic objectives.

This is the management meeting agenda, then:
- Which KPIs are most relevant to capture?
- What is the best way to capture these KPIs?
- Where will this information reside in the organization?
- How often will the sales team report on these metrics?
- What will each of the management roles involve?

- What training is needed to proceed with confidence?

With this framework, a competent social selling strategy can proceed, as it must!

Measuring your social selling impact – the SSI dashboard

For too long (well, a few years actually), social strategies were met with internal resistance by boards and senior leaders because it was a challenge to measure the KPIs and ROI of campaigns.

However, just as social business is evolving rapidly, so too are the tools to measure the impact, engagement, and returns of investments in social strategies.

The latest tool is LinkedIn's Social Selling Index – created to make it fast and easy to measure the core components of social selling success.

Fig. 6.16 is a screenshot of the Social Selling Index dashboard for Bert Verdonck:

Fig 6.16 Measuring your Social Selling Impact – The SSI Dashboard

The SSI measures a salesperson's performance based on his/her proven success at:
1. Establishing a Professional Brand with the LinkedIn Profile
2. Finding the Right People using the LinkedIn Tools

3. Engaging on LinkedIn with Insightful Posts
4. Building Relationships with other LinkedIn members.

Each category has a rating of 0-25, combining for a total score up to 100.

Until recently, the Social Selling Index was only available to companies that purchased Sales Navigator licenses. Now LinkedIn has opened access and all LinkedIn members can measure their scores.

> To see your own LinkedIn Social Selling Index score, go to https://www.linkedin.com/sales/ssi.

SOCIAL RECRUITING: HIGH-STAKES WARFARE

SUMMARY: The better your hiring, the more competitive you become – every company knows as much. Yet almost every industry today faces a critical talent shortage. The battle to secure the most promising talent has grown so fierce, and the maneuvering of opponents to gain a hiring edge has reached such intensity, that the language of recruiting is no different than warfare.

Companies either become an "employer of choice" in their industry, or risk losing the best talent to competitors. A compelling employer brand can yield powerful results, says LinkedIn's head of sales for North America, Eda Gultekin:

- *Hiring costs can be decreased by as much as 50%*
- *Employee turnover can be decreased by as much as 28%*

These are big metrics, obviously. In this chapter we'll analyze these metrics and show how, and under what conditions, they are attainable.

Oh, before we get started, it is probably a good idea to listen what Laszlo Bock, former SVP of People Operations at Google, has to say:

> "Most companies recruit the same way: post a job,
> screen resumes, interview some people and pick whom to hire.
> If they were all recruiting the same way, why would any of them
> get a different outcome than their competitors?"

So, the war for talent is ON and...

It's a Seven-Continent War For Talent

Until the mid-1990s, companies thought of their 'employer brand' as the messaging they pushed to the marketplace and occasionally refreshed.

Then leading companies such as Unilever, Nike, Microsoft, and P&G put a lens on the emerging information-based economy. They saw capital moving beyond its old manufacturing base, and even beyond its more recent financial base, to an all-new human base. And that capital was literally walking out the door every night, as the saying goes.

So these forward-looking companies began to focus on their employer brand in the same way they had previously focused on their corporate and consumer brands. They created Employee Value Propositions (EVP) to describe what they had to offer to potential employees, supported by catchy taglines:

- Microsoft – How far can your potential take you?
- Johnson & Johnson – Small company environment. Big company impact.
- AT&T – Exciting positions. Energized environment. Cutting-edge technology.
- Charles Schwab – We're looking for a different kind of employee.
- Nike – We are all about sports. And then some.

And these companies were richly rewarded for their efforts...

Comparison of Employer Value Propositions (EVPs)		
	Strong EVP	Weak EVP
Size of labor market available to source from	60%	40%
Employee turnover rate	10%	16%
Acceptable compensation level (avg.)	€859	€1,164
Salary bump required to 'poach' candidates	11%	21%
Level of commitment from new hires	38%	9%
Sources: Corporate Leadership Council; Dmitry Kucherov & Elena Zavyalova, European Journal of Training and Development; Hye Joon Park, Pin Zhou, Cornell University ILR School		

Fig. 7.1 Value of well-managed employer brand (based on multiple studies consolidated)

As Fig. 7.1 shows, companies with strong, well-managed employer brands could attract employees from a larger segment of the labor market, hold onto those employees longer, pay them less if they so desired and still keep them happy, and benefit from a far more committed workforce.[75]

---

75 Hye Joon Park, Pin Zhou, Cornell University ILR School, Spring 2013 (http://digitalcommons.ilr.cornell.edu/cgi/viewcontent.cgi?article=1023&context=student)

These early leaders looked even smarter and gained even more notoriety in 2004 when social media first took flight, and a new transparency overtook business.

In the newly open environment that came with social media's emergence, job seekers became more trusting of the online postings of a company's employees than the company's recruitment advertising was claiming.

Success in talent attraction grew beyond the HR shop. It was now tightly interwoven with all the online postings of the company's workforce, making those postings mission-critical initiatives in a global war for talent. Making them the purview of the CEO.

Either the CEO takes over the brand, or outsiders do

The employer brand is no longer something that Marketing develops and HR executes. That brand is now something that is defined, amplified, loudly questioned, torn down or built up by job candidates based on their experiences with the employees throughout the company.

The employer brand has become an employer *social* brand – a very public version of what top talent thinks, feels, and shares about your company as a place to work.

That makes it mission critical, with the primary responsibility for the employer brand resting squarely on the CEO's shoulders.

A recommended-to-read article in the *Harvard Business Review* by Richard Mosley, Global VP of Strategy and Advisory at Universum and author of the superb *Employer Brand Management*, laid out the strategic value of the employer brand going forward:

"The strength of the employer brand can have a significant effect on the quality, pride, and engagement levels of those employees involved in delivering a positive customer brand experience. And with other studies linking happy employees to happy customers, it's not surprising that most companies want to align their employer and consumer brand strategies over the next few years."[76]

---

76 Richard Mosley, "CEOs Need to Pay Attention to Employer Branding," HBR.ORG, MAY 11, 2015 (https://hbr.org/2015/05/ceos-need-to-pay-attention-to-employer-branding) (https://www.youtube.com/watch?v=ZXOXFXrzKw8)

The boldfaced "positive customer brand experience" is our doing – since nothing is more important. To strengthen their employer brands in the coming years, as we see in Fig. 7.2, companies are committing to four priority objectives. The first three will see an increased commitment, the fourth a decreased commitment:

- Build the employer brand on a global level.........17% ↑
- Secure long-term recruitment needs...................9% ↑
- Differentiate from the competition......................6% ↑
- Build the employer brand at the local level...........9% ↓

Fig. 7.2 How companies are strengthening their employer brand

On all four of these fronts, the HR and Marketing departments are involved in communicating this strengthened employer social brand. But the actual accountability buck begins and ends with the CEO now.

CEOs who understand this, and who fully embrace the mantle of social leadership, will see their companies attracting the highest number of qualified job candidates. This becomes even more crucial as the skills gap continues to widen...

A great chasm between 'knowledge required' and 'skills available'

The skills gap is, by all forecasts, expected to continue increasing in severity and creating dire new performance issues:

- Manpower Group's 2016-17 survey on the talent shortage survey found that 40% of employers worldwide reported talent shortages.[77]

---

77 https://www.manpowergroup.com/talent-shortage-2016

- The Royal Academy of Engineering reports that nearly 100,000 STEM graduates are needed this year in the UK, but only 90,000 will graduate with a STEM degree. And 25% of those will go into non-STEM careers, meaning that some 32,500 jobs are going unfilled just in the UK.[78][79]
- The U.S. Labor Department reported 5.8 million job openings (in 2015)— a 13-year high number of open jobs going unfilled. This number increased to 6.3 in 2018.[80]
- Staff turnover costs UK businesses an average of £31,808 per lost employee or £4.13 billion a year across the nation, according to Oxford Economics.[81]

None of this is news to hiring specialists. It's clear that for the foreseeable future it's going to be a candidate's market. The top job seekers will be able to choose which companies they want to work with, how much they want to be paid, and the terms of their employment.

And every company wants to hire the top 5% of talent – there is even software to assist in identifying the top rung of talent.

Did we mention that according to the World Economic Forum "AI and computer-based learning" will result in the loss of 1,000,000 sales jobs by 2020? Oh, and 800 million workers might lose their jobs because of automation.[82] Does this mean the best-of-class will be taken by the top employer brands ? Take a guess at who will still be on the job market.

Yes, it's definitely a war out there...

Adopting a "whatever it takes" attitude

With this combination of job shortages, skill deficits, and new worker demands, companies are forced into a "whatever it takes" attitude about landing top talent.

---

78 www.computing.co.uk/ctg/analysis/2320912/the-it-skills-gap-a-genuine-problem-or-just-scaremongering

79 https://www.raeng.org.uk/publications/reports/uk-stem-education-landscape

80 In a candidate's job market, the 'war for talent' is real, JILLIAN KURVERS, http://mashable.com/2015/10/04/war-for-talent/#PewM10PB58qV + https://www.bls.gov/news.release/jolts.nr0.htm

81 www.telegraph.co.uk/finance/jobs/10657008/Replacing-staff-costs-British- businesses-4bn-each-year.html

82 https://www.weforum.org/agenda/2017/12/robots-coming-for-800-million-jobs/

The competition for talent has intensified so dramatically that top-tier companies from Facebook and Intuit to Anheuser-Busch InBev and Zappos are now extending job offers to top college recruits even when they don't have a particular job waiting. These companies want to lock up the talent, and ask questions later.

Top talent is being lured away whenever there is a better reason to leave than stay. To find and hold top performers, then, companies need to create awesome cultures and also employ novel hiring strategies.

Take the example of London's online grocery supermarket Ocado. Their CTO, Paul Clarke, at some point spray-painted hiring pitches on the sidewalks outside the big IT firms, hoping to lure away some IT talent. Whether this is innovative or insane, companies are pulling out all the stops to attract and retain top talent.[83]

So who's winning and who's losing?

In tallying up various industry surveys on employer social branding and recruiting, we find something of a digital divide. About half of the companies are on the right path, with the other half lagging. Specifically:
- 1 in 3 have employees regularly posting content and interacting socially
- 2 in 3 have an Employee Value Proposition driving their initiatives
- 3 in 4 have at least some employer brand presence on social media
- 2 in 3 are measuring their employer brand activities or planning to do more.

And a survey from the recruiting platform Jobvite of 1,855 recruiting and human resources professionals – across all industries – confirms that about half consider themselves proficient, about a third call themselves a novice, and only about one in five consider themselves experts.[84][85]

83 http://www.bcs.org/upload/pdf/it-skills-gap-whitepaper.pdf
84 https://www.jobvite.com/wp-content/uploads/2014/10/Jobvite_SocialRecruiting_Survey2014.pdf
85 https://www.jobvite.com/jobvite-news-and-reports/2017-job-seeker-nation-survey-finding-fault-lines-american-workforce/

Fig. 7.3 Hiring professionals not confident in social recruiting skills

These numbers make clear that many businesses still can – and need – to strengthen their employer social recruiting skillsets. And most know it. The hurdle is not in understanding; it is in executing.

Again, that takes us back to our book title and the design of programs that REALLY are doable, and swiftly, showing ROI . . . making them golden in the dross of everyday business activity.

And so they are, as we are about to see, but first some important context...

How does top talent decide their top choice?

When people go looking for a gig, job, consulting, all of the above – where is their first stop usually?

Until very recently, they checked out employee referral programs, Internet job boards, and recruiting offices in about the same numbers.

But beginning in 2011, as Fig. 7.4 shows, job seekers turned increasingly to social professional networks such as LinkedIn.[86] And now they use these networks just as often as job boards. It follows, then, that the companies telling the best stories on LinkedIn are capturing the attention of the best talent.

More recently, it has been confirmed that 45% of job seekers search for jobs daily on their mobile device. Not using social media recruiting can lead to a great loss of potential hiring volume, as 79% of jobseekers are likely to use it for their job search.[87]

---

86 https://content.linkedin.com/content/dam/business/talent-solutions/global/en_us/blog/2014/11/global-recruiting-trends-2015-infographic.jpg
87 https://theundercoverrecruiter.com/global-stats-recruiting-trends/

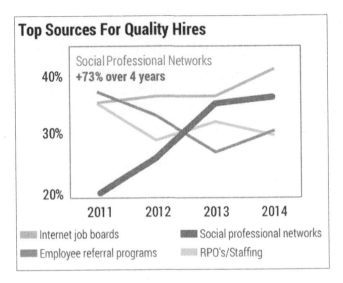

Fig. 7.4 Job hunters changing how they research employers

And we can't say it enough, but 84% of employees would consider quitting their job to take an offer from a company with a great reputation. And did you know that 69% of candidates would not accept a job in a company with a bad reputation? Even if they wouldn't have a job![88]

Let's look at the mechanics of how a savvy job hunter researches and winnows down to a short list of companies to interview at. We'll recreate what a top-of-class job seeker might go through in deciding on a job or career in retail management. The example is our client Asda, daughter company of Walmart.

CASE STUDY: Finding the perfect career at Asda

Our job candidate graduated at the top of her MBA class at the University of Leeds, and is looking to work with a great supermarket. So she first narrowed her search to a short-list of top companies including Ahold, Asda, Carrefour, Lidl, and Tesco.

Fig. 7.5 is what she first saw visiting the Asda website (www.asda.com), searching the week before Halloween.

---

88 https://www.glassdoor.co.uk/employers/blog/6-recruiting-tips-for-companies-with-bad-reputations/

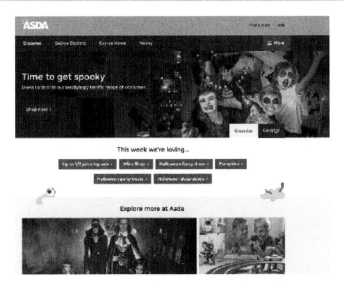

Fig. 7.5 Supermarket chain Asda's general website sets the tone of a company that is fun to work for

Our job candidate gets an instant hit: Asda could be a fun place to start a career. Asda's company website is happy, and obviously current.

The fun continues on Asda's Jobs & Careers page (www.asda.jobs) where our job seeker gets quick answers to her two top questions: What's it like to work here? What's in it for me?

Fig. 7.6 Asda's website careers page answers the top- of -mind questions of candidates straightaway

And right away, she sees job posting categories, so she can dive right in. But first she hops over to Glassdoor to see some reviews from Asda's own employees.

Glassdoor has eight million company reviews and counting, with information on C-level ratings, salary reports, benefits reviews, office photos and more.

She finds a lot of Glassdoor reviews on Asda, including some very positive ones on the people she would be working most directly with. Very good.

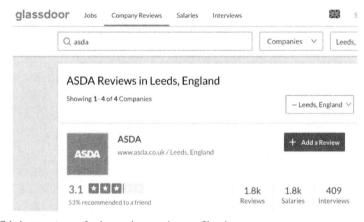

Fig. 7.7 Asda generates confirming employee reviews on Glassdoor

Her research thus far has been perfunctory. Her next stop is LinkedIn, where the real analysis begins.

She wants to research the executives and business units at Asda, to get a better sense of the company culture and social values, with whom she would be working, and how capable the team is . . . before considering an interview.

Asda's Company Page on LinkedIn brings a smile to her face – it continues the fun of the company's website. In the past even with some butt-slapping *joie de vivre* and the equipoise nod to the company's staying power on this, at the time their 50th anniversary.

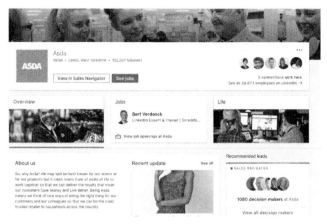

Fig. 7.8 Asda continues the 'fun offensive' on its LinkedIn Company Page

Skimming on down Asda's Company Page, she sees these posts:

- Top 10 Friendliest Workplaces – Retail Stores Dominate List | Glassdoor Blog *(which confirms her own Glassdoor research)*
- Tickled Pink, founded in 1996 by Asda, has raised £43m to treat breast cancer *(which warms her heart)*
- Asda wins best supermarket for wine at the 2015 Decanter Retailer Awards *- (which teases her taste buds, only ephemerally, but nonetheless)*
- And the award for 'Quality Food Retailer of the Year' goes to…Asda in 2016
- Grocer 33 price award for the 20th (!) time in a row in 2017
- Seven of Asda's own-brand goods have come up trumps and been voted as the Product of the Year in 2018 awards
- Interview with Asda's Chief Ice Cream Taster Louise *(again, just this looks like a fun company!)*
- And more awards, more fun posts, more jobs available *(Asda is looking good)*

Next stop is the Asda Careers Page on LinkedIn, accessible from the Company Page (Fig. 7.9).

This Careers Page really grabs her, because it's not milquetoast or generic. It has been tailored specifically to people like her looking for a rewarding career start. The taglines *"Every day matters"* and *"Let the adventure begin"* make her feel welcome. "Our people make the difference" really stands out. Who would want 'Selfie Takers, Rhymers and Long Distance Hikers, right? It affirms that Asda could indeed take her wherever she wants to go.

Fig. 7.9 Asda's LinkedIn Career Page is designed to attract a certain caliber of job seeker

She watches the video. It's brief, under a minute, enough to cement the growing sense that Asda could be the large welcoming workplace she desires.

She also notes that Asda has more than 100,000 followers – pretty good, she thinks, for a supermarket (this is not the rock star Pink, after all!).

And she sees that she has five (!) first degree LinkedIn connections at Asda. This triggers two happy-face notes to self:

- She'll have a number of warm entrées to employment decision-makers.
- The time she invested in building her network in college was well spent.

She then returns to Asda's Careers Page and looks over the current job postings in the right column. She selects the last one Engagement Analytics Manager (Fig. 7.10)

On this Position Page, she discovers not only the details of the job, but also that the job has only 10 applicants – increasing her interest. She wants to get in touch with some of her connections on LinkedIn to learn more about this position.

Further down the Careers Page (Fig. 7.11) she discovers who her team members might be, if she gets the job. A great way to get comfortable with the position and expedite her scheduling an interview.

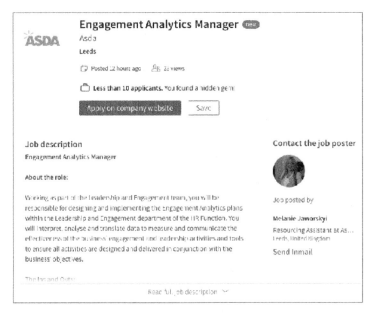

Fig. 7.10 A crisp job opening page, with some detail that helps convince the applicant this in a job to interview for

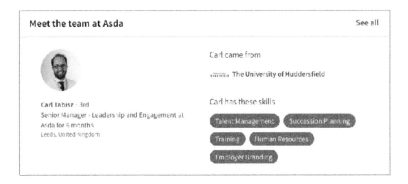

Fig. 7. 11 Further down the Careers Page, the job hunter learns more about her new team members potentially

She is getting a real 'feel' for the organization, for the people she would be working with, for the people who would be interviewing her should she apply.

She can also use LinkedIn's *Advanced Search* to pinpoint the people she wants to know more about at Asda.

For now, the takeaway from this opening section:

> The company that tells the best social business story
> is best positioned to win the recruiting battle.

Let's dig into this social business storytelling artform, and its six steps:
1. Aligning Personal, Professional and Corporate Brands
2. Developing the Social Recruiting Plan
3. Positioning as Employer-of-Choice Against the Competition
4. Turning Your Team Into Social Champions
5. Always Finding Exactly Who You Are Looking For
6. Measuring Your Social Recruiting By KPIs That Matter

Aligning Personal, Professional and Corporate Brands

In Chapter 5 we detailed how and why everyone from the C-suite down to the loading dock needs to have an aligned, consistent and socially credible brand. Let's review the high points here, beginning with why the personal, professional and corporate brands must be aligned. The reasons:
- Job seekers are looking at who they'll be working with;
- Customers and prospects want to know the people they're supporting;
- Consumers trust the employees' posts more than Marketing's claims.

The process of bringing each employee's individual and professional brands into alignment *on an ongoing basis* is far simpler than even five years ago – thanks to the evolution in social business tools.

The first principles that guide the process of branding alignment:
- Everyone's unique talents need to be surfaced.
- Each member of the team has a vital role to play.
- Changing workplace norms need to be addressed.
- Time should be prized as much as capital.
- Opportunities must be quickly seized.

Employees are already spokespersons, effectively. Since almost every employee is conversing on the social networks, they are acting as spokespersons for the company – for better or worse. So the challenge is to empower them to share their knowledge and expertise in a simple and engaging way, and to feel valued for it.

When employees do share on their social networks, they tend to reach 20 times more people than the company will reach, given the same number of followers. So it is not only *what* the employees are saying that matters, it is how *many more people* could potentially be hearing the message!

Managers need a first-rate LinkedIn Profile. It's also necessary for each manager to have an engaging LinkedIn Profile so that job seekers who go browsing through the company's employee roster on LinkedIn will see the Profiles of talented, exciting, good people – people they want to work with.

The CEO needs the best LinkedIn Profile of all. When top execs are mentioned in the media today, a link to their LinkedIn Profile is often included. When people click on that link and see an incomplete or dull Profile, they could easily conclude...
- The company is not up to date, certainly not innovative.
- The company may not be worth working for.
- The company doesn't understand today's marketplace.

178 million searches are conducted on LinkedIn every day. What is your company missing if your CEO's Profile is not among them?

All the best arguments for a CEO having an attractive and valuable LinkedIn Profile mean nothing, we understand, if the CEO has had a bad experience with stalkers and troublemakers, or fears that happening.

But ours is a transparent world now. There are dozens of ways to dig up intel on a CEO if someone is so inclined. So why not tell the very best story to the world?

This is what top CEOs do.

And LinkedIn is the platform for bringing the brands of the C-suite, managers, and employees into alignment on a personal, professional and corporate level.

Developing the Social Recruiting Plan

With the company's three branding faces all aligned and speaking in a unified voice to the greatest extent possible within your culture and organization, the next step is to draft a social recruiting plan that enjoys:

- Buy-in from the C-suite
- Solid data to support the case
- Strong cross-functional teamwork.

Here's how to make it happen:

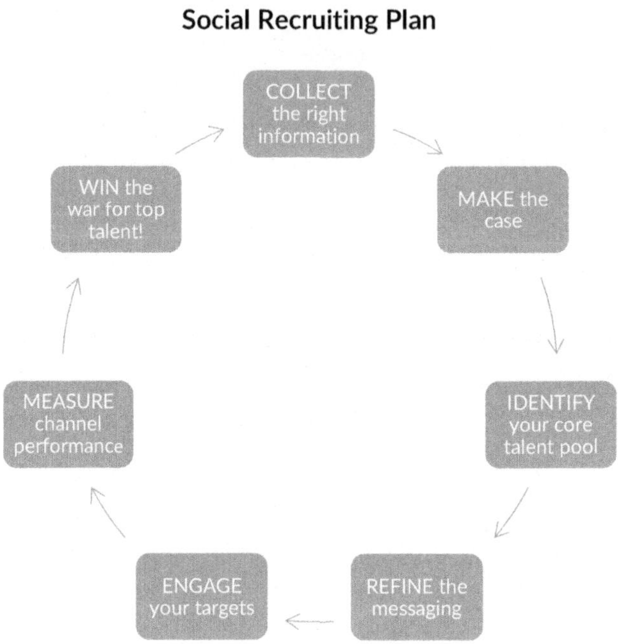

Social Recruiting Plan

Fig. 7.12 Outline of a Social Recruiting Plan

COLLECT the right information

You want to know what attracts talent to your organization, what keeps them there, and where you need to improve. And the best way to do this right is to talk to the current team. In confidential conversations and surveys with employees, you can gather the information that's an essential first step to crafting the compelling employer social brand story you will need.

Along the way, be sure to share your aggregated (names stripped out) survey results with the team – so everyone knows that they are being heard, that their input matters, and that you aim to be accountable.

Sample survey questions for current employees

- What are the primary values driving the company?
- How does the company deliver on these values in visible and effective ways?
- What values of importance does the company *not* deliver on?
- What was *originally* most attractive to you about working for the company?
- To what extent have those original expectations been met in your view?
- What's a favorite company story, something that can be shared publicly?
- How likely would you be to recommend the company as an employer?

This kind of brutal honesty (especially the last question) can be an intimidating hurdle. But without it, the social recruiting efforts become asocial, as it were, from the outset. It is nigh impossible to replicate the essential sincerity of social recruiting, no matter how gifted the individual attempting it. So be certain to poll and listen to every employee, no matter what their role or department, because in social business every opinion and view can have an impact.

Ask questions. Gather facts, opinions, and stories. Everything. And fold it into a rough battleplan to guide the next step...

MAKE the case

Armed and fortified with honest datapoints on your company, along with a rough plan of attack, you next enlist allies and make your case. You will be championing your thinking across the organization – from the lowest level to the highest.

Key elements of the battleplan

- Assessment of your company's talent strengths and weaknesses public-facing.
- Targets for the number and level of candidates that need to be sourced, shortlisted and submitted on a set schedule.
- Prioritized skillsets for the candidates so the roles are filled faster and

less expensively.

- List out/update your Employer Value Proposition (EVP). Why would people want to work at your organization?
- Stretch goals for the social recruiting initiative in KPI terms, such as *"saving $500K in recruitment fees this year"*.
- Goals translated into the business unit goals that hiring managers care about, such as *"bringing 10 people up to sales productivity in four weeks"*.

Critical importance of executive buy-in

Organizations most often lag in employer social branding because the senior executives are unsympathetic, untrusting or otherwise don't see the value.

In collecting information, you gained insight into why some executives may be pushing back. Now by linking your plan to the company's bottom line, you can build credibility for the whole venture. By making a business case for social recruiting that is clearly aligned with the company's strategic objectives, you bring the CEO and executive team on board, committed to owning and soon promoting the plan.

Something as important and transformational REALLY has to have ownership from the highest level. Wherever the social recruiting spark begins, it soon needs to become a top-down mission or else progress will be slow and success uncertain.

With the top dogs on board, every department head or business unit leader can then be shown the business case for talent recruiting projects and line up in support.

There must be support from HR, Marketing, and IT for an employer social brand to gain critical mass and lift off.

Finally, there needs to be a bottom-up mission as well, with social champions throughout the organization taking an active, energetic role.

IDENTIFY your core talent pool

With good intel about your company's talent strengths and weaknesses, and with support for social recruiting across the organization, you are best-prepared to identify the talent candidates. Targets will probably be prioritized as follows:

SHALLOW END

- Current employees – lateral moves and internal promotions
- Former employees – still have affinity, know the company
- Candidates who declined your offer – situations change
- Passive candidates (not now looking, but open to opportunity) in target functions, regions or industries – key targets.

DEEP END

- College students
- Vendors and consultants
- Customers and clients
- Competitors
- College career administrators
- Company page followers.

Make your list of target candidates using a spreadsheet or existing CRM. LinkedIn's Sales Navigator is the ideal tool for managing this step of the plan going forward. Or even better, use the LinkedIn Recruiter Seat. This tool allows you to set up talent pools, take notes, keep track of any candidate and so much more!

REFINE the messaging

Create first class messaging to appeal to candidates:
- First review your legacy print and digital assets, and your official presence on social media platforms.
- Take a measure of the unofficial conversations that are taking place online.
- Create messaging and campaign visuals that advance your talent brand, as you have identified it, and Marketing has refined and

executed it.

- Segment your messaging to different talent levels and geographic markets.
- Dry run your messaging with employees to ensure it rings true.

Checklist of talent brand materials

External facing

- Corporate website and jobs site
- Company and Career Pages on LinkedIn
- Employee LinkedIn Profiles
- Official presence on other social platforms
- Recruitment advertising and SlideShares
- Live-event collateral

Internal facing

- Direct communications with candidates and alumni
- Training and development materials
- Performance management guidelines
- Employee exit interviews

ENGAGE your targets

Many of your communications can be managed using LinkedIn's free accounts. If you do upgrade, you can reach more talent and close more offers – especially with passive candidates.

Questions for passive candidates

- What are the most important values to you in the workplace?
- How familiar are you with our company culture and working environment?
- What is your general impression of our company as a place to work?
- If your situation were to change at your current place of employment, how likely would you be to consider a job at our company?

MEASURE channel performance

Before the social recruiting campaign is up and running, lastly put in place systems to properly monitor and measure every activity you can. Track and identify the channels that produce the most quality-hires over time:

- LinkedIn and other professional networks
- Job Apps and Job Boards
- Employee Referrals

WIN the war for top talent!

LinkedIn's Employer Brand Playbook offers a good review and call to action for your social recruiting campaign. Here is an excerpt from the Playbook:

You've audited your existing talent brand materials, thought through the candidate and employee experience, and conducted research among your highest priority communities. Now...

Be real. What you say about your company must be true for your employees. If not, they'll see through you and so will the marketplace. Divide your desired messages into three buckets: what you can definitely back up, what's true in some circumstances, and what you'd like to say but can't just yet.

Be personal. Go back to the individual stories gathered during the research phase. Stories are more easily remembered and are motivational for employees. Those you feature will be proud to participate.

Be brave. Admit some negatives – people will believe you more. If you want to claim a message that you just can't say yet, identify a related one that's still enticing but can be delivered without any eye-rolling. Brainstorm options with your marketing team.

Be consistent. Think about how to align this messaging with your company's overall brand. There should be strong consistency between the two.

Set your goals. It's important to define success at the outset. Establish the baseline against which you will measure progress.

Mind the gaps. Where are the inconsistencies? Do your materials match what your research says?

Look for patterns. What themes bubble to the top? Are there any major anomalies? How does the feedback vary by audience?

Handle the truth. If you learn something unfavorable, address it. Don't attempt quick fixes: slapping a new picture on your career site or changing your tagline won't cut it. Don't get stuck on extreme comments or senior management's input if your research says otherwise.

With your battleplan fit and trim, you can begin...

Positioning as Employer-of-Choice Against the Competition

Your objective here is to use the social business networks to share your company's story, highlight your strengths and address your weaknesses, and build the most authentic and engaging employer brand reputation you can. The next step toward making this happen is...

Put your LinkedIn Company page to good use

In Chapter 5 we detailed the steps for creating a LinkedIn Company Page which allows organizations to tell their story and build relationships with customers. Here we'll skim the highlights of Company Pages, so you are certain to be putting yours to good use:

Company page > Edit tab > Overview page

Complete all fields:
- Perfunctory Information
- Company Description
- Images & Logo
- Company Specialties
- Featured Groups
- Showcase Pages
- Careers Page.

Analytics tab > Track on global LinkedIn activity

- Updates: Impressions, Clicks, Interactions, Followers acquired, Engagement
- Followers: Total, Demographics by Industry, Company size, Function
- Visitors: Pageviews by day, Unique visitors by time periods, Visitor demographics by Industry, Company size, Function.

Notifications tab > Track on latest social activity

- View all the publicly shared mentions of your company on LinkedIn
- Reach out and respond to these mentions
- Handle multiple actions across LinkedIn from a single place (all interactions will be aggregated into a single notification for easy management).

Tailor posts to your community's needs and interests

- Plan out a schedule of updates and posts that your community of fans and followers will find interesting, helpful and genuinely relevant to your industry while also demonstrating your thought leadership. Here you'll tap content provided not just from HR and Marketing, but also from sales, field support, and R&D. You can, and should, share the load of creating interesting content from each of their valuable perspectives.
- Be careful about posting anything too salesy. (LinkedIn Showcase pages are the proper places for sales pitches.)
- Choose the best times and frequency for posting. A LinkedIn Company Page shouldn't be as active as your employee's individual Profiles. An ideal schedule is one post a day at the start.
- Make it easy for employees to follow the Company Page. Ask them to click the *Follow* button and provide a list of links for them to use in their postings, which should always link back to the Company Page.
- Use LinkedIn's *Follow* button in all the places where you touch your prime communities: Your website, corporate email communications, employee email signatures, and LinkedIn Profiles.
- Use the LinkedIn plugins on your website for incremental increases in response. Key plugins are: *Share, Follow Company, Member Profile, Company Profile, Company Insider, Jobs You Might Be Interested In.*

Build the most compelling LinkedIn Career Page you can

The Career Page augments your LinkedIn Company Page, and is a premium service. It sits tabbed behind the Company Page and is set up to run social recruiting campaigns that target specific pools of talent. You can...

- Speak directly to prospective employees about specific job opportunities.
- Share the warmth of personality and culture of your company.
- Give candidates a genuine feel for their 'fit' in your organization, among your employees, and within your culture.
- Strategically engage candidates by giving them information about employees they'd likely be close to, as well as general company news and evidence of your industry leadership.
- See a dashboard of analytics on the success of your campaigns.

Top-line value of a Careers page

- Your content will be adapted to viewers, based on their LinkedIn Profiles (and depending on the type of paid Careers page you choose).
- Job seekers will see jobs tailored to their backgrounds.
- With multiple-page and/or multi-lingual versions, you can target individual candidates.
- Use videos and employee interviews to bring out your culture.
- Recruiter Profiles connect candidates directly with your company.
- You can run your own custom ads with a branded look (such as a LinkedIn *Work With Us* campaigns).
- Detailed analytics show you who is engaging with your brand.

To see a well-executed Career Page, visit some of our clients: Deloitte, Microsoft, RBS, The Adecco Group or BNP Paribas.

Key elements on your Careers Page

- Your Header Image. LinkedIn lets you use a different header here, and you should. Choose a photo or image that specifically relates to your company culture and hiring efforts and reinforces your brand positioning with prospective employees.
- Your Posts. *Your Company Page posts auto-populate here, but* you also have the ability to post separately. *Focus on* roles that you are trying to fill, team-building activities, employee testimonials, and company

perks *that tell the 'human side' of your company. Did we mention that video works really well?*

- Your Openings. Your available openings auto-populate on the right side bar if you use LinkedIn Talent Solutions to post your openings. Make the most of this benefit by keeping your openings up-to-date. Also make sure that if you have a lot of openings available, they all appear on LinkedIn. (It looks bad to have 10 jobs listed on LinkedIn but 100 on your corporate website!)

Constantly publish your thought leadership

In Chapter 5 we detailed how LinkedIn has taken its Pulse product uptown, going beyond a place where only top influencers in an industry are publishing to a place where anyone with great ideas and writing talent can have their posts shared broadly with millions of LinkedIn members in relevant industries.

So LinkedIn becomes an excellent way to put the best of your company's thought leadership in front of candidates. Read all about publishing articles on LinkedIn in Chapter 5.

Take advantage of LinkedIn's New 'ProFinder'

Since 2015 the number of job openings listed on LinkedIn tripled to more than one million, with more than 10 million in 2018[89], as LinkedIn began a pilot called ProFinder (Fig. 7.13) connecting businesses with local freelancers.

Fig. 7.13 ProFinder extends LinkedIn's assistance into the gig sector

---

89 http://fortune.com/2017/04/24/linkedin-users/

The pilot project is being run in the US, as we write. The idea is to organize job openings in some 15 categories ranging from the highest-paid software engineers to the hardest-working pizza delivery drivers.

ProFinder is the latest step on LinkedIn's path of becoming the economic graph of the world, a digital map of every employee, company and school with integrated tools for networking, AI-driven learning, career development, business product purchasing, and a decade out, presumably . . . simply retiring.

This step with ProFinder takes LinkedIn for the first time into the contingent workforce space which includes:
- Freelancers
- Independent professionals
- Contract workers
- Independent contractors
- Specialized consultants.

The step-by-step of ProFinder is in Fig. 7.14:

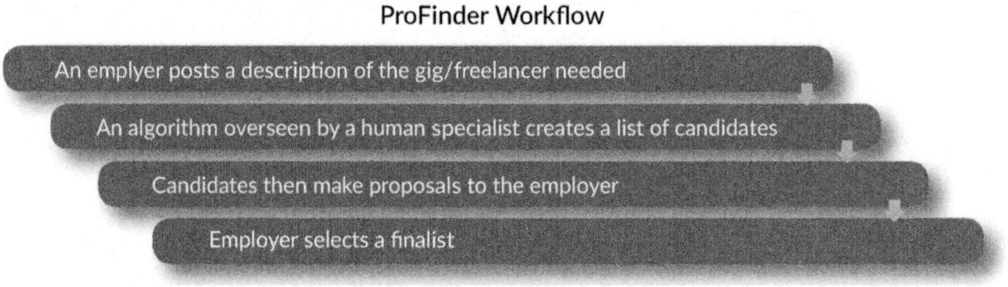

ProFinder Workflow

An emplyer posts a description of the gig/freelancer needed

An algorithm overseen by a human specialist creates a list of candidates

Candidates then make proposals to the employer

Employer selects a finalist

Fig. 7.14 Summary of ProFinder Workflow

With ProFinder, LinkedIn hopes to validate the idea that contingent workers – who are becoming the largest segment of the workforce in many countries – can secure new work contracts with employers with the same ease that full-time employees have been able to.

LinkedIn transformed the marketplace for professionals seeking full-time positions and career development. Will it succeed as well with gig seekers?

Well, smaller networks have tried to build and scale online platforms like this. Think Freelancer.com, Craigslist, Elance, Guru, Upwork, SimplyHired, and Fiverr.com. But none have tried on the global-to-local scale that LinkedIn envisions.

And while most online networks aim to help freelancers who can usually work remotely for any client, ProFinder matches local freelancers with local employers. That should open up opportunities in staff recruiting.

So when you are looking to hire contingent workers in a specific area, ProFinder could become a tool of choice for finding and vetting candidates.

If the pilot is successful, as we expect it to be, LinkedIn will roll into every market.

Passive candidates become active in LinkedIn Groups

We talked about LinkedIn Groups extensively in Chapter 5. These Groups are ideal places to develop relationships with passive candidates who aren't currently in the job market but just might move with the right offer or circumstance.

Passive candidates are most motivated by a better working environment, training for career advancement, and compensation, in that order (according to a LinkedIn survey). And 85% of them are open to switching jobs; the other 15% say they would not move.[90] This suggests a very large pool of passive talent to tap.

An idea place to hold informal conversations with these passive candidates is in the Groups, where both you and a candidate have an opportunity to demonstrate your more attractive qualities, with little pressure. It's ideal for incubating relationships.

Use a 'Company Insider' window to welcome talent

Place a *Company Insider* window on your company's webpage so that job candidates who visit your page will get some valuable information fast:
- A friendly welcoming view of your employees
- Who in your company they are connected to
- Insight into how quickly others move up your career ladder.

---

90 https://www.ziprecruiter.com/blog/7-keys-to-finding-passive-job-candidates/

See a sample *Company Insider* window in Fig. 7.15:

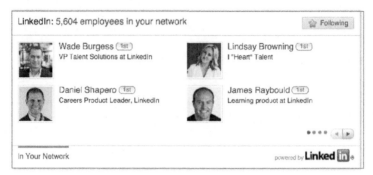

Fig. 7.15 A cutaway of the Company Insider page Bert Verdonck sees for LinkedIn, showing his connections within LinkedIn

This window is installed with a plugin, most commonly on a jobs/careers page. It can be set up to face job candidates and show valuable information in three ways:

1. Show all of the company's employees that are in their LinkedIn networks.
2. Show the latest new hires in your company.
3. Show any changes in your employee structure.

You have the option to hide any of these features, but it's generally best to show all.

Get the plugin for the Company Insider: http://developer.linkedin.com/plugins.

Follow your company's followers

As you fill your pool of job candidates, you can use LinkedIn to also see which of them is following your company on LinkedIn.

(The list of companies they follow is at/near the bottom of their profile.)

They could be following you for a number of reasons. Perhaps you are a competitive company they are tracking. But just as likely, you are a company that interests them and they may someday wish to work for you.

By reaching out casually and nurturing an on-going relationship with these people, you deepen your talent pool with 'prequalified' candidates.

We've now covered the basics of positioning as an employer of choice in your industry. There are even more social recruiting strategies coming into play, and we dig into them at LinkedIn Learning if you want to see more. But for now, let's continue onto the next big social recruiting initiative...

Turning Your Team Into Social Champions

In Chapter 5 we detailed the strategy for turning an entire team into social champions for the company, advancing the brand across the social channels. Here we will summarize the strategies as they apply to social recruiting.

We have seen how today's consumers are twice as likely to trust what an employee says over what the company PR or CEO say, and how a 12% increase in brand advocacy can generate 2x revenue growth, so conscripting employees to publicly share their own confidence and trust in the organization makes good sense.

And this happens most certainly when employees are shown how they and the company will both benefit from their participation. Specifically, how they can...
- Become better known as experts in their specialty
- Build their social credibility on the networks
- Learn new things through new social connections
- Help attract talent like themselves to the team
- All of which impacts the company's social brand.

Here is a summary of the Social Champion training we give:
- C-Level Leadership. Like any business initiative, a social champion program requires buy-in from the highest levels to ensure acceptance across the corporate culture.
- Clear-cut Objectives. The objectives of the program must align with corporate objectives so that results can be measured.
- Companywide Training. It's impossible to unleash your people on the social networks without first training them on the social tools that deliver the maximum advantage.

- **Content Sharing.** There must be content developed by Marketing and by the employees themselves to share. Using an app (such as Scredible) that automates and simplifies social sharing is ideal.
- **Monitor and Measure.** There is no sense in proceeding if KPIs are not set and the company is not prepared to measure the benefit; this is a must do.

How to develop a companywide 'recruiting' mentality

First identify a natural champion, someone from HR, ideally, who is enthusiastic about LinkedIn and believes in the program's potential; someone who can motivate the team to participate. Have the leader recruit a couple of confederates who will help build the program and later join in encouraging the entire team to participate.

Make clear the vision: For every employee to have a real stake in the company's future by sharing messages that attract quality talent like themselves.

Assuming that your team's LinkedIn Profiles are all up to snuff (they are, or will be, right?!) then ask your employees to begin sharing the content that is ideal for the social business channels.

It's common for employees to share aggressively in the beginning, then lose interest as other pressing tasks take priority. But social recruiting is not a run and gun endeavor. It takes time, and you must keep a firm hand on the initiative until it gains the momentum of routine.

A good idea is to put reminder alerts on your team's calendars, so they stick to the program long enough to ingrain the activities and soon, before long hopefully, you will have a routine in place and social champions that are becoming known in your industry and beyond.

CASE STUDY: 60% sales referral increase in one week

Few companies have had the disruptive impact of Salesforce.com. This company has been a big innovator since unseating Siebel and joining Oracle and SAP as one of the three leaders in the CRM space. So it's no surprise that it was among the first to transform into a social recruiting juggernaut. But given its massive size, it's hard to believe that a LinkedIn employer branding initiative could spur an astonishing 60% increase in sales referrals in just one week.

Yet that's precisely what happened.

Salesforce.com had deep openings to fill for account executives and sales engineers. At the urging of Kate Israels, Senior Program Manager responsible for the Global Recruiting Operations, CEO Marc Benioff fired off an email to the team rallying them to a LinkedIn offensive (Fig. 7.16).

Salesforce.com CEO Marc Benioff fires up team for social recruiting

To: # All Sales World Wide
Subject: Get Social and Spread the Word!

As we work to become a $10 billion company, we need to grow our world-class sales team—and you can help us do that by connecting us to amazing people like yourself. We've put together a few posts that we'd love for you to share with your networks. This is a great way for you to help us build our first-rate team *and* receive a nice referral bonus.

Post #1:
Attention sales rockstars: salesforce.com is hiring! Join a world-class team at the most innovative company in the world. [Ping me if you're interested.] http://www.salesforce.com/careers/sales/

Post #2:
salesforce.com is growing! Join our amazing team. We're hiring for sales positions across the board and around the world! Find open jobs here: http://www.salesforce.com/careers/sales/ - [reach out to me if you'd like a referral]

Post #3:
I'm in my #dreamjob at salesforce.com and we're hiring! Check out open positions here: http://www.salesforce.com/careers/sales/

Aloha.
Marc

Fig. 7.16 CEO takes action to spur 60% increase in social sales referrals

As reported by LinkedIn, Salesforce.com's sales team was inspired by their CEO to *double* the number of LinkedIn *Status Updates* they were producing, as a result reaching potentially 38,000 sales professionals. Referrals from those employee posts spiked 60% in just one week.

That was 2012. Since then Salesforce.com's market share has continued to rise; its stock price nearly doubled to $80 a share in 2015 and in 2018 has continued the growth to $118, as we write. This is a smart company that is committed to advancing their employer social brand . . . for better social recruiting.

CASE STUDIES: Cutting out the middleman

The updated LinkedIn recruiting tools have made it very convenient for companies to marshal their employees behind social recruiting initiatives. In so doing, they have bypassed the traditional recruitment agency for all but the most senior of positions. In those cases, a discreet tap on the shoulder from a headhunter such as Korn/Ferry or DHR International is still expected. Some top examples of LinkedIn platform successes:[91]

- Rajesh Ahuja, the talent acquisition leader for the Indian software outsourcers Infosys, says that two years ago he *used recruiters to fill 70% of his open positions in Europe; but now, only 16%.*
- Steven Baert, head of human resources at pharmaceutical giant Novartis, says he *hired at least 250 people through LinkedIn*[92], instead of using a recruiter as they had previously.
- Hubert Giraud, head of people management and transformation at the French consulting firm Capgemini, says he used LinkedIn to hire 33 managers in India *at substantially lower cost.* (By the way, Capgemini has the highest number of LinkedIn certified recruiters in the world.[93])
- Glenn Cook, director of global staffing at Boeing, says that LinkedIn is even a good source for finding aviation engineers. He is now *swiftly filling jobs* that used to remain vacant for 6–8 months.

Clearly social recruiting is becoming the way to win the war for talent. So let's recap what we've covered thus far:

> With your company's three brand components in alignment, a social recruiting plan fully developed, the company positioned as the employer of choice against your principal competition, and a program in place to convert your employees into social champions, the next step is to use LinkedIn to find precisely the name talent you're looking for...

---

91 "Workers of the world, log in", *The Economist*, August 17, 2014 (http://www.economist.com/news/business/21612191-social-network-has-already-shaken-up-way-professionals-are-hired-its-ambitions-go-far)

92 https://www.businessinsider.com.au/linkedins-plan-for-the-future-2014-8

93 http://www.slideshare.net/linkedin-talent-solutions/capgeminis-journey-transforming-global-social-sourcing-through-accelerating-linkedin-certification

Finding Exactly Who You Are Looking For

Your experience in recruiting and hiring may be similar to our own.

In the good old days (as recently as five years ago) when we needed to hire someone, we would paste job ads onto a couple dozen websites and then gird our loins for the flow of incoming email applications.

We'd next spend hours with a finger poised over the delete button, giving a yea or nay based solely on the quality of the cover email.

Then we'd open up the resume PDFs of the remaining few, and email back a list of questions for each candidate to complete, adding a 'fast deadline' as a further filter.

This would net us 10-15 interviews, most of which would be disappointing. That's because the best prospects had good positions already, and didn't need to be scanning the jobs ads.

We knew that the people who were responding to online job ads weren't always the best candidates. But we needed to hire, and we couldn't always justify forking out over 20% of the new hire's first year salary to a recruiter.

That's why we were early adopters of, and in fact became training specialists in, LinkedIn's *Advanced Search* tool. In our view it is the fastest, easiest and cheapest way to find exactly who you are looking for – whether it is a vendor, customer prospect, or as here, an employee.

In Chapter 6 we ran through each of the filters available in *Advanced Search* to find the one in 550+ million LinkedIn members you are looking for.

We noted that less than 50% of our training session attendees over the years have used *Advanced Search* – even though the free version can yield significant results, and the low-cost premium version can save any organization substantial hiring costs and turnaround time.

Find internal talent as well

Many companies, especially those organized in a matrix structure, can have a difficult time locating the ideal staffers needed for a given project. And the larger the organization, the more difficult it is to know whether or not the needed expertise is already in-house.

As a consequence, the same tedious and time-consuming talent hunts are often repeated over and over again for the very same resources inside the very same organization, business unit, or even within departments.

Companies recognize this problem, of course, and have built databases or turned to cloud platforms like Slack or Workplace by Facebook to capture the skills profiles of their employees. But there are shortcomings to these approaches:
1. Not everybody keeps their data up-to-date since it doesn't always serve their own needs (many think of it as bureaucratic hassle to be handled mañana).
2. In these company databases, usually only the skills and knowledge related to the projects within the organization are stored. So valuable achievements at former employers might not be known inside the current organization.
3. Even if a project manager finds someone with the right skills, it is unknown whether this person will be a good cultural fit with the rest of the team.

LinkedIn can overcome these issues:
- Many people don't update their Profile in internal databases, but they do on LinkedIn. Showing their peers in other companies, their colleagues and friends about their professional career is a higher priority.
- On LinkedIn most people list their current skills and knowledge, and also courses they took in the past, and other possibly relevant information.
- LinkedIn knows no borders. Thus, it's very easy to find colleagues all around the world. (Note: This works only when everybody links his or her personal Profile to the same international parent Company Page, as well as the national one where they work most of the time).
- Because LinkedIn shows how you are connected, it is easy to check references to colleagues. You can easily run fact-finding missions

with people who used to work on the same project about the person you are considering for the project.

LinkedIn's Search aims to be a logistical nightmare solver. After poring over user data LinkedIn discovered that about 30% of the searches done each month were for coworkers. In a survey of 814 members, LinkedIn confirmed:[94]

1. 38% of professionals say their company intranet is a serviceable way to learn about coworkers – but at a low level of satisfaction.
2. 58% say they could perform better if they could find coworkers with specific skills – so they go looking elsewhere.
3. 46% say they look up coworkers on LinkedIn – because it's easier, faster, and LinkedIn Profiles are more up-to-date.

LinkedIn says it is *"the fastest way to learn about your coworkers"*. In larger companies with distributed workforces and only adequate HR systems in place, that may be especially true.

Big Fat Fails: What not to do in social recruiting

In working with 650+ companies since 2004, we've seen seven employer social branding screw-ups pop up time and again, in companies of all sizes, in every industry.

Some of these screw-ups are obvious ones, others not so much. But both can cost companies dearly:

1 Viewing employer branding as merely a recruitment strategy or a near-term job-filling campaign instead of a KPI.
2. Creating recruitment advertising that doesn't build memory associations on what it's like to work for the company.
3. Promising a workplace culture in the recruitment advertising that doesn't really match the actual employment experience.
4. Failing to collaborate across departments responsible for corporate, consumer, and employer branding initiatives (e.g. HR, Marketing, Communications), resulting in a disjointed approach.
5. Using a different recruitment message across multiple channels and changing the message for each campaign in the name of creativity (or

---

94 https://blog.linkedin.com/2015/08/19/introducing-linkedin-lookup-easily-find-learn-about-and-contact-your-coworkers

simply to win an award!)

6. Derailing progress because of an untrusting company culture and a reluctance to embrace the openness of social media.
7. Failing to conduct research with the internal and external audiences to determine what makes the employer brand distinctive.

At this point in the book, you should know if (1) your team is committing any of these screw-ups and (2) how to remedy them. If not, please let us know and we can talk about a custom plan for moving beyond old screw-ups to new successes.

Measuring Social Recruiting By KPIs That Matter

When you create a social recruiting strategy, you want to know how and why your strategy is working. You want both quantitative and qualitative metrics of your performance, to prove the ROI of your on-going efforts and plan for the future.

Benchmark improvement in four key social recruiting metrics

In our training sessions, we find companies are most interested in improving performance on four key metrics. We find that when companies follow the strategies detailed in this chapter, they can expect to see improvements of between 30% and 50% in these top four benchmarks (as shown in Fig. 7.17).

Benchmark Improvement in four Key Social Recruiting Metrics		
	Low-End Improvement	High-End Improvement
1. Time-to-hire	28%	44%
2. Quality of candidates	38%	55%
3. Employee referrals	32%	60%
4. Quantity of candidates	42%	63%
(These figures are averages seen across hundreds of companies and industries, and can range higher in highly motivated companies with dedicated teams and capable coaching.)		

Fig. 7.17 Improvements expected from social recruiting initiatives

Beyond the top four benchmarks, we have found that companies also want social recruiting programs that deliver on these success measures:

1. Increase offer acceptance rate
2. Reduce employee attrition
3. Improve employee on-the-job satisfaction
4. Increase familiarity with employer social brand
5. Increase the number of employees with an optimized social brand

We recommend using all nine metrics, in addition to your own industry-specific metrics, to manage your progress.

What is the cost of not having these metrics in place?

Learn from the Virgin Media case...where a bad candidate experience is costing Virgin Media £5,000,000 annually![95]

Why? When a fan of the Virgin Media brand with very limited qualifications applies for a job and against the odds is granted an interview. Obviously, (s)he prepares extremely well, including asking interview tips from friends, maybe following a few online courses to upskill, arranging child care and even buying a new outfit.

So, when that applicant has a bad candidate experience, like dealing with a grumpy receptionist, followed by an interviewer, who keeps him/her waiting for more than one hour (after the agreed time) and then after five minutes (!) rejects him/her on the spot, because (s)he is not qualified, you can imagine how that the applicant feels. Confused and disappointed at least. And what is the true impact on his/her brand experience? Changing from an ambassador to a detractor (not willing to recommend the brand) and even canceling his/her Virgin Media cable subscription (or whatever product(s) they have).

Surely, that must be an exception, right? No! When the Head of Resourcing dug deeper and found out that about 18% of rejected candidates were also Virgin Media customers, it became clear there was a real problem.

About 6% of the rejected candidates actually switched providers within a month! Let's bring in the rest of the numbers... Virgin Media rejects

---

95   https://business.linkedin.com/talent-solutions/blog/candidate-experience/2017/bad-candidate-experience-cost-virgin-media-5m-annually-and-how-they-turned-that-around

about 123,000 candidates each year. Let's multiply that by an average £50 subscription fee per month. This brings us to a total of £4.4M!

Please be mindful that these numbers did not take into account candidates who switched after one month, and more importantly how candidates shared their bad experience with friends and family. Long story short, you can easily see this number going over £5M.

Obviously, Virgin Media took the necessary steps to fix this problem. Read their astonishing approach and results: http://ht.ly/s2Pd30jwMq8 .

LINKEDIN RELEASES NEW HIGH-VALUE TOOLS

8

Let's now take stock of the tools and applications offered by LinkedIn that are most useful for business sales and development. Some are free to use; others require a subscription. We focus only on the tools that have proven with our own clients to:

- Increase online visibility
- Generate high-quality leads at lower cost
- Improve recruiting numbers
- Generally enable social business success.

Plus, since LinkedIn is constantly upgrading their existing tools and adding new ones, you can keep up-to-date on high-value developments at https://how-to-really-use-linkedin.com

Free-to-Use LinkedIn Tools

Voyager - LinkedIn App bundles LinkedIn tools

LinkedIn spent time revamping its App portfolio, keeping their desktop experience robust with functionality but streamlining the App for quick access to tools that are more relevant on the go, as well as fun and friendly (for iOS and Android). The main App is "Voyager" and it comes with five simple buttons:

1. Home – the main news feed with personalized news articles
2. My Network – for monitoring the activities of your connections
3. Messaging – simple chat interface
4. Notifications – activity on your Profile from connections and interested people
5. Jobs – find your dream job

And, of course, the top Search Bar – find connections, follow companies, access other info available on LinkedIn.

Fig. 8.1 Screenshot of LinkedIn's mobile app – Voyager

Voyager is ideal for downtime, e.g., waiting for a meeting to start, standing in line at the market, enduring the ads if watching TV in real time. Voyager uses popular "card based" design to make it easy to:

- Check your inbox to see if anything needs immediate attention
- Catch-up on all the updates of people in your network, to stay current
- Check out Profiles of people in your network, and look to deepen the relationship
- Look through LinkedIn's suggestions for people to connect to.

You can also sync your phone contacts and calendar to find new connections, and Voyager helps you prepare for meetings by bringing-up a snapshot of the parties' profiles.

The streamlined App *does not* give you access to all of the LinkedIn features and tools.

Most people are surprised when they discover that LinkedIn has separate apps for different functionalities, like:

- LinkedIn Groups – for networking
- Job Search – for job tracking and hunting
- Slideshare – for viewing and publishing presentations
- Lynda – for upgrading skills
- Linkedin Learning – for upgrading skills
- LinkedIn Elevate – for sharing smart content.

LinkedIn is now constantly upgrading its desktop and multiple Apps, so expect this information to require regular updating. More info about the latest Apps can be found on https://mobile.linkedin.com.

SlideShare – Millions of stunning presentations at your fingertips

SlideShare is LinkedIn's global hub for professional content, with more than 80 million users finding and sharing expert content each month.

It's a visual format (usually done in PowerPoint) that resonates with today's audiences and, in turn, generates greater brand exposure, higher-quality leads faster, and more business opportunities.

Importantly, in today's video-motivated and savvy world, the average consumer is thought to be capable of processing visual images 60,000 times faster than text.[96] As a result, according to LinkedIn[97]:

- People are 44% more likely to engage with images
- Visual presentations are 4x more viral than text presentations.

Conventional marketing materials and sales pitches do not usually work on SlideShare, and should be avoided.

The best SlideShares capture your company's insights and offer helpful tips to customers and prospects. These trigger people to follow you, sign-up for your newsletter, or just make a mental note to learn more about you.

Why SlideShare is a go-to communications tool for businesses

- SlideShare has more professional viewers than platforms like Facebook, Twitter, and Google+
- LinkedIn loves SlideShare! Even before they acquired it, they featured it highly and ranked its content prominently in search results. So using it results in great SEO.
- Adding SlideShares to your Company Page and employee Profiles on LinkedIn ratchets up interest in the brand and product lines.
- SlideShares can also be embedded in your company's website and

---

96 http://blog.hubspot.com/marketing/visual-content-marketing-infographic
97 https://business.linkedin.com/marketing-solutions/blog/best-practices--content-marketing/2016/new-linkedin-research-reveals-how-to-create-engaging-content

blog, and there is no limit to how many you can use.

Upload a SlideShare: www.slideshare.net. You can use your LinkedIn credentials, so you don't have to setup yet another account.

Summary of SlideShare

- Strong professional context
- Delivers excellent SEO reach
- Can be embedded in a blog or website
- Does take time to grow a following, but worth the investment
- Ideally cross-promoted with Facebook or Twitter.

Premium LinkedIn Tools

LinkedIn offers many more premium business tool than most people realize, beginning at $30 a month (as of 2018).[98] These tools can be smart investments for some of the social business hiring, marketing and sales situations a company faces. We'll look more closely at them to help you determine if a further conversation with a LinkedIn sales representative makes sense.

NOTE: If you don't have a LinkedIn representative yet, get in touch with us connect@reallyconnect.com and we will connect you with the right person for your needs.

Summary of Premium Plans

What follows is *not* an exhaustive overview of all that LinkedIn has to offer. Instead, we'll review the tools that (1) we've found most useful and (2) can be readily purchased with a credit card. In addition to this, LinkedIn has a full suite of enterprise products in three areas:
1. Talent Solutions
2. Sales Solutions
3. Marketing Solutions.

---

98 Scredible does not sell LinkedIn products. Please check with LinkedIn for the latest pricing.

LinkedIn's Premium Career Plan ($29.99/month when billed annually)

- Three InMail messages (for reaching out to recruiters found on LinkedIn)
- See who's viewed your profile in the last 90 days (not just the last five)
- Display at the top of recruiters' applicant lists
- See how you compare to other candidates
- View salary insights while browsing jobs
- Get access to LinkedIn's online video courses

LinkedIn's Premium Business Plan ($47.99/month when billed annually)

- 15 InMail messages (for reaching out to prospects found on LinkedIn)
- Additional search filters (for more targeted searches)
- Unlimited searches in your extended network (for finding who you need)
- Join the OpenLink network so non-first-degree contacts who have upgraded accounts can message you directly (and not have to use paid InMail)
- Show the "Premium" badge on your Profile, making clear that you take LinkedIn seriously as a professional (this badge is not right for everyone, and you should follow your intuition in displaying it)
- See business insights (e.g. "Employee distribution and growth by function")

LinkedIn's Sales Navigator Professional ($64.99/month when billed annually)

- Lead-builder tool
- Premium search filters
- How you are connected
- Lead recommendations
- Real-time insights on existing accounts and leads, on LinkedIn and beyond
- Synced App

LinkedIn Premium Recruiter Lite ($99.95/month when billed annually)

- Automatic candidate tracking and integrated hiring
- Unlimited visibility into your extended network

- Additional search filters
- 30 InMail messages

LinkedIn Elevate ($25/mo. per seat)

- Curate high-quality content and suggest it to employees for sharing.
- Employees can share on desktop or mobile to their LinkedIn and Twitter connections.
- Analytics measure impact on company hiring, marketing, and sales goals.

Sales Navigator – Must-have tool for social selling

We talked at length about Sales Navigator in Chapter 5 because we have found it to be an indispensable tool for budget-conscious sales teams.

In an era of social selling where a great portion of the buying decision has been concluded before the deal is closed, Sales Navigator helps salespeople meet their prospects early-on in the social buying decision-making process, building high-value connections and trust earlier when it matters most.

This early-on meeting is made possible through the trove of data LinkedIn collects. As we said earlier, members make 10 million comments a week on each other's Profiles but these members also post two billion updates per week.[99] That's a lot of data to mine. And with Sales Navigator in-house, your team can have these member updates sliced and diced to just about any kind of business need.

Your team can know what your target accounts are talking about, and what's going on in their lives, revealing connection paths between your company and your targets that can be leveraged for warm introductions.

Revealing the right set of data is just as important as filtering out the irrelevant data. Sales Navigator does this by bringing in just the relevant network data and news sources, joining this information on the same page as your accounts, leads, and preferences so you can better connect and build relationships with your highest-value buyers.

---

99 https://lss.csod.com/clientimg/lss/MaterialSource/10_2015061702324683_503360437_PDF.pdf

Why Sales Navigator is an essential tool

✓ Pinpoints the right people on social networks and recommends ideal contact based on preferences and social sharing *(all in real time).*

✓ Produces prospect information at the top of the sales funnel (*crucial since 57% of the buying process is complete before people even reach out).*

✓ Establishes a two-way relationship based on authenticity *(without cold calls or generic sales pitches).*

✓ Gives creative tools to establish credible thought leadership *(that opens up new opportunities).*

✓ Tells who within the company is already connected with a prospect or lead (to avoid embarrassing overlap and to allow one rep to pick up from another) (=TeamLink).

✓ Eliminates the tedium of manually searching through second- and third-degree connections to identify prospects.

✓ Replaces a scattershot approach to social selling with a single platform that keeps track of prospects and records activity for future action.

Value of Sales Navigator *(LinkedIn Data)*	
Increase in success over free version	
Finding prospects	+119%
Generating opportunities	+52%
Securing meetings	+128%
Winning deals	+70%

Fig. 8.2 Performance metrics for LinkedIn Sales Navigator

CASE STUDY: Microsoft boosts productivity 38% as it grows its Sales Navigator user base from 15 users to 3,000+ in two years.

Phil Amato was Marketing and Communications Manager at Microsoft from 2013-2016 (long before LinkedIn was bought by Microsoft). He saw the launch of the company's Azure cloud computing solution as a reason to shift sales tactics because the sales team had to find their own customers for the SaaS solution, and build up solid relationships with buyers, rather than just work the leads sent over from Marketing. So it was an ideal pilot opportunity.

The pilot began with just 15 people using Sales Navigator. When it came time to analyze results, Mr. Amato found that the whole series of small actions driven by Sales Navigator (looking up people's profiles, sending messages, sharing content, and engaging online) had a cumulative effect that resulted in 38% more sales opportunities than traditional Microsoft sales teams tallied.

From there, the program grew organically. As Mr. Amato reports:

"Our team of sellers had tremendous passion and saw tremendous results. They started to tell all of their friends, 'Hey, go talk to Phil, he can give you a Sales Navigator license for LinkedIn.' We got so many requests, soon managers reached out to get on board, then mid-level managers, and it organically worked its way up the chain. By the time it made its way up to the executives, we had a group of rabid users and overwhelmingly positive results. Everyone agreed to scale up the program with more infrastructure and executive support behind it."[100]

To ensure that the social selling initiative scaled successfully, Microsoft also made sure to train the users in how best to leverage Sales Navigator to make the most of social selling and transform their sales business.

Let's look closer at Sales Navigator...

Quickly build a high-quality pipeline

Salespeople waste hours a day trying to find the right people to talk to. But with Sales Navigator on their desktop or device, they have an automated tool doing this for them in the background.

As salespeople run searches on LinkedIn for target companies, Sales Navigator is learning from those searches and in turn sifting through a vast storehouse of LinkedIn data for lead recommendations that could be relevant, based on the search criteria. Hours can be saved – since pages of the wrong targets are not reviewed and carefully culled pages of the right prospects are fed into the pipeline.

This time-saving is only the start, because the result is almost always going to be a higher-quality pipeline, and an accelerated sales process as well.

---

100 https://business.linkedin.com/content/dam/business/sales-solutions/global/en_US/site/pdf/cs/linkedin-microsoft-case-study-en-us.pdf

It's certainly possible to do much of this search filtering with a basic LinkedIn account. But the fine-toothed filtering is only on Sales Navigator – enabling salespeople to be substantially more efficient and productive, as per the earlier chart (Fig. 8.2): 119% more successful at finding prospects, 52% more successful at generating opportunities, 128% more successful at securing meetings, 70% more successful at winning deals.

Key tactics...

Use Premium Search filters

- Sort by a number of factors including geography, sector and company size — and scope the size of each opportunity by filtering for company revenue.
- Look for names on accounts where you have a second-degree connection or good introduction opportunity. This becomes your list of target companies.
- Load the list into Lead Builder and filter further by titles to identify decision-makers. Filter for director-level sales and business development titles.

Use Lead Recommendations to automatically receive leads

- Receive pre-vetted leads based on presets and historically saved leads.
- See similar decision-makers and influencers at recommended companies.
- Look at the recommended decision-makers and influencers within your target accounts that Sales Navigator sends, and identify potential new leads.

Keep informed on key changes in target accounts

- Get alerts when there's a trigger event in a key account – perhaps a change in the contact's personal or professional life that suggests a new need, or a company change that yields a new, potentially valuable connection.
- Quickly generate custom-tailored content when a connection needs it most, so that content is held in higher esteem, building greater trust.
- StandOut against other salespeople who routinely fire off non-tailored information that has little immediate value to the prospect.

Use the CRM Widget

- Sales Navigator is compatible with a number of popular CRMs, including Salesforce and Microsoft Dynamics, allowing you to build relationships using pre-existing CRM contacts, while leveraging LinkedIn's network and features.
- Account and contact information from CRM systems port in, with automated daily syncs that keep data fresh.
- Salesforce users can also view LinkedIn information (including insights, messages and InMail) from within the CRM system.

Go out-of-network

- *Out-of-Network Profile Unlock* helps uncover hidden leads outside your network. By unlocking profiles from search results, salespeople gain visibility into prospects beyond third-degree connections.

Use TeamLink to make connections through peers

- *TeamLink* taps the credibility of another person's connection, allowing one team member to make an introduction for another in a leveraged way (as shown in Fig. 8.3).
- Because the connections are made on Sales Navigator, they carry the added credibility of the LinkedIn brand.

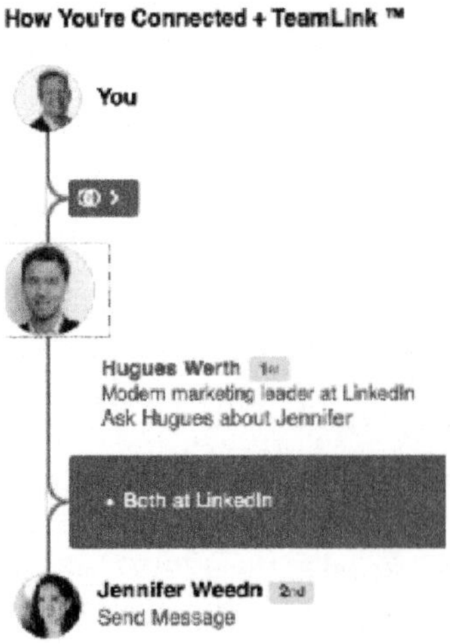

How You're Connected + TeamLink ™

You

Hugues Werth 1st
Modem marketing leader at LinkedIn
Ask Hugues about Jennifer

• Both at LinkedIn

Jennifer Weedn 2nd
Send Message

TeamLink in 3 steps:

1. In this example, Bert Verdonck wants to connect with Jennifer Weedn at LinkedIn, but doesn't know her.

2. Bert can see that his 1st degree connection Hugues Werth, also at LinkedIn, can make a socially credible introduction to Jennifer.

3. Bert can meet Jennifer on the best of terms.

Fig. 8.3 How to use TeamLink to meet someone you don't know through someone you do

Use InMail to get through the email storm

- We all receive too much email and ignore a lot of it, but InMail from LinkedIn enjoys a higher open rate.
- InMail is optimized for viewing on all devices.
- The ability to send InMail can separate you from other B2B vendors – suggesting more of a peer-like level of engagement.

Used together, LinkedIn and Sales Navigator are the perfect way to manage B2B lead generation. In just minutes a day, your salespeople can build up knowledge on existing accounts, read all of their updates, comment on those updates when appropriate, and build up credibility, so that when they reach out to a client company they are more warmly welcomed.

Summary of the value of Sales Navigator

- Extended Network Access – to see deeper into your leads' Profiles
- Advanced Search – to build a better pool of leads
- Saved Searches – to keep leads and accounts handy for follow-up
- Lead Recommendations – to have more leads to consider
- Custom Updates – to get just the information on leads that you want
- Team Link – to leverage the connections of your colleagues
- InMail – to reach out to leads with more effective LinkedIn messaging
- Email Notifications – to make sure you don't miss anything

LinkedIn offers a free trial of Sales Navigator, which you can sign-up for: https://business.linkedin.com/sales-solutions/sales-navigator.

Recruiter – find clones of your best performing employees

In 2018, LinkedIn began updating its Recruiter tool to speed up the process of finding candidates with the right skillsets. This people-matching algorithm was born out of a challenge facing recruiters on the LinkedIn platform:

It has not always been easy to find the right person in an efficient way.

But with the rebuilt Recruiter, an employer can simply select the profile of its 'rockstar' employees, and LinkedIn's algorithms will crunch through billions of data points to pinpoint a list of similar people.

Employers can view the criteria and filters the system uses to pinpoint these potential hires, allowing adjustments as part of the winnowing process.

Or if the company doesn't have a 'rockstar' model, Recruiter has pre-made search tags that generate a list of potential hires that meet threshold recruiting criteria, such as:

- Are connected to the company's employees
- Have liked the LinkedIn company page
- Have interacted with company updates on LinkedIn
- Have applied for previous positions at the company

Let's use Recruiter to look for an architect in the Greater Seattle Area, for example. As in Fig. 8.4, LinkedIn will suggest *top trending skills* for the title "Architect". This allows you to fine-tune your search faster and easier, because you are not looking for just any type of architect, right? Think about an industrial architect versus a computer hardware architect, etc.

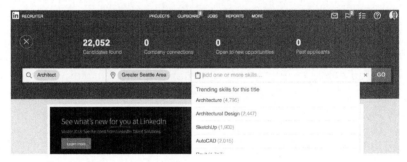

Fig. 8.4 LinkedIn suggests certain skills for any given title in the search

In the search results the Recruiter delivers to you, even more suggestions are offered. As in Fig. 8.5 under *Titles* you get suggestions as well for 'Project Architect' and 'Senior Architect.' You also get some additional locations to look at. And you get additional skills such as 'Design Research' and 'Architectural Drawings.'

Fig. 8.5 Recruiter search results include suggestions to help you find the right person

Recruiter's most-valued benefits on the web and mobile App

1. Setup campaigns and build talent pools
2. Zero in on the right person with 25+ search filters
3. View complete Profiles of *every* LinkedIn member
4. Candidate searches can be saved so there is always a shortlist at hand
5. Use up to 150 InMail messages per month per team member
6. Entire team can access or manage the talent pipeline on a single platform
7. Powerful reporting and analytics tools are built-in.

With the souped-up capabilities of Recruiter, we expect the numbers of companies using it to shoot well past the current 50,000 in 2018. There is just too much of a talent and skills shortage in companies, and tools like Recruiter cost little in comparison to the rewards of quality hires, brought in faster.

> TIP: If you are using LinkedIn Recruiter, make sure you use the Inside Opinion feature. This helps your internal recruiters by finding colleagues who may know a candidate based on a shared experience or education. So, let's say you are recruiting a Java Developer. And you believe one of your candidates worked (or studied) with one of your colleagues in the past. Now you can ask that colleague for his/ her thoughts on the candidate by sending them a message. Their reply is confidential and will only be sent to you and the recruitment team. This feedback helps to make better hiring decisions!

Elevate - Turn employees into social sharing professionals

Sharing content on LinkedIn helps employees strengthen their professional brands, of course, but seeing is believing. If employees can't see how they benefit from their posting, their attention can wane.

So *Elevate* sends employees email highlights of the profile views that result from their sharing. Employees can thus see which influential people in their networks viewed, liked, commented on, or shared their content with others.

Employees also receive push notifications when shared content receives a large number of likes, comments, or shares, or is re-shared.

Elevate goes beyond *Pulse* in that it not only allows employees to post to LinkedIn and Twitter, but also to Facebook.

Elevate is only available for larger organizations, starting with 1,000 licenses.

See who is engaging with employees' content

Elevate shows the demographic information on the recipients – job functions, companies, industries, etc. – so you know precisely who your content is reaching, and whether or not it is resonating with that audience.

In early surveys of *Elevate* users, LinkedIn was understandably pleased to see that people were in fact sharing more frequently than before – because it was easier to do so on *Elevate*. LinkedIn's data crunchers then did some digging and in their words *"discovered that across all the companies using Elevate, employees have shared four times more than they did before"*.[101]

VISA is using Elevate to hire and retain talent

Credit card company VISA reports that its employees have shared 7x more often since using *Elevate*. That has resulted in a 5x increase in job-opening views and Company Page followers, and together with other VISA

---

101 https://business.linkedin.com/talent-solutions/blog/2015/09/hire-market-and-sell-better-using-linkedin-elevates-new-features

activities on LinkedIn, influenced a significant number of new hires. Says VP of Corporate Social Media Lucas Mast:

"As a leading technology company, we compete for talent not only with traditional financial services companies, but also with startups and technology companies . . . Elevate helps our best advocates – our employees – endorse our brand, which makes Visa a more attractive employer. Additionally, it helps us retain employees because they value Visa helping them build their own professional brand on LinkedIn, which is a win-win situation."

Fortinet is using Elevate for social selling

Fortinet sales reps are now sharing 4x as often. As a result, their profile views have nearly doubled, and they've made 3x the number of new connections, positioning themselves as experts and resources for customers and prospects. Michael Perna who worked as Fortinet's social media strategist said:

"Elevate increases sales serendipity . . . makes it easy for sales reps to quickly learn about what is going on in their industry, and then share content on social networks that showcases their expertise and establishes them as the first resource customers and prospects will turn to when they need help."[102]

To learn more from LinkedIn about how *Elevate* can in fact elevate your team's social sharing, see at: https://business.linkedin.com/elevate#.

LinkedIn Developer Tools

LinkedIn also provides a number of Developer Tools (https://developer. linkedin.com/).[103] Since LinkedIn changes these tools frequently, here is a short overview of some of the tools we currently find useful:
  1. Sign in with LinkedIn. Enhance the sign-in experience on your own website or app, by allowing people to sign in with the LinkedIn credentials.
  2. Share on LinkedIn. How would you like to share on LinkedIn? Several APIs and SDKs are made available: REST API, JavaScript

---

102 https://business.linkedin.com/talent-solutions/blog/2015/09/hire-market-and-sell-better-using-linkedin-elevates-new-features
103 https://developer.linkedin.com

SDK, Android SDK, Customized URL, Plugins, iOS SDK

3. Manage your Company Page(s). Maximizes your company's presence on LinkedIn.

4. Add to Profile. With a single click, graduates can add a degree to their LinkedIn Profiles.

This completes our review of the LinkedIn tools that we find most useful. If you have further questions about any of them, we'll keep updating our reviews and answering questions at https://how-to-really-use-linkedin. com

WHAT'S THE VALUE OF ADVERTISING ON LINKEDIN?

Companies committed $51.3 billion to social media advertising globally in 2018, a figure that's on track to hit $76.5 billion by 2022[104]. Yet consumers have proven adept at tuning out brand-related content on the networks. Consumers not only glaze over social media ads, according to surveys from Gallup and Nielsen, they also place greater trust in TV, print, radio and billboard ads.[105]

It should be no surprise, but when advertisers resort to the old-time 'harder sell' in the softer social medium, consumers tune out or even turn against. Yet the news for advertisers just got worse...

Ad blocking – the rising threat to online advertisers

Advertising on social networks enjoys begrudging acceptance in a desktop setting, because the ads don't usually sit on top of the content, but around it.

In a mobile setting, however, due to having only 10% or so of the real estate of a desktop monitor, things are different. Advertisers have (or have had to) put roadblocks in place requiring users to X out the ad, with an X that's too small for big thumbs to strike. Or they have used the "*Skip ad in 4... 3... 2... 1*" countdown, annoying people with such ugly and intrusive sales techniques that a growing number of people avoid mobile browsing altogether.

So when Apple's mobile software upgrade enabled third-party ad blockers, the marketplace cheered. Apple's move quickly spawned a cottage industry of mobile ad blocking companies. One such company, Purify, with their

104 https://www.statista.com/outlook/220/100/social-media-advertising/worldwide#market-revenue
105 http://www.emarketer.com/Article/Social-Network-Ad-Spending-Hit-2368-Billion-Worldwide-2015/1012357   ...
http://www.wsj.com/articles/companies-alter-social-media-strategies-1403499658   ...   https://www.wsj.com/articles/companies-alter-social-media-strategies-1403499658

$1.99 ad blocking app, made $150,000 in their first month in the App store.[106]

Jason Calacanis, the Silicon Valley angel investor, trendsetter and founder of Launch, summed up the thinking of most people that ad blocking is not only welcome, it will keep growing in popularity:

"Using two Apps called Adblock Fast and Crystal for the past week and surfing the web on my iPhone has become delightfully fast and uncluttered. Blocking ads on your mobile phone is like moving from a crowded apartment complex in a polluted, violent city to a peaceful lake house."[107]

With the growth in mobile use and more than 50% of all online searches being done on mobile devices, advertisers have to be concerned. But LinkedIn isn't.

There are no "ads" on LinkedIn mobile, only textlinks and sponsored updates.[108]

LinkedIn is trying to deliver on Seth Godin's refrain from his seminal 1999 work, Permission Marketing, recently updated in his blog:

"When ads are optional, it's only anticipated, personal and relevant ones that will pay off . . . the new generation of ad blockers is starting from the place of, 'delete all' . . . This reinforces the fundamental building blocks of growth today:

The best marketing isn't advertising, it's a well-designed and remarkable product.

The best way to contact your users is by earning the privilege to contact them, over time.

Making products for your customers is far more efficient than finding customers for your products.

---

106 http://www.wsj.com/articles/propelled-by-apple-ad-blocking-cottage-industry-emerges-1443115929?mod=djemCMO Today&alg=y
107 http://calacanis.com/2015/09/24/apples-brilliant-assault-on-advertising-and-google
108 https://help.linkedin.com/app/answers/detail/a_id/719/~/ad-positions-on-linkedin

Horizontally spread ideas (person to person) are far more effective than top-down vertical advertising...[109]

LinkedIn is executing on Godin's credo, enabling one-to-one relationships between advertisers and members by asking members to share their data in order to:

- Serve the most appropriate ads, making them more and more relevant.
- Otherwise hold down membership costs, keeping most elements of the platform free, and others at lower cost.

So let's look closer at LinkedIn's approach to advertising, beginning with...

Why Many Advertisers Fail with LinkedIn Ads

It is not uncommon for marketing execs to walk away from the LinkedIn advertising platform after an initial test for two, feeling dispirited and unhappy with their performance results. This usually happens for one of three reasons:

1. Don't understand the platform's unique traits

The LinkedIn platform often tests poorly on *traditional* online advertising metrics such as clickthroughs, conversions, and direct sales increases. That's because it is not a direct marketing platform, it is a professional engagement platform designed to build and nurture relationships with fellow professionals...

...which leads to deeper relationships...
...which then leads to traditional measures of business success such as conversions and increased sales.

So if an advertiser is looking to push out solutions or products on LinkedIn and then compare results, such as clicks and conversions, on Google Adwords, they will often be disappointed.

---

109 http://sethgodin.typepad.com/seths_blog/2015/09/ad-blocking.html

In Google searches, users are actively looking for product information, often with the intent to purchase. Those potential buyers are deeper into the sales funnel.

On LinkedIn, the members are making connections, expanding their professional expertise, not necessarily focused on buying anything.

These members tend to be better prospects for most products and services because of a higher socioeconomic status, but they need to be approached with an entirely different 'top of funnel' strategy, with a campaign consisting of multiple layers, rigorous testing, and continual refinement.

2. Don't manage the campaigns effectively

LinkedIn ads are run on an auction basis, so the highest bidder gets the lion's share of impressions and follow-on clicks and conversions. But when testing a new online platform or campaign, advertisers typically enter the smallest bid possible in the auction – to test results, and adjust from there.

On the LinkedIn Campaign Manager Ad tool, the minimum bid is $2 (with a $10 daily budget per campaign). But the bid minimum is usually well below the current bidding range of other advertisers, so the bid is not entered into many auctions, and thus not seen by the target audience.

The campaign creative and offer structure may be good, may be not – but at the minimum bid price, the advertiser never finds out.

Compounding the problem is the ticking clock. When bidding for eyeballs, which is what's essentially happening, the pace moves fast and an ad must be getting traction or LinkedIn's algorithm will sideline the ad. And the advertiser will lose confidence.

3. Haven't seen the revamped "Campaign Manager"

LinkedIn's Campaign Manager was upgraded in July 2015 and again in 2018, and it was overdue. The old tool had a reputation for being slow and unwieldy, certainly as compared to Google Adwords and Facebook's Ad platform.

Now the Manager has a snazzy interface, user-friendly design, and an Account Overview page that makes it easy to keep tabs on multiple accounts and run extensive A/B testing to continuously improve ad performance.

Getting familiar with the unique nature of the LinkedIn platform, and intricacies of advertising on it, is absolutely essential. Let's look more closely at the programs LinkedIn provides.

Array of Ads on LinkedIn

There are two main ways to advertise on LinkedIn:
- Self-Serve Platform with one-stop capability, ideal for smaller companies
- LinkedIn Advertising Partner with traditional insertion order programs

And there are four kinds of advertisements on LinkedIn:
- Self-Service Ads. These include display ads, text ads, and sponsored content.
- Display & Text Ads. These appear across the platform and include images and video along with minimal text.
- Sponsored Content. These can be *Status Updates* or 'news stories' that appear in the news stream of members, and can be finely targeted.
- Dark Posts. These are Sponsored Content but are *not* published to a company's LinkedIn page (ergo, dark), so advertisers can test offers and messaging to targeted audiences without interfering with other campaigns underway or ending up overloading the same audience with multiple posts.

LinkedIn's Self-Serve Advertising Platform

Self-service advertising lets you create and place ads to appear in a number of places, such as a member's inbox, on the side and bottom of the homepage, and across the web through LinkedIn's 2,500 publisher sites.

Summary of self-serve ads (as per Fig. 9.1 example)
- You create ads to drive prospects to your landing page and campaign.
- You specify which LinkedIn members view your ads by selecting a

target audience based on granular criteria such as *Company, Job Title, Job Function, Seniority, School, Skills, Groups, Age, Gender.*

- You control your costs by setting a budget and pay only for the clicks or impressions you receive.

To create a campaign...

- On the top menu, click *Work* and then *Advertise.*
- You will see an overview of options. LinkedIn is often testing copy here, so the format may be different. But click *Get Started.*
- You will now be taken to a personalized Campaign Manager and given a choice of ad formats:
  - I want to drive targeted leads across multiple LinkedIn pages with *Text Ads.*
  - I want to reach LinkedIn members right in the LinkedIn feed with *Sponsored Updates.*
- (For our walkthrough here) Select *Text Ads.*

Walkthrough of creating 'Text and image ads'

NOTE: If you have ad campaigns going, you will see them first. We assume here that this is your first use of the self-serve ad platform.)

When you select *Text Ads,* you will be taken to a page that could change, as noted above, but the fields will be the same as or similar to:

Open a fresh ad account for your new campaign:

1. Enter an *Account Name* for your campaign
2. Choose the *Currency* you will use
3. Tell LinkedIn if you have a Company or Showcase Page
4. Enter a *Campaign Name*
5. Choose a *Language* for the campaign to run in
6. Choose a *Landing Page* option
   a. (One of) your LinkedIn page(s)
   b. Your website or dedicated landing page
7. Create your basic ad
   a. Headline (up to 25 characters)
   b. Two lines of body text (up to 75 characters)
   c. Image
8. Choose ad format

a. Square
b. Tall
c. Horizontal
d. Long
9. Save your ad
10. Preview your ad, and make any edits with the blue pencil
11. You can create another ad – it's ideal to create 15 variations for testing.

Choose Target Audience

LinkedIn now walks you through a precise targeting program, allowing you to include or exclude viewers based on location and 13 other filters (shown in Fig. 9.1). Simply follow the prompts and answer LinkedIn's questions for each of the targeting criteria. Using autocomplete, LinkedIn makes it a breeze.

Fig. 9.1 LinkedIn self-serve ads – targeting filters

LinkedIn will keep a summary description of your targeting decisions, and tell you your estimated target audience as you go, helping you plan and budget.

At this point, you can also use the *Audience Expansion* feature:
- This instructs LinkedIn to expand your campaign to also reach members who, according to their algorithms, are similar to your target audience.
- This nifty tool lets you increase your campaign 'reach' by showing

your ads and updates to audiences with similar attributes to your targets.

- For example, if you target members with the skill 'Online Advertising,' your campaign might also be shown to members who list the skill 'Interactive Marketing' on their Profile.

Campaign Budget

- Choose the type of bid
  - Cost per click (CPC)
  - Cost per thousand (CPM)
- Choose a bid range – LinkedIn suggests a bid, but the choice is yours. *(See below for how to optimize your bidding).*
- Choose your daily budget
- Choose the start date
  - Immediately
  - Enter date to begin
- Enter account details for credit card billing
- Review order and launch campaign

Your ad will be placed in a box of three in the right column of member pages that meet your targeting criteria, as per Fig. 9.2:

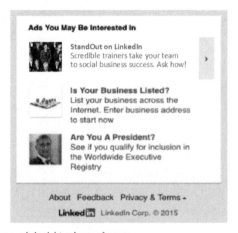

Fig. 9.2 LinkedIn self-serve ads in right column of pages

Walkthrough of creating 'Sponsored Updates'

When you select *Sponsored Updates*, you will be taken to a page similar to...

Create a Sponsored Update campaign:

1. Enter a *Campaign Name*
2. Choose a *Language* for the campaign to run in
3. Because you earlier told LinkedIn that you have a Company Page, LinkedIn will now show you a list of your past company updates – tick the box for the one you want to feature in this campaign and preview it to make sure you like how it will look
4. Scroll to the bottom of the page and click *Next*
5. You can now target your audience, using the same screens we reviewed above in *Text Ad*. The rest of the process is also the same.

An example of a completed Sponsored Update is in Fig. 9.3, along with captions:

Fig. 9.3 LinkedIn Sponsored Update with notes

You can also sponsor a post from your Company Page:

- Go to your Company Page *Statistics* tab.
- See the engagement with some of your Company Updates.
- Updates with a minimum of 3% to 5% engagement are eligible for a *Sponsored Update*.

- With one click you can indicate which Company Update you want to be used as a *Sponsored Update.*
- The rest of the process is similar to the above.

Optimization

Since LinkedIn ads are run on an auction basis, the highest bidder gets the lion's share of clicks and conversions. To optimize for this auction format and make the best use of your advertising spend:

Run several campaigns at once

- Take advantage of LinkedIn's demographic detail to craft different campaigns that test variations in the offer and the messaging to different audiences.
- Experiment with your images, subject lines, ad text, everything. This will help you discover your audience's preferences, fine-tune the relevancy of your ads, and increase response rates.

Change content one to two times a week

- Continually rotate in fresh ads to maintain audience interest. Even if the company has strict branding guidelines in place requiring consistency of messaging, LinkedIn ads should keep changing or risk being judged as yesterday's news.

Visuals matter greatly, of course

- Make your visuals eye-catching to improve clickthrough rates. (Just having an image drives 20% more clicks, according to LinkedIn.)
- Image dimensions should be square (ideally 50 x 50 pixels) and the three best image types tend to be people, product, or logo.
- LinkedIn also promotes company videos in the sidebar space of the page. When clicked, a window opens with an ad up to 20 seconds long.

Sharp copy is critical

- You have 25 characters in your subject line to grab viewers – make it count!

- Subject lines of 'how to' or 'lists of' tips tend to perform better; that is, *"How to explore Mars"* and *"Seven tips for exploring Mars"* will probably earn more clicks than *"Why explore Mars?"*
- In the body copy you have just 75 characters to make a compelling offer and include an essential call to action.

Post moderately

- You don't want to under- or over-deliver to your audience. As with unpaid posts, one to two paid posts a day is a good maximum for most companies.

LinkedIn Advertising Partner Solutions

LinkedIn's premium display ads allow for the same targeting as the self-serve ads. But they differ in size and placement, and come with more sizing and placement options. These are the available formats and placement opportunities:

- Textlink – Appears on Homepages, Profile Pages, Company Pages, Group Pages, and Messaging Pages.
- Medium Rectangle (300 x 250 pixels) – Appears above the fold in the right sidebar on Homepages, Profile Pages, Company Pages, Group Pages, and Messaging Pages.
- Wide Skyscraper (160 x 600 pixels) – Appears on Connections Pages and Messaging Pages.
- Leaderboard (728 x 90 pixels) – Appears at the bottom of some feeds.

Sponsored InMail

Sponsored InMail is different from regular InMail. The sponsored ones go right into LinkedIn's new messaging system with a "Sponsored" tag. These can be targeted to any one of 550 million members, using the same granular segmentation filters that LinkedIn offers for its display ads.

You write the copy for your Sponsored InMail, and LinkedIn offers tips on making it more engaging. You can send it from the company, or an individual within.

LinkedIn promises 100% deliverability with Sponsored InMail. They can do this because the message is delivered when members are signed on.

These messages can also feel more personalized because of their placement in the messaging stream, though in fact they are not more personal.

Note in Fig. 9.4 that the Sponsored InMail sample from American Express also carries an ad in the right column. This option maximizes the touchpoint.

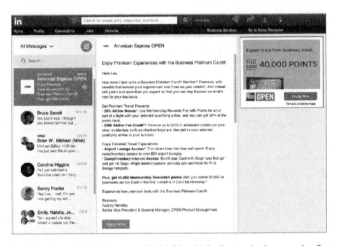

Fig. 9.4 Sample of American Express Sponsored in Mail in a LinkedIn member's messaging flow

LinkedIn limits the number of Sponsored InMails to one every 60 days, so members are not overwhelmed and advertisers have a clear medium for messaging.

Follow Company Ads

Follow Company ads help organizations grow a LinkedIn following and increase the brand's credibility on the platform (Fig. 9.5).

These *Follow Company* ads appear on the pages of members who should be most interested, based on LinkedIn's targeting filters. A big blue Follow button makes it easy for any interested member to follow the company – for a relatively friction-free start of a relationship.

Fig. 9.5 Follow Company ads – ideal for keeping the employer brand strong among likely job prospects

Advertisers often use these ads as remarketing tools, placing them on the homepages of people who have *Followed* the company, as a way to keep the follower up-to-date and the engagement continuing.

Recommendation Ads

These ads appear across the LinkedIn platform and are ideal for credentializing a new or specific product (Fig. 9.6).

Recommendation Ads feature:
- Company name
- Product name and image
- Number of people who have recommended the product, including some photo thumbnails of recommenders
- Buttons for recommending or sharing the product

Fig. 9.6 LinkedIn Recommendation ads – ideal for credentializing a product

Join-Group Ads

For companies looking to increase the number of members in their LinkedIn Groups, Join-Group ads can be ideal (Fig. 9.7):

Join-Group ads feature:
- Name of the Group
- Brief description of topics being discussed
- Prominent call-to-action button

Fig. 9.7 LinkedIn Join-Group ads – for building membership in a Group

New Ads

LinkedIn is constantly updating its ad platform, and working to make those ads perform better for marketers (win-win). To see any new updates on LinkedIn's Solutions page, go to: https://business.linkedin.com/marketing-solutions/native-advertising.

LinkedIn's Premium Solutions

We covered the most popular of LinkedIn's paid programs in Chapter 6 (Social Selling) and Chapter 7 (Social Recruiting). Here, let's look at some additional LinkedIn solutions that are proving valuable for advancing employer social branding and sourcing top talent.

Job Posts

Job Posts (https://business.linkedin.com/talent-solutions/advertise-jobs) are designed to promote job listings on the Profiles of a precisely targeted group of candidates, based on an algorithmic match. Your posts are seen by the candidates that should have the right sets of skills and experience you are looking for – even if these people are not active job seekers.

Job Posts program features:
1. Curated list of active and passive candidates for your talent pool.
2. Up to five InMails to reach out to prospective candidates.
3. A single interface for swiftly posting job openings, tracking applicants, and sharing top picks with your team.
4. Insights on how your job posts are performing.

Job Slots

Job Slots (https://business.linkedin.com/talent-solutions/advertise-jobs) are different from *Job Post* ads which go onto Profiles only. *Job Slots* go all across the LinkedIn platform, in email, and in the *Job Search* app. Again, LinkedIn's algorithm recommends your job openings to members with the relevant skills and expertise, resulting in a better-filtered talent pool.

Job Slots program features:
- Find passive candidates that are qualified but might otherwise be missed by using the *Jobs You May Be Interested In*.
- Integrates with LinkedIn's *Job Posts, Career Page and* mobile *Job Search* app.
- Manage applicants, outreach, commentary, analytics and reporting from a single dashboard.

Work With Us Ads

Work With Us ads are placed on your team's LinkedIn profiles so that potential candidates will think of your company when researching or connecting with your employees. These ads can be personalized with highly relevant job info so the candidates know you're looking for professionals like them.

LinkedIn claims that these recruitment ads outperform typical banner ads with up to 50x higher clickthrough rates. *"Higher than what?"* we ask, but the ads can be very effective at driving interested professionals to your jobs listings, Career Page, and other landing pages.

Fig. 9.8 LinkedIn *Work with Us* ads – another way to attract top talent

Work With Us program features:

- Grabs the attention of prospects in a highly credible way since they are positioned on the Profiles of your employees.
- Each candidate can receive a customized job recommendation based on his or her Profile.
- Candidates who respond can be sent to a special jobs page, or to your LinkedIn Career Page.

SUMMARY

The advertising industry faces a genuine threat to its wellbeing from the new ad blocking apps that are expected to proliferate in years ahead. It's smart, then, to develop advertising campaigns that meld organically with the content and connections that LinkedIn members are seeking on the platform.

In our view, a company should ideally first optimize for engagement across LinkedIn, then put LinkedIn's various advertising programs to the test.

CAN WE HELP YOU FURTHER? 10

At this point, you may be thinking:

> There is a lot more to LinkedIn and social business
> than I ever imagined!

It's sure an understandable conclusion to reach. Not five years ago, most people thought of LinkedIn as a place to post your resume when looking for work. Now the Sunnyvale company is becoming the economic graph of the entire professional world.

So yes, we've had a lot to cover.

Now in this concluding chapter we'll talk briefly about the value – the when, how and why – of outsourcing certain elements of your social business to service providers such as ourselves.

Your authors are Bert Verdonck, Michael (Mike) Clark and Caleb Storkey.

Bert is a worldclass LinkedIn expert, international speaker and master trainer, and a passionate lifehacker. In addition to this book, Bert has (co-) authored *The Power of LinkedIn*, *Little LinkedIn for Dummies* (in Dutch), *Little WhatsApp for Dummies* (in Dutch), *Your Book in 100 Days*, *150 Lifehacking Tips*, and *The Wealth Garden*.

Some of Bert's additional achievements:
1. Certified by LinkedIn Corporation as a LinkedIn Trainer, 2010
2. Speaker at TEDxGhent (2012)
3. First Speaker at the launch of the Professional Speakers Association (PSA) Belgium, 2012
4. Speaker at the PSA Holland General Assembly, 2011
5. Speaker at the Global Speakers Summit (Global Speakers Federation), 2011
6. Winner of the PSA Holland "Elevator Pitch" contest (Professional

Speakers Association), 2010
7. Global Training & Development Leadership Award, 2017

More about Bert can be found on his LinkedIn profile (where else?): https://www.linkedin.com/in/bertverdonck

Since 2004, Michael (Mike) Clark has been highly entrenched in entrepreneurial businesses across the globe. After moving from Australia to the UK to launch a business that went from complete start up to £3M+ within two years, Mike then expanded the World's 1st certified LinkedIn training company from Belgium, turning it into Europe's largest LinkedIn training business where they secured an exclusive two year EMEA partnership with LinkedIn.

This company grew to 25 trainers that delivered training in over ten languages and rolled out organisation-wide LinkedIn training projects for multi-billion euro brands such as Barclays, Canon, American Express, Deloitte and Accenture. His company was then acquired in 2015 by a Silicon Valley start up.

The techniques you're about to learn in this book are based on the experience gained through this period where Really Connect trained over 65,000 employees across 650+ companies.

Caleb Storkey is a serial entrepreneur, international speaker and consultant, in disruptive technologies, change management, marketing, entrepreneurism and leadership. Co-author of *Futureproof – How To Get Your Business Ready For The Next Disruption* and Founder of Storkey Media (an integrated marketing agency), Caleb has worked with a wide range of businesses, from multinationals to highly disruptive and rapid growth tech startups. Caleb is also one of the principle trainers at Really Connect.

About "How To REALLY Use LinkedIn"

Our company, Really Connect, is headquartered in the UK with offices in California, London and Antwerp. Through Bert Verdonck and Jan Vermeiren we were the first certified LinkedIn training organization globally (back in 2010!) and since 2004 we have trained 650+ clients with 65,000+ professionals in 15 countries and eight languages.

Our training is bespoke, driven by client objectives and built on a five-part competency model that has reliably proven to achieve the highest performance results:

1. Initial Assessment
2. Pre-Training Prep
3. Training Syllabus
4. Routine Creation
5. ROI Evaluation

1. Initial Assessment

A week before training begins, participants take an online questionnaire that does double duty:

1. Gets everyone into the proper mental state for the training ahead
2. Helps our trainers assess skill levels, identify areas of strength and weakness, and customize the training accordingly.

2. Pre-Training Prep

Shortly before training begins, when appropriate, participants receive a preparation pack so they can familiarize themselves with the syllabus, become acquainted with the expected outcomes, and ultimately learn and retain more – driving ROI.

3. Training Syllabus

Attendees learn and are able to demonstrate subject mastery much more reliably because the presentations are strictly limited and the primary focus is on practicing in real-life simulations that include:

- Lively interaction between participants and trainer
- Tools to facilitate networking and overcome fears
- Plan of action that's co-written by the participants so all are invested.

Training Comparisons		
	Common Approach	Scredible
Presenting	70%	20%
Discussing	10%	10%
Practicing	10%	40%
Reviewing	10%	20%
Maintaining	0%	10%

Fig. 10.1 Traditional training vs. Scredible training

4. Routine Creation

According to Harvard psychologists, we forget 80% of what we learn within 48 hours, no matter how well presented originally. Clearly, training is not a spectator sport. So we bake in a methodology *that makes the learning memorable:*

- **First Give** – *Share the knowledge the participants need in fast, fun format*
- **Then Reinforce** – *Return to the elements of the training, imprinting with routines*
- **Lastly Maintain** – *Follow-up with evaluations that keep the learning fresh and valuable.*

5. ROI Evaluation

After each training session, the evaluation begins at once. The "smile sheets" that participants fill out give management immediate feedback. Then at one-month and three-month intervals we check back with participants to measure progress against pre-agreed metrics.

It's the "How To REALLY Use LinkedIn" difference:
ROI-driven social business training.

Our Master Training Courses

OUR MASTER TRAINING COURSES
• Social Business Awareness & Strategy
• Employer Branding in the Digital Age
• Socially Credible Sales Teams
• Social Recruitment Team Development

OUR SPECIALTY PROGRAMS
• Optimizing LinkedIn Profiles
• Building Vibrant Social Communities
• Launching Social Campaigns
• Employee Social Activation
• The Socially Savvy Executive
• Mastering LinkedIn's Sales Navigator
• Formulating Social Media Policy
• Credible Content Creation Workshop

Fig 10.2 Our Service Offerings

Social Business Awareness & Strategy

SUMMARY:
Gain an understanding and company-wide support for ROI-driven social business.

SITUATION:
Most companies have some form of LinkedIn Company Pages, Twitter accounts, Facebook Fan Pages, YouTube channels and the like. But often their own employees are not sharing them, or even aware of them. And people at all levels of the company remain skeptical of social business. This is often because employees don't fully understand (1) the value of social business and (2) how critical is it to the company's future.

SOLUTION:
This five-part workshop takes key team members through the hierarchy of social business to gain a working understanding of the benefits realized at each level.

SESSIONS:
Up to five half-day workshops (no limit on participants)

Employer Branding in the Digital Age

SUMMARY:
Create a powerful social presence for your company by aligning all personal, professional, and corporate branding activity.

SITUATION:
Many employees are aware of the social tools and strategies available to them, but they are not adopting because they don't understand how to use them *productively*. Other employees are conversant in social media and are out there speaking about the company ... but without coordination, they speak haphazardly. The challenge for all is the same: show how to align the personal and professional brands with the company's brand in the social realm so that everyone prospers.

SOLUTION:
- Assess the company's social branding and outline the tools and strategies that will align the entire company's brand interests and deliver on KPIs.
- Optimize the team's LinkedIn Profiles and practice applying the most effective social business networking strategies tailored to the company.
- Co-write with the team a results-driven plan to hold everyone accountable to KPIs and motivated to turn the training into a winning routine.

SESSIONS:
Typically three half-day workshops (up to 12 participants)

Socially Credible Sales Teams

SUMMARY:
Your sales team learns to engage socially with prospects and customers to generate more leads, appointments, conversions, and sales.

SITUATION:

All selling is now socially enabled selling as salespeople use social media to find customers, engage with them and help solve their problems which, in turn, leads to increased sales. But even knowing this, many sales teams approach the social tools and strategies with a mix of confusion, apprehension, even fear.

SOLUTION:

- Assess the company's social selling activity to date and outline the social strategies that will deliver on the sales objectives and KPIs desired.
- Conduct social selling simulations with role-play to perfect best-practice strategies with competency-based feedback.
- Co-write with the team a results-driven plan to hold everyone accountable to the KPIs and motivated to make the training part of a winning routine.

SESSIONS:

Typically three half-day workshops (up to 12 participants)

Social Recruitment Team Development

SUMMARY:

Work with HR and recruiting to develop social recruiting that sources the right talent for the right positions – less expensively.

SITUATION:

When people go onto the job market, their first stop is usually an Internet job board or social professional network, and most often LinkedIn. So the companies that are telling the best story on LinkedIn capture the attention of the best talent. What story are you telling? When people research your executives and your business units, do they get a strong sense of your company's culture and values, who they'll be working with, and how capable you are? Do job seekers get a compelling narrative?

SOLUTION:

- Answer the above questions in order to formulate the recruiting KPIs that matter to the company (quality of hire, time to fill, hiring manager satisfaction, etc.) and then co-write an action plan to deliver

on those metrics over 6, 12, and 24 months.
- Role-play with the recruiting tactics in a real-world simulation, then practice, practice, practice – with real-time feedback.
- Review progress to fill holes in training and imprint best practice performance against KPIs going forward.

SESSIONS:
Typically three half-day workshops (up to 12 participants)

Our Specialty Programs

Optimizing LinkedIn Profiles

Our social business experts work with the entire team to optimize LinkedIn Profiles, handling all aspects, requiring only a small time commitment from the team.

We also set up booths at company events (job fair, conference, etc.) and work with attendees to touch-up, fix-up and polish their LinkedIn Profiles.

Building Vibrant Social Communities

We build successful social communities with highly engaged fans to drive membership retention, acquisition, and monetization.

Launching Social Campaigns

We bring together the digital agency resources to manage social business campaigns to drive market awareness, customer engagement, and website traffic.

Employee Social Activation

We develop a blueprint for transitioning the organization and its employees into genuinely motivated social champions, and then we help manage the transition.

The Socially Savvy Executive

We coach the C-suite on the social business technologies that will support the company's strategic vision and drive performance.

Mastering LinkedIn's Sales Navigator

We teach the sales team to use *Sales Navigator* to find prospects, generate opportunities, secure meetings, and win deals faster and less expensively.

Formulating Social Media Policy

We guide the development and implementation of sustainable policies and governance to support the company's strategic objectives.

Credible Content Creation Workshop

We develop a strategy to drive social engagement and build the brand across the social networks – spanning ideation, strategy, execution, and measurement.

CONNECT WITH THE AUTHORS

To learn more about our social business training, feel free to contact us:

Bert Verdonck
https://www.linkedin.com/in/bertverdonck
@bertverdonck
bert@reallyconnect.com

Michael (Mike) Clark
https://www.linkedin.com/in/mikeclark3
@mikeclark03
mike@reallyconnect.com

Caleb Storkey
https://www.linkedin.com/in/calebstorkey
@calebstorkey
caleb@calebstorkey.com

We've enjoyed sharing the social business knowledge we've gained over the last decade, and would equally enjoy hearing your thoughts, feedback, or questions going forward.

All the best to you,

Bert, Mike & Caleb

MORE FREE INFORMATION

Social business is advancing at such a rapid clip, and LinkedIn is now updating its platform almost daily, so the information in these pages can become outdated.

To guard against that, we have used Adobe Digital Editions so that the eBook version is always current with seamless updates.

 But the print version enjoys no such advantage. So we advise bookmarking https://how-to-really-use-linkedin.com where we've posted all the follow-on materials talked about in this book.

Discover it all at https://how-to-really-use-linkedin.com

If you have access to LinkedIn Learning or Lynda.com, feel free to check out Bert's courses as well.

LinkedIn Profiles for Social Business Success

 Unlike a simple business card or résumé, your LinkedIn profile can help you reach millions of other business professionals. So, how do you make your profile stand out from the pack? In this course, I show you how to create a winning profile. I share how to select a professional profile photo, craft a compelling summary, highlight past experience appropriately, develop and enhance your personal brand, showcase skills and education, and ultimately develop a powerful LinkedIn profile.

Recruiting Talent with Social Media

Social media is changing the way recruiters source talent. In this course, social recruiting expert Bert Verdonck shows how to leverage the top social media platforms—LinkedIn, Twitter, and Facebook—to find and attract top talent. Learn how to find qualified candidates, make a compelling company profile, and write articles, posts, and tweets that attract talent. Plus, find out how to post job openings on LinkedIn and Facebook, and get time-saving tools and techniques that will help you spend more time on people and less time on tech.

Social Recruiting for Recruiters

Recruiting talented candidates via social channels has become an important part of a recruiter's job. But how does one best tackle this channel? In this course, instructor Bert Verdonck shares strategies that can help recruiters efficiently and successfully recruit top talent on social platforms. Bert explains how social recruiting fits into the overall recruiting process, which social platforms to focus on, and how to jump-start your social media recruiting presence. He also shares how to find and approach ideal candidates, collaborate with hiring managers, and drive referral recruitment.